Best Practice in Team Excellence

Also available from ASQ Quality Press:

Journal for Quality and Participation

The Quality Improvement Handbook, Second Edition
ASQ Quality Management Division

The Magic of Self-Directed Work Teams: A Case Study in Courage and Culture Change
Paul C. Palmes

The Quality Toolbox, Second Edition
Nancy R. Tague

Quality Improvement Made Simple . . . and Fast!
Matthew J. Maio

Root Cause Analysis: The Core of Problem Solving and Corrective Action
Duke Okes

The Executive Guide to Understanding and Implementing Employee Engagement Programs: Expand Production Capacity, Increase Revenue, and Save Jobs
Pat Townsend and Joan Gebhardt

The Executive Guide to Understanding and Implementing Lean Six Sigma: The Financial Impact
Robert M. Meisel, Steven J. Babb, Steven F. Marsh, and James P. Schlichting

Lean Kaizen: A Simplified Approach to Process Improvements
George Alukal and Anthony Manos

Root Cause Analysis: Simplified Tools and Techniques, Second Edition
Bjørn Andersen and Tom Fagerhaug

The Certified Manager of Quality/Organizational Excellence Handbook,
Third Edition
Russell T. Westcott, editor

To request a complimentary catalog of ASQ Quality Press publications, call 800-248-1946, or visit our website at www.asq.org/quality-press.

Best Practice in Team Excellence

Using the International Team Excellence Award Framework to Improve Your Organization's Results

Laurie Broedling
Vern Goodwalt

ASQ Quality Press
Milwaukee, Wisconsin

American Society for Quality, Quality Press, Milwaukee 53203
© 2012 by ASQ
All rights reserved. Published 2012
Printed in the United States of America
18 17 16 15 14 13 12   5 4 3 2 1

Library of Congress Cataloging-in-Publication Data

Broedling, Laurie A.
  Best practice in team excellence : using the international team excellence award framework to improve your organization's results / Laurie Broedling, Vern Goodwalt.
      p. cm.
  Includes bibliographical references and index.
  ISBN 978-0-87389-832-4 (hard cover : alk. paper)
  1. Teams in the workplace. I. Goodwalt, Vern. II. Title.

HD66.B757 2012
658.4'022—dc23   2011050721

ISBN: 978-0-87389-832-4

No part of this book may be reproduced in any form or by any means, electronic, mechanical, photocopying, recording, or otherwise, without the prior written permission of the publisher.

Publisher: William A. Tony
Acquisitions Editor: Matt T. Meinholz
Project Editor: Paul Daniel O'Mara
Production Administrator: Randall Benson

ASQ Mission: The American Society for Quality advances individual, organizational, and community excellence worldwide through learning, quality improvement, and knowledge exchange.

Attention Bookstores, Wholesalers, Schools, and Corporations: ASQ Quality Press books, video, audio, and software are available at quantity discounts with bulk purchases for business, educational, or instructional use. For information, please contact ASQ Quality Press at 800-248-1946, or write to ASQ Quality Press, P.O. Box 3005, Milwaukee, WI 53201-3005.

To place orders or to request ASQ membership information, call 800-248-1946. Visit our website at http://www.asq.org/quality-press.

∞ Printed on acid-free paper

Quality Press
600 N. Plankinton Ave.
Milwaukee, WI 53203-2914
E-mail: authors@asq.org

ASQ   The Global Voice of Quality™

Without the support of our families, we could not have created this book. They have supported us throughout the writing process and also in our professional team excellence endeavors that led us to embark on this ambitious undertaking. We sincerely dedicate this book to them.

He that feels important to a job will make every effort to be on the job. He will feel important to the job if he can take pride in his work and may have a part in improvement of the system.

—W. Edwards Deming, *Out of the Crisis*

Table of Contents

List of Figures and Tables . . . . *xvii*
Foreword . . . . *xix*
Preface . . . . *xxi*
Acknowledgements. . . . . *xxv*

Chapter 1   Introduction. **1**
   Purpose of the Book 1
   Foundation of the International Team Excellence Process 7
   When to Use the Team Excellence Framework 8
   Why Use the Team Excellence Framework? 8
      Improve the Level and Consistency of Improvement
         Teams' Results 8
      Improve the Level of Employee Engagement 10
   Overview of the Team Excellence Framework. 11
   Which of These Organizations Are You In? 14
   Organization of the Book 15

Chapter 2   Benefits of Using the Team Excellence
   Framework. **17**
   Types of Benefits That Result from Using the Team
      Excellence Framework. 18
   Project Results and Benefits. 26
   Organization-Wide Results and Benefits 28

Chapter 3   Team Excellence Criteria. **45**
   Description of the Criteria Summary. 46
      Section 1. Project Selection and Purpose 50
      Section 2. Current Situation Analysis 51
      Section 3. Solution Development. 51

Section 4. Project Implementation and Results......... 51
Section 5. Team Management and Project
   Presentation 52
Rationale for the Criteria in Terms of Continuous
   Improvement Models and Approaches, Including
   PDC/SA and DMAIC 54
Rationale in Terms of Teamwork and Collaboration 57
The Criteria's Emphasis on Methods That Produce Good
   Results 62
Conclusion 71

Chapter 4   Team Excellence Assessment...................   73
How to Assess Project Presentations 76
   The Basic Elements of Scoring Project Presentations 76
   Understanding the Various Dimensions of the
      Criteria 77
   The Team Excellence Criteria Three Dimensions
      and Dimension Detail 77
   Exceeds Criteria—Scoring Integration and
      Cross-Linkage 82
   How to Write Effective Non-Prescriptive Actionable
      Feedback Reports (Dimension 3 of the Scoring
      Guidelines) 86
   Examples of Good Comments on Strengths and
      Opportunities for Improvement 88
How Organizations and Teams Can Best Use the
   Feedback 89
   Customers for the Feedback 89
   Sources of Feedback 90
   Understanding and Applying the Feedback Report 91
   Conclusion....................................... 92

Chapter 5   Application of the Criteria and Related Tools.....   93
How to Use the Criteria As a Project Checklist............ 94
Techniques and Tools to Meet and Exceed the Criteria....... 94
   Data and Metrics 101
   Project Management 102
   Starting New Teams 102
Best Practice Examples of Using Tools to Exceed the
   Criteria.. 102
Must-Do's for an Effective Project Presentation 112
Advice from Experienced Assessors 115
Conclusion 116

Chapter 6 Relationship of the TEF to Broader Performance Excellence Programs 117

An Integrated Enterprise System of Best Practices for
    Organizational Sustainability and Team Excellence....... 118
        Enterprise Architecture for Sustainability 119
        Enterprise Strategy for Sustainability................ 120
        Value Creation Chain Framework for Enterprise
            Sustainability 122
        Best Practices for Sustainability 123
Integrating the Framework's Use with Use of the Baldrige
    Criteria.. 125
        Organizational Profile............................. 125
        Performance System 126
        System Foundation 126
        Criterion Structure................................ 126
        Implications for Integrating the TEF into an
            Organization Using the Baldrige Criteria 128
Integrating the Framework's Use with the Shingo Prize
    Model... 129
        Implications for Integrating the TEF into an
            Organization Using the Shingo Model.............. 131
Integrating the Framework's Use with ISO 9001:2008
    for Quality and Standardized Processes 131
        ISO 9001:2008 Quality Management System........... 132
        ISO 9001:2008 Clauses............................ 133
        Implications for Integrating the TEF into an
            Organization Using ISO 9001:2008 134
Integrating the Framework's Use with Information and
    Knowledge Management Using Integrated Enterprise
    Management System Software 134
        Implications for Integrating the TEF into an
            Organization Using Enterprise Resource Planning
            Systems...................................... 135
Integrating the Framework's Use with Metrics, Key
    Performance Indicators, Balanced Scorecards, and
    Dashboards...................................... 136
        Activity-Based Costing 136
        Performance Data 137
        Performance Metrics.............................. 137
        Key Performance Indicators 137
        Balanced Scorecard............................... 137
        Dashboard 138

Implications for Integrating the TEF into an
Organization Using Various Metrics 138
Conclusion..................................... 139

Chapter 7 The ITEA Process............................ 141
History 142
Why Enter an ITEA-Sponsored Event? 142
Why Attend an ITEA-Sponsored Event? 145
Description of the Structure........................... 145
The International-Wide Process 146
Regional Showcase Recognition Programs 147
Education Team Excellence Recognition (ETER)
Program 149
Recognition....................................... 150
Recognition Received from Participating in the
International-Wide Events 151
Recognition Received by Participating in Regional
Showcase Events............................... 152
Connecting Internal and External Team Recognition 154
Other Opportunities for Participation 156
Learn from Participating Teams 157
Volunteer to Support the Assessment and Recognition
Process 157
Volunteer As a Judge.............................. 158
Volunteer in Program Administration. 159
Volunteer to Provide Sponsorship and Other Support 160
Conclusion..................................... 160

Chapter 8 Next Steps 161
Organizations New to Either CI Methodology or the Use
of Teams.. 162
Organizations Already Using Teams Equipped with
Systematic CI Methodology.......................... 165
Organizations Recognized as High in Overall
Performance Excellence 168
Closing Thoughts on the Merits of Promoting Team
Excellence 170

**Appendix A International Team Excellence Award
Process—Criteria 173**

**Appendix B International Team Excellence Award
Process: Scoresheet Example.......................... 187**

Appendix C   Assessment Worksheet and Scoring Guidelines **191**

Appendix D   Assessment Team's Consensus Scoresheet **201**

Glossary of Terms and Acronyms *203*
References *213*
Index. *219*

List of Figures and Tables

Figure 1.1	When the team excellence framework is most beneficial.	4
Table 1.1	Major reasons that improvement teams fail.	9
Figure 1.2	Team excellence framework components.	11
Figure 1.3	Putting it all together: a standardized, systematic organizational approach to team projects.	13
Table 3.1	International Team Excellence Award (ITEA) criteria (2011).	47
Figure 3.1	Cycle of continuous improvement—PDC/SA.	55
Figure 3.2	DMAIC model.	56
Figure 4.1	Criterion 3 × 3 dimension tree.	74
Table 4.1	Criteria Summary example.	78
Figure 4.2	Criteria process flow.	79
Figure 4.3	Criteria progressive structure.	80
Table 4.2	Assessment option score for item requirements.	82
Figure 4.4	Assessment notes and scoresheet.	83
Table 4.3	Alternate scoring method.	84
Figure 4.5	Assessment panel consensus scoresheet.	85
Table 5.1	Team Excellence Criteria as a project planning and management checklist.	95
Table 5.2	ASQ quality tool kit.	96
Table 5.3	DMAIC-V methodology and aligned quality tools.	97
Table 5.4	Lean tools.	100
Figure 5.1	PowerPoint slide example.	113
Figure 6.1	Enterprise architecture for sustainability.	119

Figure 6.2	Enterprise strategy for sustainability.	121
Figure 6.3	Enterprise sustainability tree.	122
Figure 6.4	Best practice systems for organizational sustainability.	124
Figure 6.5	Baldrige framework.	125
Table 6.1	Baldrige categories and items.	127
Figure 6.6	Shingo Prize model.	130
Table 6.2	Shingo Prize criteria categories and items.	132
Figure 6.7	ISO 9001:2008 framework.	134
Figure 6.8	Enterprise system framework.	135
Table 7.1	Summary of Showcases: feeder programs in the ITEA Process.	148
Table 7.2	Organizations with ITEA Gold Award–winning teams 1985–2011.	153

Foreword

I just love "how-to" books and books that assemble lots of related materials and package them in one place for easy reference and access. Laurie and Vern have done just that for *team excellence*, which is a favorite subject of mine. They cite many organizations that are benchmark organizations with regard to team excellence, including the Boeing C-17 program with which I am very familiar, having been there from 1991 until 2000. In 1992 we were introduced to *employee involvement* (EI), often called *employee engagement* elsewhere, as achieved through the development of a team-based culture. As evidence that it still exists today, it fills me with pride to see C-17 teams still well represented at ASQ's World Conferences, 20 years later, as part of the International Team Excellence Award (ITEA) competition and still receiving awards! This demonstrates the power of teams, EI and *continuous improvement* (CI) in helping to sustain high performance in organizations over long periods. As quoted by Laurie and Vern in their book, the C-17 team developed a wonderful relationship with the United Auto Workers union, in my opinion, all attributable to EI and the team-based culture.

The foundation of the approach to team excellence is the Team Excellence Framework (TEF), which is the subject of this book. While the concepts involved in the TEF appear simple, as with many CI methodologies, following them requires lots of hard work plus the all-important leadership to get it started and to sustain it. The authors provide compelling evidence to help leaders understand why it should be used, including both verbiage as well as extensive case studies. Universally, team excellence improves business outcomes, internal operations, and my all-time favorite, organizational culture! The authors go on to explain the Criteria, how it can and should be used, and how it can facilitate integration with other initiatives including Baldrige, Shingo, and enterprise and performance management systems, which avoids the issue of using it as a stand-alone program, and how to assess organizations against it. Its versatility allows it to be used to facilitate project planning, and integration with ASQ quality and CI tools. And lastly, but not least, they address how to seek external recognition through the ITEA Process to further drive CI and culture. As with many initiatives, it is often difficult to know how to get started. The authors have anticipated this and provide "next steps" for beginners, practitioners, and high-performing teams!

I encourage you to read, enjoy, study, and learn from this book, and go forth and empower your teams to lead you and your organization to world-class results.

—E. David Spong

ASQ Past President

Former president of Aerospace Support
for Boeing Integrated Defense Systems,
and former vice president and general manager
of Airlift and Tanker Programs for Boeing
Military Aircraft and Missile Systems

Preface

In this book we provide a valuable approach to implement and enhance the way to use teams of people to make improvements in your organization. The Team Excellence Framework has been proven over many years to vastly increase an organization's success rate with improvement projects done by teams. Its unique focus is the subject of teams that are assigned improvement projects. The framework's foundation is the American Society for Quality's International Team Excellence Award Process. As such, its effectiveness has been validated through 25 years of use by thousands of teams in a wide diversity of organizations. While the framework was initially developed to support an external recognition program, it has become much more broadly useful as a guide for improvement teams. This framework can be used by anyone associated with improvement teams at any organizational level and from any type of organization. In this book we cover the three essential elements for its use: why to use it, how to apply it, and how to integrate its use into your organization.

Assigning a team to do an improvement project represents a significant investment, and many organizations have had mixed returns on this investment. Teams that have effectively used the Team Excellence Framework to guide their improvement projects have consistently achieved extraordinary benefits for their organizations.

VOICES

In organizations, voices come from everywhere, giving us requirements and suggestions for change. To stay in business we must listen and decide how to respond. High-performing organizations exceed those demands. Average organizations meet them. Organizations that do not respond adequately fade into history with a bang or a whimper.

These voices come from three major sources:

- *Voice of the customer* (VOC)—Those who receive the organization's products and services.
- *Voice of the business* (VOB)—Those who "own" the organization in some form, such as shareholders, boards of directors, taxpayers who fund government organizations.
- *Voice of the employees* (VOE)—Those who execute the organization's work.

These voices are rarely in harmony. In fact, they are sometimes a cacophony representing conflicting demands. Customers of healthcare services want diagnoses from state-of-the-art test equipment, but owners are reluctant to take the hit on profits and share value from having to discard functional equipment for more expensive devices. Customers want cheap energy, but employees do not want exposure to safety hazards of deep mining and drilling. Employees want job security, but owners want to maintain staffing flexibility to adjust to market demands. To further complicate matters, harmony is sometimes lacking within these voice sources. Some customers want the same product but at a cheaper price, while others want the organization to discontinue the existing product in favor of the latest gee-whiz model. Some employees want to forgo pay raises for more vacation time, and some do not. And so it goes. If you come home after a particularly hard day at work, chances are it is as a result of such challenges.

CONTINUOUS IMPROVEMENT

What these voices tell us changes over time, and they usually increase their expectations and demands. This is known as progress! In today's global marketplace, there is no geographic or market niche immune to competitive pressure. So, continuous improvement is a requirement of every organization. The quality revolution, with its genesis in the contributions of intellectual giants such as Walter Shewhart, W. Edwards Deming, Joseph Juran, and Kaoru Ishikawa, has blessed our world with knowledge about how to effectively analyze and improve any process, product, or service. This body of knowledge has had major positive impacts on customer satisfaction, operating efficiency, and/or quality of work life everywhere that it has properly been used.

TEAMWORK

Important improvement challenges can rarely be met by a single person; it takes a team. One reason for this is that the voices are rarely in alignment, so all the significant, relevant stakeholders must be represented in developing and implementing a particular improvement. The other is that engagement of employees in continuous improvement has become a distinct competitive advantage. The difference in organizational performance over time between having an engaged versus a complacent workforce is profound. One means to engage employees is to assign them to improvement teams. A team is a very special entity, and a high-performing team is an entity to be truly cherished. It is important to note that all teams are groups (two or more people), but all groups are not teams. All too often, a manager labels a group a "team" when it is anything but.

In this book we explain the Team Excellence Framework in terms of its three major components: the criteria, the assessment process against the criteria, and assessment methodology and feedback. Throughout the book we also provide numerous examples of resulting real-world project experiences and successes of those using the framework.

Both of us have been associated with use of the Team Excellence Framework for over a decade, initially through the California Team Excellence Award program. As long-time quality and performance improvement professionals, we have repeatedly seen firsthand the power of this framework. We have seen the business results it has produced. Equally important, we have seen the extraordinary impact it has had on team members, some of whom have never before been meaningfully engaged in their workplaces. There is a transformational impact from allowing employees to apply the full capacity of their intellect, skills, and knowledge as part of teams to solve important organizational problems and succeed in doing so. We have observed this impact countless times, and each instance is compelling. When done properly, improvement teams are truly win–win scenarios. We believe that, after reading the best practice success stories included in this book, you too will be impressed.

Acknowledgements

First, we want to acknowledge the dedication of ASQ's International Team Excellence Award Process staff and volunteer committee members for making the program such a success. Over the years they have contributed countless hours developing and refining the program criteria and running a highly professional and beneficial award program. Similarly, we want to acknowledge the dedication of the volunteer members of the California Team Excellence Award Council and the volunteer members of the Board of the California Council for Excellence for its continuing success.

We thank all those who talked to us during the time we wrote this book, sharing their observations, experiences, and advice. Their particular contributions are captured in the book.

We especially want to thank the following people for their significant input: Geetha Balagopal, Jim Bianchetta, Barry Bickley, Mindy Corcoran, Eugene Kirsch, Patti Trapp, Glenn Walters, and Michael Whisman.

We also want to express appreciation for the encouragement of several ASQ Presidents, past and present: Peter Andres, Deborah Hopen, Jerry Mairani, James Rooney, and E. David Spong.

1
Introduction

The Team Excellence Framework (TEF) is a proven way for teams to consistently perform excellent improvement projects. This framework enables organizations to harness the power that comes from coupling teamwork with systematic continuous improvement methodology. People who have effectively used this framework attest to how helpful it is in improving organizational results as well as employee engagement. Most leaders would prefer an engaged workforce over a complacent one, but they often struggle with the means to accomplish it. The TEF has been validated over many years by positive outcomes from team improvement projects. It has evolved to become the international standard that defines excellence in team-based improvement projects. High achievement against the TEF's criteria is recognized as world-class, best practice performance. The TEF is useful to anyone involved in team-based improvement, including management; team sponsors, champions, leaders, facilitators, and members; and continuous improvement support staff. Because the framework is generic, it applies to all types of organizations and work.

One of its many advantages is that the TEF criteria are written at several levels of detail. This allows organizations to tailor their use to their organization's level of competency in using improvement teams to drive organizational results. Moreover, because it is generic, the option exists to tailor it to your particular business sector with relevant language.

PURPOSE OF THE BOOK

The purpose of this book is to explain the TEF and how to leverage it to ensure the success of your improvement teams. This framework is based on the approach developed by the International Team Excellence Award (ITEA) Process. Established in 1985, the process is run under the auspices of the American Society for Quality (ASQ). It has a long-standing track record of providing the means by which teams can produce highly successful outcomes for their organizations.

Primary ways to benefit from the Team Excellence Framework. The framework itself offers three ways to benefit:

- *Guide.* Use it as a guide for teams doing improvement projects.

- *Assessment.* Use it to objectively assess completed projects.

- *Feedback.* Use it to provide feedback to improve how future projects are done and the competency of employees to do so.

The framework's criteria are "A world-class systematic guide to successful team-based projects" (Whisman and Levenhagen 2011). Improvement teams that have effectively employed these criteria to guide their projects have achieved extraordinary results.

Benefits come in the form of improved customer satisfaction, mission accomplishment, cost, timeliness, product quality, employee quality of work life, employee commitment to the organization's values, and other results important to the organization's goals. They also come in the form of significant impacts on team member engagement, skills, and overall motivation.

Organizations can use this framework to great advantage, apart from any decision to involve their teams in an external assessment. However, ASQ's ITEA Process also offers the opportunity for external assessment, recognition, and benchmarking for your improvement teams. Therefore, one of the TEF's strongest points is that it has been validated by the superior project accomplishments of teams that have scored high in ASQ's objective assessment process. These teams' approaches and results, as you will learn in this book, speak for themselves. Employing the framework can give your organization results of the caliber demonstrated by these highly successful teams.

Secondary ways to benefit from the Team Excellence Framework. These benefits derive from the fact that ASQ has documented many of these successful projects in the form of PowerPoint presentations and written case studies. At its annual conference it also offers an opportunity to hear team presentations and network with team members:

- *Education.* Exposing employees to this knowledge base provides them information about more tools, new and better ways to use them, and better ways to engage team members. It opens up their minds to new possibilities and perspectives.

- *Benchmarking.* The ITEA's highest-scoring, award-winning teams serve as validated best practice examples. Exposing employees to these projects provides them with tangible examples of what constitutes world-class team improvement projects. They can see how others have used approaches and tools that have enabled those organizations to generate outstanding results. Benchmarking provides value from learning how these organizations and their teams performed their projects and also from seeing the gaps between how you are doing your projects and how world-class projects are done.

In Box 1.1 and Box 1.2 are case examples from leaders who have supported widespread use of the TEF in their organizations and achieved major organizational benefits as a result. Case studies have been written describing some of their many projects (Kryzkowki 2010; Adrian 2007; Adrian 2008a; Edmund 2009; Adrian 2008c; Krzykowski 2011).

BOX 1.1: A TOP LEADERSHIP PERSPECTIVE FROM A MANUFACTURING ORGANIZATION IN THE UNITED STATES—THE BOEING COMPANY

Boeing's Airlift and Tanker Program that produces the C-17 aircraft has won more awards from the ITEA Process than any other organization, defining it as a benchmark in team excellence. Four successive top leaders of this large organization have used teams to perform improvement projects as a major means to drive business results: Donald Kozlowski, David Spong, Howard Chambers, and David Bowman. The C-17 aircraft was a breakthrough in aerospace technology, being a large transport with very short requirements for takeoff and landing, including on unpaved landing strips, enabling it access to many more locations than other large transports. It has been instrumental in thousands of missions for national security and humanitarian relief around the world. In 1998 the organization won the Malcolm Baldrige National Quality Award.

In 2001 when Howard Chambers was placed in the top job as vice president and general manager, he was confronted with a new and daunting business reality. While the U.S. Air Force customer was very happy with the C-17's performance, they could not afford to buy more at the existing price. Boeing and the Air Force negotiated a new contract at a 25% price reduction accompanied by strict delivery schedule requirements. To add pressure, the contract was *firm fixed price*, meaning if the cost or schedule requirements were missed, the penalties would be subtracted from Boeing's profit margin. This extraordinarily ambitious target required major efficiency gains. Chambers believed there was only one way to reach this target. "It required every piece of ingenuity that existed throughout the whole workforce. That meant we had to get everyone jumping in the boat, all rowing at the same angle and in unison. They all had the same goal—get the cost out of the production process" (Chambers, pers. comm.).

Upon his arrival, the organization had already established the two basic elements shown in Figure 1.1—continuous improvement (CI) and teamwork. They had programs to perform CI and also to create a team-based organization through employee involvement, meaning that the entire organization from top to bottom was to consist of teams. The need for cost reduction was his burning platform to spur faster deployment of these programs and integrate them. The TEF proved to be a perfect vehicle to do so. The organization came upon the framework through its affiliation with the California Council for Excellence, which sponsors the California Team Excellence Award program. After his organization used the TEF with selected improvement projects and got excellent results, Chambers required all teams to use the TEF's criteria to guide their improvement projects. He sold the concept internally with the rationale that using the TEF involves benchmarking. This gave him assurance that all teams were applying best practice requirements in accomplishing their projects. This meant the framework was applied to hundreds of improvement projects each year, and that practice has continued to the present. According to Rick Payne, Manufacturing Analyst who is the coordinator for the organization's team improvement projects (based on a

Team Excellence Framework

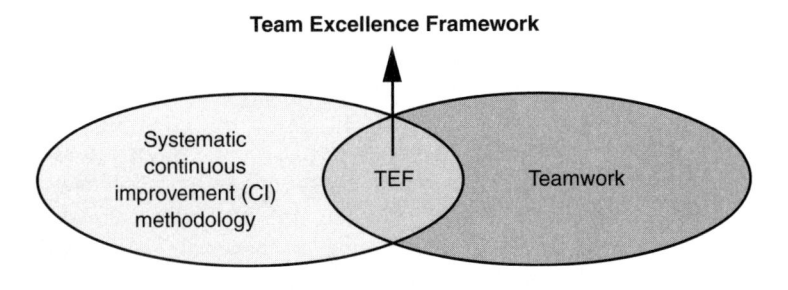

Systematic continuous improvement (CI) methodology — TEF — Teamwork

Figure 1.1 When the team excellence framework is most beneficial.

program called "Lean Plus" at Boeing), at any given time there are about 600 improvement projects underway. He and his predecessor, Ed Schaniel, have been instrumental in ensuring use of the TEF by all the teams. Payne attributes their organization's significant results from team-based improvement to consistent leadership support. The top leadership support filtered down to other senior leaders such as Don Pitcher, who affirmed that his reason for using the TEF is business success. "We have experienced so much success that, whenever we have a problem, we use it" (Pitcher, pers. comm.).

The business results of this story speak for themselves. The contract was fulfilled on time and within budget. This is not quite the end of the story, however. According to Chambers, "To get good performance you need people who think highly of themselves." Achieving success is a guaranteed way to get people to think highly of themselves. Success is made possible by having a team use CI methodology with the TEF as a guide. A striking example of this principle is to watch a shop floor team professionally present and defend a sophisticated business case to top management when, up to that point, their work was focused on turning wrenches or calibrating equipment. At the same time there were transformative effects on the culture, moving it from a functional organization to an entirely team-based organization and ingraining CI as a core expectation (Chambers, pers. comm.). It is a testament to the power of leaders, such as Howard Chambers and his colleagues, to transform the self-concepts of their workforce and the culture of their organization.

BOX 1.2: A TOP LEADERSHIP PERSPECTIVE FROM A SERVICE COMPANY IN ARGENTINA—TELEFONICA/MOVISTAR

Telefonica is a large mobile phone service company that has emerged as a benchmark in team excellence, as evidenced by winning Gold-level ITEA awards in 2010 and 2011. Eduardo Caride, President of Chile, Columbia, Argentina, Uruguay, Peru, and Ecuador Mobile and Landline Operations, is the top leader responsible for mobile and landline operations in these countries. He has fully supported his company's involvement with the International Team Excellence Award, including their teams' use of the TEF.

According to Mr. Caride (pers. comm.):

Many times we ask ourselves, which is the thing we most care about in our jobs? Why we do what we do? Every morning, everyone wakes up with the intention of giving their best! If we look back to our best experiences at work, many people mention that those experiences are related to our pride of doing things the right way! That our work is important for someone. That our organization is recognized for dedicating its best effort to improve things. One way we imagined to spread that spirit in the whole company was "seeding" a great number of improvement projects, where lots of people can participate and help to have a better company. The ITEA competition and our national team competition are important milestones that help us generate the will to participate and enthusiasm to show the great effort we are doing to Argentina and the world. Besides the teams that compete every year, there are lots that make their best [effort] to qualify for the competitions, developing their projects for more than one year, enjoying the same team and fair competition spirit. I think the results obtained reinforce to us the importance of doing things the right way, and change others we don't like. Ultimately, we get proud of our work and we feel part of an organization that focuses on improvement every day.

Luciana Barrera, Quality Director of Telefonica Group, Argentina, has also been instrumental in encouraging and supporting involvement in team excellence:

Actively participating in the ITEA competition with the world's best improvement teams challenges us more every day. I'm really proud to see how our teams prepare and improve their projects' presentation quality to represent Telefonica Group and Argentina. Dedicating time to prepare different projects for the ITEA competition drove us to review different important aspects of our quality program. For example, the structure and rigor to identify different stakeholders and assure their involvement and commitment through all the projects. Personal and group development of all team members through the project and ITEA competition preparation process reinforces my commitment with the Quality program (Barrera 2011, pers. comm.).

Matias Gadda-Thompson, Improvement and Innovation Chief for Telefonica, shared that the company had embarked on a vigorous program using the DMAIC model a number of years before becoming aware of the TEF. However, once they started using it, they realized how well the framework complemented and strengthened what they were doing in CI and building teamwork: "We found the TEF very helpful. For example, one error we were commonly making was to wait until the end of the project to involve stakeholders. Using the TEF has helped us avoid that mistake." The company does many team improvement projects each year, and the TEF is now embedded in its training program for its Six Sigma belts. It has helped move the company culture away from competition and toward collaboration (Gadda-Thompson and Barerra 2010). He attributes its spread to top leadership, who has deployed it and invested significantly in formally recognizing teams that have used the framework to greatest benefit for the company (Gadda-Thompson, pers. comm.).

FOUNDATION OF THE INTERNATIONAL TEAM EXCELLENCE PROCESS

The particular strength of the TEF is that its represents the foundation of the ITEA Process. As such, the framework has been continuously improved and validated by recognized experts on the subject of team-based improvement projects over many years. The ITEA Committee, made up of ASQ member volunteers, collaborates with ASQ in managing the ITEA Process. Their vision is to "support ASQ in making the ITEA Process *the* world recognized program for benchmarking excellence in teams," and their mission is to "achieve the ITEA Vision by continually improving the ITEA Process with the support of the ASQ staff" (Geetha Balagopal, pers. comm.). According to Eugene Kirsch, Chair of the ITEA Committee, the TEF provides an easy-to-understand, practical approach for management and teams to use, one which helps them learn not only the requirements for team-based improvement projects but also "why" these requirements exist (Kirsch, pers. comm.).

ASQ provides detailed information about the ITEA Process through its website and the process administrator. The web address is http://wcqi.asq.org/team-competition/index.html. This website is directly accessible to the public; you do not have to be an ASQ member to access any of this content.

WHEN TO USE THE TEAM EXCELLENCE FRAMEWORK

The TEF is useful when both of the following conditions apply, and Figure 1.1 reinforces this point graphically:

1. The problem or process to be tackled is sufficiently complex that a systematic CI methodology should be applied. Most significant problems in today's world are complex ones. However, some issues are simple enough to have obvious solutions. In the language of Lean Six Sigma (LSS) these are called "Just Do Its" and do not warrant detailed analysis.

2. The issue to be tackled requires more than a single individual or a simple group. In today's complex world many, but not all, issues require a team of people. An important point to note is that a team is always a group, but a group is not necessarily a team.

Another way of expressing these conditions is (see Figure 1.1):

$$\text{Team excellence} = \text{Systematic continuous improvement methodology} + \text{Teamwork}$$

WHY USE THE TEAM EXCELLENCE FRAMEWORK?

Let's face facts. Assigning a formal team of people to do an improvement project that requires CI methodology poses an organizational risk. Will this substantial investment pay off?

Improve the Level and Consistency of Improvement Teams' Results

When leadership assigns a team of people to do an improvement project, one of three things happens with the team:

- It produces a positive *return on investment* (ROI).
- It breaks even.
- It produces a negative ROI.

Leaders need a way to reduce the risk of teams producing marginal or negative project ROI. According to Brian Joiner (1994, 203), the hallmark of a rapidly improving organization is that it is capable of "improving how we improve." The TEF provides a means to do just that.

How many ways do improvement teams fail? More than we can cover here, but Table 1.1 summarizes some major ones. If you have had extensive experience with improvement teams, chances are you have observed one or more of these situations and perhaps could even add to this list. Beyond just avoiding project failures, however, using the TEF enables organizations that already have consistently successful projects to do even better.

- The project was selected in a vacuum.
- The project team was not given clear responsibility and accountability.
- The solution did not address the observed gap.
- The team did not plan the implementation of the solution well.
- The results were not sustained—either from resistance or poor systems.
- There was a loss of support and buy-in due to poor communication within the team or to stakeholders.
- The project was considered a special assignment, not an integral part of the job.
- Participants were not given enough (or any) dedicated work time or other necessary resources to adequately execute their project. Management's expectation is that the effort must come "out of hide."
- Participants were assembled and labeled a team when in fact they were only a group. As a result, they worked at cross-purposes, had low mutual trust, and engaged in implicit or explicit "blame game" behaviors.
- The project became primarily the responsibility of one person in the group.
- The purpose of the project leader was primarily to obtain a certification, meeting some mandated requirement.
- At a given project stage, the team skipped one or more requirements for success. Management let the team move to the next stage, either out of ignorance or for expediency's sake—hoping for the best.
- The team's hard work was not recognized, rewarded, or celebrated.

Table 1.1 Major reasons that improvement teams fail.

Note: The first six reasons on this list are taken from Whisman and Levenhagen (2011).

Improve the Level of Employee Engagement

An engaged employee is one who is committed, collaborative, competent, and excited. How many employees in your organization are committed to improving organizational results versus simply compliant to management direction? How many work collaboratively by building relationships with others to achieve mutual success versus working just to build their own success? How many are continuously improving their professional competency levels versus stagnating? How many feel excited and even inspired by working in your organization? How many have fun while working hard to meet a challenging goal? Lindborg (2011, 58) shared the definition of employee engagement from the U.S. Baldrige Performance Excellence Program as "the extent of workforce commitment, both emotional and intellectual, to accomplishing the work, mission, and vision of the organization." In his book on the famous Toyota Production System, Liker (2003, 6) points out that Toyota's extraordinary capacity in using lean and other quality tools to achieve operational excellence "stems from a deeper business philosophy based on its understanding of people and human motivation. Its success is ultimately based on its ability to cultivate leadership, teams, and culture, to devise strategy, to build supplier relationships, and to maintain a learning organization."

With respect to using the TEF specifically, it has important impacts beyond simply making each of your improvement projects successful. It also affects those employees who participate in teams, sometimes profoundly. For most people, being associated with an improvement team is a memorable experience. Being associated with one that employed good CI methodology and used true teamwork, thereby achieving a successful project outcome, makes people more committed, collaborative, competent, and excited. However, being associated with a team whose results do not justify the effort, or a group that never coalesced into a mutually supportive team, is an experience no one wants to repeat. Most importantly, the members' work colleagues will hear about their experiences with improvement projects. If their experiences were good, employee engagement will spread. If their experiences were poor, employees will avoid getting involved with improvement teams. This book contains examples of how using the TEF supported achievement of these conditions that constitute employee engagement.

What is an improvement team? With respect to the definition of a team, there are many academic definitions. According to Katzenbach and Smith (1994), "A *team* is a small number of people with complementary skills who are committed to a common purpose, performance goals, and approach for which they hold themselves mutually accountable." For our purposes we define an *improvement team* as one that has been assigned a commonly understood objective, assumes mutual accountability, and applies teamwork skills of mutual trust and support to achieve that objective. To further explain an important point made above, not every group (two or more people working together on a task) in the workplace is a team. In fact, many of them are not, which is why genuine collaboration is in such short supply in organizations.

There is no hard line between when a group can be considered a true team or not. Also, there is a continuum between being a basic team (one whose members demonstrate the basics of teamwork) and one often referred to as a *high-performance team* (HPT). The organization must invest resources to turn a group into a basic team, and even more resources to develop them into an HPT. It is also very important to note that not every problem requires a team to tackle it. Sometimes a group or even a single individual is adequate. However, if the circumstances do require it, which is the case for most improvement projects, then the TEF gives guidance about some of the necessary conditions that must be addressed. Teams produce both tangible and intangible results for the organization, but they also produce transformative intangible impacts on team members and their supporting management. There are several types of improvement teams. Some are permanent entities while some are temporary. Some work within functional areas while others are cross-functional. The TEF is applicable no matter what the type of improvement team.

OVERVIEW OF THE TEAM EXCELLENCE FRAMEWORK

The TEF comprises three components, and Figure 1.2 illustrates this composition:

1. The *criteria* for achieving project success. See Table 3.1 in Chapter 3 for the Criteria Summary and Appendix A for the full version of the criteria.

2. The *assessment* method to objectively determine the extent to which the criteria were met.

Criteria	Assessment methodology	Non-prescriptive feedback

Figure 1.2 Team excellence framework components.

3. The *feedback* method to enable teams and their organizations to continuously enhance how they do improvement projects.

These components are described and explained in Chapters 3, 4, and 5. Here we provide a summary description. The basic logic behind these components is simple. In order to improve human performance on any task, one must take three fundamental actions:

1. Describe the specific *expectations* for the task. This includes both what constitutes a successful outcome and what behaviors are required to achieve that outcome.

2. *Assess* their performance against these specific expectations.

3. Provide them actionable *feedback* on how they performed relative to the expectations for outcomes and behaviors.

The TEF components directly reflect these three actions:

1. The *criteria* describe expectations for doing a successful improvement project, both in achieving positive project outcomes and in the behaviors based on CI and teamwork required to produce those positive outcomes. Figure 1.3 provides a useful schematic describing the major sections of the criteria and how they fit together, which was presented by Michael Whisman and Michael Levenhagen (2011).

2. The *assessment* method is an objective and valid way to evaluate how well a project team addressed each of the criteria.

3. The *feedback* method provides information to the team and its organization on how the team addressed each of the criteria, both the aspects in which they did well (strengths) and aspects on which they could have done better (opportunities for improvement). Its purpose is to enable the organization to continuously improve its success by using improvement teams.

The framework's criteria are deliberately non-prescriptive. In other words, the criteria do not require the use of specific tools or techniques to satisfy what is stated. This enables teams to apply the particular techniques and tools that are most appropriate to their projects. In this way the criteria are analogous to the Baldrige National Quality Program's Criteria for Performance Excellence (http://www.nist.gov/baldrige/index.cfm). The Baldrige criteria consist of non-prescriptive items that guide an organization's journey toward achieving overall organizational excellence. Both frameworks are based on state-of-the-art knowledge. The TEF's criteria are based on

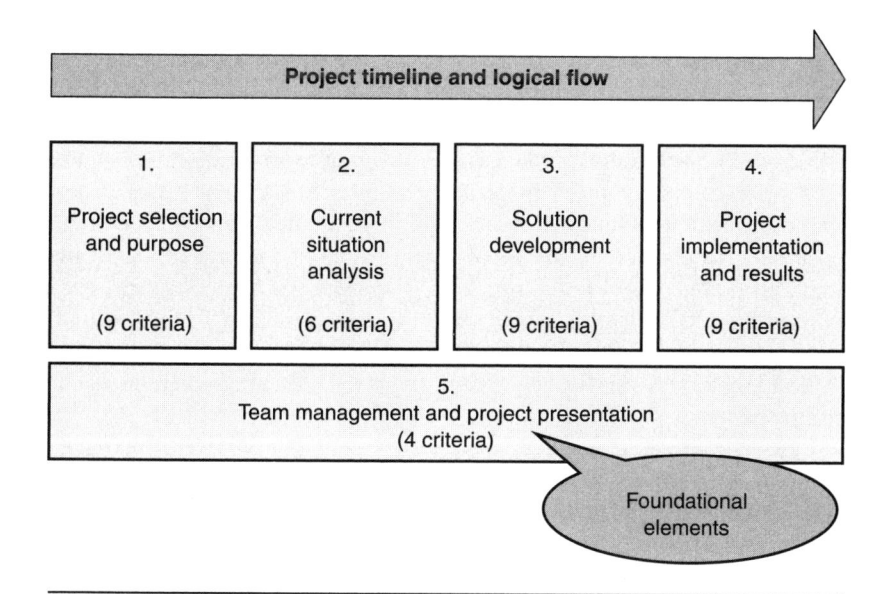

```
┌─────────────────────────────────────────────────────┐
│         Project timeline and logical flow  ──▶      │
└─────────────────────────────────────────────────────┘

┌──────────────┐ ┌──────────────┐ ┌──────────────┐ ┌──────────────┐
│      1.      │ │      2.      │ │      3.      │ │      4.      │
│              │ │              │ │              │ │              │
│   Project    │ │   Current    │ │   Solution   │ │   Project    │
│  selection   │ │  situation   │ │ development  │ │implementation│
│ and purpose  │ │   analysis   │ │              │ │ and results  │
│              │ │              │ │              │ │              │
│ (9 criteria) │ │ (6 criteria) │ │ (9 criteria) │ │ (9 criteria) │
└──────────────┘ └──────────────┘ └──────────────┘ └──────────────┘

┌─────────────────────────────────────────────────────┐
│                        5.                           │
│     Team management and project presentation        │
│                   (4 criteria)                      │
└─────────────────────────────────────────────────────┘
                                      ( Foundational elements )
```

Figure 1.3 Putting it all together: a standardized, systematic organizational approach to team projects.
Source: Used with permission, Whisman and Levenhagen, 2011.

the knowledge in two areas, CI and teamwork, while the Baldrige criteria are based on the knowledge about organizational excellence and improvement. Another similarity is that both frameworks include a professional methodology for assessing the extent to which the criteria have been met.

It is important to note that since the TEF is non-prescriptive, it accommodates the use of any of the conventional CI analytic models or any systematic approach that makes sense for the project. CI methodology is based on some type of improvement model or approach. Commonly used generic models/approaches include define–measure–analyze–improve–control (DMAIC) from LSS, plan–do–check/study–act (PDC/SA), total quality control (TQC) (Ishikawa 1985), total quality management (TQM) (Besterfield, Besterfield-Michna, Besterfield, Besterfield-Sacre, 2003), theory of constraints (TOC) (Goldratt 2004), balanced scorecard (Kaplan and Norton 1996), or some combination. Many organizations have developed their own tailored methodology based on the logic of one or more of these generic approaches.

In summary, the TEF can be applied proactively as a guide for teams in executing projects, retroactively as a company internal self-assessment tool to evaluate the projects, and, ideally, both ways.

WHICH OF THESE ORGANIZATIONS ARE YOU IN?

An organization new to either CI methodology or the use of teams. The TEF offers you the perfect opportunity to get off on the right foot. It provides an ideal first step. Applying it as guidance for all your teams will ensure that you avoid mistakes that organizations and their teams typically make in doing improvement projects. It enables you to start small, even with a single team, and not overcommit to an expansive CI program until several teams have consistently generated positive results. The feedback given to the first team will be particularly valuable in improving the results for the next team, and so forth.

An organization already using teams equipped with systematic CI methodology. If you are in this situation, then chances are good that you have attained some project successes. However, chances are also good that you have had some teams that have achieved mediocre results and/or projects that had to be abandoned or rescued along the way. Using the TEF will substantially improve the success rate of your teams as well as enhance the value of the results they generate. Since the TEF is generic and easily accommodates use of a variety of CI approaches, no change in your CI approach is necessary. This is further explained in Chapter 3. More importantly, the framework enables you to overcome some of the cultural barriers so typical to attaining widespread acceptance of the power of CI. The history of CI initiatives is replete with ones that come and then go because they were dependent on the backing of a few key leaders and never became institutionalized into the culture and daily work. In those cases, when key leaders turn over, CI sometimes loses its priority. Since the quality revolution outside Japan began in 1980, many organizations have gone through two or more cycles of introducing, dropping, and reintroducing CI initiatives, usually disguised with new labels and terminology in an attempt to prevent the workforce from realizing it is based on the same concept as previous CI initiatives. (The ruse rarely works.)

An organization recognized as high in overall performance excellence. Organizations are recognized as excellent in a number of ways. One is being a sustained market leader. Another is being judged by impartial evaluators against a set of criteria, for example, performance excellence awards (the U.S. Baldrige Performance Excellence Award and its equivalent in other countries) or "best company to work for" awards. A third is being nominated by peers, for example, the Forbes list of most admired companies. One of the essential qualities of an organization that intends to sustain excellence is that it has a CI culture. It recognizes that, even though it is at the top of its game today, change from outside and inside is ever present, and it must adapt. At its essence, CI is the systematic, intelligent method of adapting. If you are in this type of organization, your leadership is always looking for ways to improve the amount and quality of its improvement efforts, that is, improving how it improves. They are also aware that one of the underpinnings of the organization's success is continuing to engage and develop its workforce, including increasing the degree to which they collaborate as teams. In a recent study of the eleven healthcare organizations that earned the Baldrige Award between 2002 and 2010 it was found that they all demonstrated high levels of collaboration, employee empowerment, and ongoing development of their people (Bodinson and Kendall 2010). Use of the TEF is a synergistic fit into this type of organization. In essence, it is a method for sustaining continuous improvement. It keeps energy and enthusiasm generating at all levels in the organization by keeping tangible and intangible improvement flowing from engaged employees. Also, this type of organization usually has employee recognition programs, and the TEF can provide an excellent supplement to them.

ORGANIZATION OF THE BOOK

This book is organized to help you first understand why the TEF is beneficial and then provide knowledge based on best practice to enable you to successfully apply it. This knowledge is derived from two major sources: experts who have been involved in improving and assessing the performance of improvement teams by using the TEF, and those who have been associated with successful teams that used the TEF.

In Chapter 2, "Benefits of Using the Team Excellence Framework: How Your Teams and Organization Can Achieve Outstanding Improvements," we go into more depth about the benefits of using the TEF. We cover how having consistently successful improvement teams has major impacts on organizational success. We describe both the tangible and intangible benefits achieved, as seen by organizational management and team champions, leaders, facilitators, and members.

In Chapter 3, "Team Excellence Criteria: How the Criteria Are Organized and Why," we cover the first of the three TEF components: the criteria. We provide the Criteria Summary that comprises the basic framework and the rationale behind it. We link the criteria to the core philosophy and models of CI, including PDC/SA and DMAIC. We also link them to the core principles of employee engagement through teamwork.

In Chapter 4, "Team Excellence Assessment: How to Score the Criteria and Provide Useful Feedback," we cover the second and third of the three

TEF components: the assessment and feedback methods. First, we show how the criteria are scored. Then we describe how assessors write useful feedback. Finally, we cover how organizations and teams can best use that feedback to benefit future improvement projects and support development of a CI culture.

In Chapter 5, "Application of the Criteria and Related Tools: How to Successfully Apply the Criteria," we describe how to apply the criteria, both the summary version and the detailed version. Included is advice from experienced assessors since the choice of appropriate tools and techniques does depend to some extent on each project. Then we explain how to choose the appropriate tools and techniques to meet the criteria.

In Chapter 6, "Relationship of the TEF to Broader Performance Excellence Programs: How Organizations Can Integrate It," we cover how to fit the use of the framework to support broader initiatives that your organization may already have for achieving overall performance excellence. This means using it synergistically with broader initiatives. Specifically, we cover integrating it with use of the Baldrige Performance Excellence framework for organizational management, Shingo Model, ISO 9001:2008—Quality management systems—Requirements for operations and process management, enterprise systems/ERP for information and knowledge management, and using metrics, key performance indicators (KPIs), balanced scorecards, and dashboards for performance management.

In Chapter 7, "The ITEA Process: How to Participate and Obtain External Recognition for Your Teams' Achievements," we cover material for those organizations that are also considering having their teams participate in ASQ's ITEA Process, which provides external assessment and recognition. We describe the ITEA's history, how it operates currently, the judging and recognition procedures, and the formal recognition given. In addition to the international-level award process, there are some Showcase programs in other countries and U.S. states that function as feeders to the international process. Some organizations also run internal team assessment and recognition programs using the TEF. Lastly, other opportunities for individuals to participate in the ITEA Process are described.

In Chapter 8, "Next Steps: How to Apply the Team Excellence Framework in Your Organization," we recommend next steps to take in using the TEF, depending on the maturity level of CI and teamwork in your organization.

In summary, using the TEF as a guide leads teams and their management sponsors to consistently high levels of success. In today's competitive global marketplace, continuous improvement of organizational results and the workforce who generates them is not optional.

2

Benefits of Using the Team Excellence Framework

How Your Teams and Organization Can Achieve Outstanding Improvements

"Free money" for the organization is one of the most compelling benefits from using the TEF, according to Peter Andres, a longtime professional in aerospace quality and past ASQ president (pers. comm.). As coach of the Ramp Operations Improvement Team at Boeing, Pete helped that team apply the criteria at each step of their project to guarantee a substantial ROI. The project was complex, involving many sub-operations. He saw numerous benefits result from using the criteria. It was a way to engage employees, motivate them by giving them a venue in which to get their ideas heard, and empower them to implement their solutions. Interestingly, he observed that it was only because the people were operating as a team that management listened to them. If the same ideas had been promulgated by a single individual, that person would have been ignored. Another advantage he saw was that it required the team to perform the cost–benefit analysis themselves, a task normally done by an outside staff group such as finance or business management. So it required the team members to consider the project from the vantage point of business, not just operations. It also required them to consider the impact on all other stakeholders. In sum, the criteria required that the team be responsible for the project from beginning to end. Andres emphasized the importance of the recognition component of team excellence. His team received great recognition from Boeing management for the outstanding results they achieved. To put the icing on the cake, the Ramp Operations Improvement Team won the Silver Medal in the 2003 ITEA Process—an external validation of their outstanding accomplishment.

In Chapter 1 we noted that management always takes a risk whenever it invests in a team to undertake an improvement project. Labor hours and other significant resources are required. Unfortunately, the world is littered with improvement projects that either did not reach their full potential or were abandoned before completion. In this chapter we first describe the

18 Chapter Two

types of benefits that accrue to organizations that use the TEF. We then describe benefits that accrue as a result of the individual projects. Finally, we describe additional ones that accrue to the overall organization. To put this chapter's message in a nutshell, an organization that systematically applies the TEF will reap the best possible impacts from its team-based improvement projects.

TYPES OF BENEFITS THAT RESULT FROM USING THE TEAM EXCELLENCE FRAMEWORK

What benefits do teams that effectively use the TEF provide their organizations?

- *Better organizational outcomes* in terms of customer satisfaction, profitability, market share, mission accomplishment, delivery times, and/or product performance and value.

- *Improved internal operations* through more efficient use of all types of resources, including human, physical, financial, technological, and intellectual.

- A *more motivating organizational culture* that includes more skilled and engaged employees who have adopted CI as a way of organizational life.

In their article "Evidence-Based Management" Pfeffer and Sutton (2006, 63) pose the following question: "Executives routinely dose their organizations with strategic snake oil, discredited nostrums, partial remedies, or untested management miracle cures. In many cases, the facts about what works are out there—so why don't managers use them?" Among other benefits, the TEF is founded on the principle of using fact- or evidence-based management. It is no wonder the teams that follow it produce consistently good results.

How would you feel to have projects that accomplished the magnitude of improvements described in Box 2.7 at the end of the chapter? These examples report the benefits from the ITEA finalist teams from 2010–2011. They are just a few examples of the outstanding results achieved by actual teams scoring high on the TEF criteria. The examples also show that the TEF has been employed by all types of organizations around the world and applied to all types of problems and processes. Many more of these examples are available on ASQ's ITEA website in the form of top-scoring presentations and case study articles. The examples show tangible and intangible benefits achieved by high-scoring improvement teams. These projects vary widely in their scope, meaning some tackled modest-sized improvement opportunities while others tackled major ones. It is sometimes said that CI comprises base hits and home runs. Base hits are the many small improvements made that, when added up, collectively have a big impact on organizational performance. Home runs are ambitious projects that take on ambitious goals. Box 2.7 at the end of the chapter contains examples of both. With respect to home runs, when was the last time you heard of the cost of attending business school dropping with no impact on program quality? Not only did the Ramaiah Institute of Management Studies project have a remarkable impact on its own educational institution, but the project's outcome also has the potential to transform the face of college-level education across all of India. Southern California Edison's team successfully guided a huge and technologically advanced system development and implementation of smart meters, impacting energy conservation in a substantial way. A Ford Motor Company team solved a very complex analytical problem in two weeks, avoiding postponement of a major new product launch. Team excellence can make the impossible possible.

In Boxes 2.1 through 2.6 we provide some expanded case examples of benefits achieved.

BOX 2.1: CASE EXAMPLE—RELIANCE INDUSTRIES LIMITED

The Reliance Industries Limited team, winner of the 2006 ITEA Gold Award, successfully tackled an important problem directly tied to the organization's mission and goals. Their compelling story highlights not only positive impact on business results but also on external stakeholders, including people in the community for whom even a small improvement in their lot makes a big difference in their survival. Reliance Industries Limited is a Fortune Global 500 company and is the largest private sector company in India. It is the flagship company of Reliance Group, with businesses in the energy and materials value chain. Reliance is the world's top polyester producer, with manufacturing facilities in India and abroad. Since Reliance is the world's largest polyester producer, the company also generates the largest quantity of polyester waste; therefore, the company also operates the largest international polyester recycling facility, which produces polyester fiberfill used for filling and stuffing applications. Of course, every effort is made to reduce the overall quantity of waste generated in the manufacturing process, but the company's use of recycled materials is an essential step in making it possible for Reliance to serve society by eliminating non-biodegradable polyester waste from the environment and converting it into value-added products. In fact, the company not only recycles its own waste but also purchases waste from external sources. In order to achieve Reliance's quality and productivity targets, the company must carefully control the materials put into the polyester production process; therefore, the quantity of recycled waste being used was trending down, and high-cost oligomer was used instead. The price of oligomer was rising in conjunction with the escalating price of crude oil, exacerbating the need to improve the quality of recycled fiber. Additionally, the poor quality of polyester waste feedstock required higher doses of high-cost toners, raising the conversion cost even more. All of these factors affected profit margins adversely, as well as reducing the company's ability to protect the environment with its recycling efforts. Product quality was slipping because of contaminated feedstock, and customer satisfaction issues were also occurring. The company was growing increasingly concerned about the problem, particularly given its mission statement, which includes the following two aspects:

- To produce polyester staple fiber and fiberfill per market requirements in the most economical way while achieving total customer satisfaction.

- To work constantly to encourage employees to develop professional competency and to accept social responsibility through the company's safety, environmental, productivity, and quality efforts.

Furthermore, Reliance's four foundational values—trust, environmental friendliness, responsible care, and ecological harmony—all supported the team's work to reduce the production cost of polyester fiberfill and maximize the use of recycled polyester waste materials (Bhatt, Dhingra, Jain, Kale, and Vakil 2006, 34–35). "The project favorably affected the company's overall business objectives. Raw materials cost dropped by 10%, usage of recycled waste increased by 15%, chemicals cost dropped by 20%, and production cost dropped by 11%. Productivity, process capability, and plant yield increased appreciably. Market complaints dropped by more than 70%, product quality increased by 3%, and product exports increased by more than 50%. Additionally, the project contributed $4 million (U.S. dollars) per annum in monetary benefits. Intangible benefits included increased awareness of stakeholders' needs, increased employee morale, and a positive effect on society. Reliance engaged in a meaningful partnership with an unorganized group of rag pickers, who would collect post-consumer use waste PET bottles for recycling. The project also had a positive effect on the community by increasing earnings of rag pickers and improving the quality of collected bottles, creating a win–win situation for all. In fact, the partnership with the rag pickers resulted in their earnings shooting up 150%! Most important, the changes improved the local environment by adding value to the littered PET non-biodegradable waste." (Bhatt, Dhingra, Jain, Kale, and Vakil 2006, 39–40)

BOX 2.2: CASE EXAMPLE—HD SUPPLY FACILITIES MAINTENANCE

The Voice of the Customer project team, winner of the 2009 ITEA Gold Award, designed a new process to address customer requirements, significantly reducing customer defects and increasing customer loyalty, at the same time saving $3 million. HD Supply Facilities Maintenance is in the service business, providing maintenance, repair, and operations for the multifamily, hospitality, and healthcare industries, so customer satisfaction is critical. The company was growing rapidly, so a major organizational goal was to not "fall into the trap of turning customers off while its business grew . . . . Before the VOC approach, there wasn't a standard procedure for what to do with customer feedback . . . . The ritual of gathering and evaluating customer data and taking action has become a 'cultural mind-shift' at HDS FM. 'VOC is part of our daily life,' Basheer said" (Edmund 2010, 51).

> *While most of HD's teams use quality tools like run charts and Pareto diagrams, Espinoza said there has been an increased awareness of another important method: root cause and defect analysis. In the past, many people were intimidated by the concept. This has now changed. "It's part of the thought process now," said Espinoza, "Everyone's thinking in terms of what the root cause problem is. I now hear the term 'root cause' and 'defect' more regularly and amongst various levels/areas in the organization than I did a few years ago." There has also been much more*

interest in benchmarking. While HD Supply-FM is a top contender in its industry, management and staff are starting to benchmark their processes against the top companies outside the industry. It has been a positive shift for the company and makes sure they are always focusing on continuous improvement (Ayesha Basheer, pers. comm.; Sheri Espinoza, pers. comm.).

BOX 2.3: CASE EXAMPLE— FIRSTSOURCE

Firstsource is a major global provider of *business process outsourcing* (BPO), offering a wide variety of services across banking and financial services, telecommunications and media, and the healthcare industry. Headquartered in Mumbai, India, it has business units located in several places around the world. This company has been a regular participant in the ITEA Process and has had numerous teams reach finalist status. A few examples of the benefits in the form of great individual project results are:

- For credit card company clients, a team significantly reduced the rate of bounced checks for their credit card company clients, saving $400K.

- For a bank client, a team improved the speed of delivering mortgages to its clients, from 69% of meeting its fourteen-day obligation to 80% of meeting its fourteen-day obligation, while continuing to meet lending standards. This achievement also brought them new clients.

- For the benefit of the company, a team significantly improved the productivity and profitability of its purchase order processing services in the healthcare industry, moving the gross profit margin from −1.5 to +1.2.

- For both the company and end users, repeat calls from the same customer for the same reason are non-value-added. A team reduced the rate of repeat calls from 15.8 % to 10%.

In addition, Firstsource has experienced a variety of organization-wide benefits. According to Nathanael Anderson, Process Excellence

Manager, using the TEF has had several organization-wide benefits. One is that it helps ensure that the projects selected are aligned to overall organizational goals, something that is especially valuable in a large, dispersed company. Second, organizational learning and improvement have been impacted. Among other things, they have linked attainment of LSS belt certifications to leading a successful team improvement project. As a result, the belt candidates learn about use of the TEF. A third benefit is standardization. As a global company, the fact that ITEA's TEF is a recognized international standard has made it easier to gain acceptance for implementing it as their internal standard team excellence framework across all their business units. A fourth benefit is replication. In some instances, the improvement has been taken from one part of the business and implemented in the same processes elsewhere (Anderson, pers. comm.).

BOX 2.4: CASE EXAMPLE—MWM INTERNATIONAL MOTORES

MWM, a wholly owned subsidiary of Navistar, produces diesel engines for the vehicular, agricultural, industrial, and marine sectors. One of their team projects, a 2009 ITEA finalist, not only improved the company's ability to purchase one particular type of part but also is an example of additional significant benefits through replication. The company recognized it had an inefficient purchasing strategy for the more than 400 different bolts used in manufacturing. The relationship between their price and the steel from which they are made is expressed in an index called *linear price performance* (LPP). By reducing LPP the team could lower waste and cost. Using a Six Sigma approach, the team went through the cycle of identifying CTQs (critical to quality factors) and root causes, and then applied design of experiments (DOE) to determine the relationships among the four root causes and LPP. They ran a simulation entailing purchasing volumes in three levels and four separate suppliers and then drafted a model, including LPPs from the suppliers' returned quotes. The team developed solutions using brainstorming, benchmarking, stakeholder interviews, and process waste assessment. Using additional methods they refined the solution set. The results were: a cost reduction of 13.6% in annual purchase price of bolts, saving almost $1 million

USD; 90% reduction in process variability; elimination of audit gaps; factoring in price reductions in the next round of price negotiations with customers; elimination of non-value-added steps, and a ten-day reduction in process lead time. "Lopes explains that the team's yearlong process improvement effort will continue to pay dividends into the future as the company applies the process to other commodities: 'With their project we found a way to optimize the results of the purchasing process, and it can be used for every kind of material purchased by MWM Interational. We are planning to replicate these analyses for other commodities to achieve a new level of quality in every purchasing process'" (Jacobsen 2009d, 4).

BOX 2.5: CASE EXAMPLE—HUMANA, INC.

Humana, Inc. offers group and individual health insurance and other associated services such as a mail-order pharmacy. It has 37,000 associates. It has entered teams in several ITEA cycles. According to Kanchan Barve and Ryan Kruer (pers. comm.), members of the Quality Engineering team, they have found that using the TEF has been a very useful supplement and complement to the strong internal structure they have been developing to support team-based CI. The results of Humana's recent teams are shown in the Box 2.7 at the end of the chapter and speak for themselves. Their Quality Engineering team is a central shared resource to deploy lean methodology and lead culture change through teaching, coaching, and facilitating. Barve points out, "Associate engagement is one of the core methods of influencing culture." They describe how the benefits of the TEF have come from using the feedback to improve and the opportunity to benchmark against other excellent teams. As a result, their standard for what they consider as team excellence has gone up. An example is that they now have adopted stakeholder involvement at every project stage as standard practice. Since the company has been acquiring other companies, it also helps that the TEF is an external validated standard, which makes it more credible to new organizational units, as well as to Humana's existing management.

BOX 2.6: CASE EXAMPLE—ANHEUSER-BUSCH INBEV METAL CONTAINER CORPORATION

Anheuser-Busch InBev's Metal Container Corporation has been using structured process improvement teams to solve problems, reduce variability, and drive innovation in its plants since 1991. A few years ago they introduced use of the TEF as a supplement to these efforts. In addition, they solicited external recognition by participating in the ITEA Process in three consecutive years, each team from a different plant. Each of these plants has fewer than 200 people. With little support staff in general, the TEF has helped guide their improvement teams to success. They have used it by constructing a checklist derived from the criteria but in a format and language easily understandable to the people on their improvement teams. According to Don MacGavin, Director Quality Systems of the Metal Container Corporation, the TEF has been useful in these plants for several reasons. One is that the criteria are generic and fit with their different types of teams. Another is that they used the criteria to identify some gaps in their team processes and made improvements based on their analysis. Yet another is being able to benchmark their team process against the best in the world. This organization has gone beyond just internal use of the TEF to also engage in the external recognition process of the ITEA as another method for recognition beyond that of their internal award process. As a result, they had significant impact on employee development. "Almost all our presenters are hourly employees from our manufacturing plants. Presenting to 50–100 people at ASQ's World Conference definitely takes them outside their comfort zone. However, over the years each person has done an outstanding job delivering their part of the presentations. This provides our teams with an opportunity to see teams from other organizations" (MacGavin, pers. comm.). Metal Container Corporation, Oklahoma City, Oklahoma, which produces in excess of 13 billion lids per year for the beverage industry, was a 2011 ITEA finalist. One of their most recent teams had project results that reduced annual maintenance costs by 20% while having no negative impact on quality or operational performance. Through continued use of improvement teams, this plant's overall operational efficiency has significantly improved over the past few years. Also, placing the hourly workforce on improvement teams has engaged them in feeling involved with the success of the business.

PROJECT RESULTS AND BENEFITS

When a team uses the criteria to guide their project, the results turn out better than if the team did not. This is because the criteria are crafted to ensure achievement of the following key elements necessary for project success:

- Selecting projects that clearly support organizational goals.
- Identifying root causes, not just symptoms.
- Selecting solutions that address root cause.
- Implementing and institutionalizing the improvements.
- Creating and managing a team, not just a group.
- Garnering adequate support from the stakeholders for the change. Stakeholders are anyone who is impacted by the improvement that is being proposed.

Benefits from improvement projects can be in the form of one or several of the benefits listed in the previous section. However, for any given project a team should focus on achieving just a subset of the types of results since one hallmark of a successful team is to set a specific goal and limit the project scope accordingly.

The criteria require that all the project's results are clearly documented in the form of tangible and intangible benefits (criterion 4Ca). Therefore, high-scoring teams make it crystal clear what benefits were realized from their project.

How do these benefits accrue from using the criteria as a guide? People experienced with the criteria agree that it helps ensure that no essential actions are overlooked during project selection, formation, or implementation:

- *Beginning-level teams* find it very helpful in holding them to a logical sequence of actions. It keeps them on the path of accepted CI practice of project phases. Often, such teams get confused about the order in which to tackle their project. A common mistake is to get lost in the weeds of measurement before very clearly defining the project goal and outcomes. Then they waste time and energy collecting data they do not need and/or in inappropriate forms. In other words, in their rush to move on with the project, they miss the forest for the trees. They do not appreciate that the "plan" or "define" stage is the foundation for any project. Like any foundation, if there are faults, it affects the rest of the project irreparably.

- *Intermediate-level teams* find it very helpful in ensuring that they do not skip any essential step. People who have used the framework frequently cite two examples. One is the requirements to validate findings at two different stages of the project. Preliminary findings provide information, but validation reduces the uncertainty of that information and thereby reduces the risk of incorrect solutions. The other is the requirements to ensure stakeholder involvement at every phase of the project in order to create stakeholder buy-in. Of all the types of requirements, this set is most often mentioned as especially beneficial. A common mistake is for a project to move forward without identifying and involving all the key stakeholders from the very outset. If at all, an attempt is made to get their buy-in right before the implementation stage. A fundamental principle of organizational behavior is as follows: *people who are affected by change support change that they have had an opportunity to create, and do not support change that someone else does to them.* This means that even highly valid project recommendations for change are sometimes rejected by key stakeholders. Human beings operate only partly on logic. Emotion, ego, and power are dynamics that also affect organizational behavior. In addition to the need for their buy-in, stakeholders can be very useful sources of ideas for improvement. Because they represent different perspectives, they have the potential to offer insightful information about the causes of the problem and also potential solutions.

- *Advanced-level teams* demonstrate very sophisticated tool sets carefully assembled to be appropriate to their particular projects. They do not use the same set of tools for each project. This makes the difference between adequate project results and outstanding ones. People associated with such teams have found that the criteria drive them to very thorough and thoughtful consideration of which tools to select during each phase of their particular project. It drives them to advanced levels of CI competency by encouraging them to learn highly advanced tools and to recognize when a simple tool is just as good or better than an advanced tool. Using the appropriate mix of tools that do not constitute analytic overkill is one hallmark of a team that scores high on the criteria.

ORGANIZATION-WIDE RESULTS AND BENEFITS

There are numerous benefits to the broader organization:

Achievement of major organization goals. This benefit accrues when an organization requires all its improvement teams to use the criteria. The collective impact of a systematic set of successful projects substantially helps achieve organization-wide goals. If a whole series of successful projects is done that address an important and complex challenge, this can be a game-changer for the organization. It also has a substantial impact on organizational culture. In other words, it is an essential element to becoming a high-performing organization.

Employee engagement. Success builds enthusiasm and competency. When an organization requires a single team to use the criteria, the members' increased engagement serves as a model that encourages both them and their colleagues to support CI. Moreover, according to Rob Bryant (2011), Senior Vice President of Quality and Lean Six Sigma, Computer Sciences Corporation, "engaged customers come from engaged employees." If employees are assigned additional team projects and continue to learn from the TEF-based feedback, they will gradually develop the capacity to be a member of not just a basic team but of an HPT. From the team members' perspective, feeling "successful" depends on two conditions. One is creating a set of excellent improvement recommendations. The other is seeing these recommendations actually implemented and the benefits come to pass. If management decides not to adopt the recommendations, they should give the team feedback as to why. However, if they approve the recommendations, they should implement them and document the improved results. Sadly, there are many instances in which management approves the team's recommendations but never fully implements them, or never even starts. So, no benefits to the organization result even though the team was recognized by management as having done an excellent job. No one wants to put forth a major effort, and be told it was an excellent job, only to see nothing happen as a result. This important condition is often overlooked, but people desire to have a positive impact on their world. "The (ITEA) program can improve the communication necessary to turn a team's recommendations into reality. Since a team rarely controls all the resources or procedures that will be affected, the approval by some set of management and other stakeholders is almost always required for the recommendations to be implemented. One of the most potent motivators for teams is to see their recommendations adopted" (Broedling 2003, 440–41). Teams also want to see the benefits that resulted. This justifies their hard work and also demonstrates their competency to others in the organization.

Organizational learning about how to better improve. Using the TEF enables the organization to learn how to better continuously improve processes and products. Because the TEF requires the assessors to provide feedback on the project's strengths and opportunities for improvement, organizational management and team members both benefit by learning lessons from those aspects where the project highly conformed to the criteria and those aspects where their project fell short. Management learns lessons to guide them in improving their policies, practices, and training regarding team-based improvement projects. Team members learn valuable lessons about how to better perform improvement projects in the future, building their competency and confidence. Also, ASQ's ITEA Process offers additional learning opportunities both through studying its database of presentations and case studies (see Chapter 1) and networking as part of its recognition process (see Chapter 7).

Organizational learning about its processes. Using the TEF enables the organization to capture, retain, and apply critical knowledge about how its processes actually work. Many organizations are too dependent on "tribal knowledge," knowledge that disappears when employees retire, leave for other organizations, or are laid off. A whole discipline called *knowledge management* has emerged to address this problem (O'Dell and Hubert 2011). Information collected from an organization's TEF-based improvement projects can be incorporated into the organization's knowledge management repositories for application in training, further process improvement, and product development.

Changing the organizational culture to ingrain improvement as a way of life. There is an extensive knowledge base on the subject of changing organizational culture to create improvements in organizational performance (Schein 2010; Cameron and Quinn 2010; Kotter 1996). One aspect of their culture many organizations would like to modify is to make continuous improvement a routine expectation rather than an ad hoc activity only instituted when there is a noticeable problem. Most organizations that do team-based improvement projects struggle with making this important transition. There is a need to move from a situation where team improvement projects are viewed as outside or extra work apart from the participants' regular jobs to one where CI and collaboration are an integral part of everyone's work responsibilities. While many leaders recognize the need to make this transition, they are not always clear on ways to accomplish it. Requiring use of the TEF across all team improvement projects will help make this transition. Lastly, if the organization recognizes and rewards the successes of improvement teams, it will positively shape the culture. "Reward systems express and reinforce the values and norms that comprise corporate culture. A careful consideration of reward system design can help decision makers successfully modify the organization's culture. Reward systems are, in effect, powerful mechanisms that can be used by managers to communicate desired attitudes and behaviors to organization members" (Kerr and Slocum 2005, 137).

Changing the organizational culture to support teamwork. Another aspect of culture many organizations want to enhance is to strengthen teamwork and collaboration. Most have "turf" issues that interfere with overall mission accomplishment. Use of the TEF teaches and reinforces many of the principles necessary to teamwork and collaboration.

Standardization. Many of today's organizations are complex, containing a variety of departments and business units. Frequently, the business units are dispersed, and increasingly multinational, being located across different parts of the world. What sometimes results is use of different frameworks to guide team-based CI. Use of the TEF across the organization provides a standard that ensures consistency. It is the only international standard in existence for achieving successful team-based improvement projects. Due to its widespread use, it has evolved to become the accepted international standard on this topic. Its credibility is backed by the fact that it is managed by ASQ. When an organization applies the international standard for team excellence, it overcomes the difficulty of gaining acceptance for the framework in its different geographic locations.

Replication. One of the biggest sources of ROI from team excellence is when the opportunity exists to replicate the improvement in similar processes elsewhere in the organization. This is powerful leverage because the only investment that management needs to make is in implementing an already proven solution. Having used the TEF adds credibility to the solution when it is taken to others in the company who might be skeptical. It helps overcome the "not invented here" reaction that sometimes occurs.

In summary, this chapter has presented the numerous types of benefits organizations receive from using the TEF. Also presented were selected examples, and they only represent the tip of the iceberg of excellent team accomplishments. The body of achievement from twenty-five years of application is a strong testament to the power of using this accepted international standard for team-based improvement projects.

Next, we turn our attention to describing and explaining the foundation of the TEF—the Team Excellence Criteria.

BOX 2.7: EXAMPLES OF PROJECTS AND THEIR RESULTS

Organization: **Littelfuse Phils, Inc.**
Location: Lipa City-Malvar, Bantagas, Philippines
Team Name: TR-TE Soldering Team
Benefits: This team achieved a 50% reduction in fuse soldering defects, from 24,500 ppm to 12,300 ppm. This greatly contributed to scrap reduction and significant material cost savings. It wove the group into a more tightly knit team and won back customer confidence.

Organization: **North Broward Medical Center**
Location: Deerfield Beach, Florida, USA
Team Name: Total Joint Program
Benefits: This team of highly trained orthopedic surgeons and healthcare professionals designed a destination joint replacement center utilizing the latest technologies and techniques to increase elective joint replacement procedures and provide optimal clinical outcomes. Surgical volumes increased from 29 to 56 per month, increasing net revenue to over $4.8 million. Length of stay was reduced from 5 to 3.2 days, saving $724,000. Patient satisfaction went from 46% to 99%. It was the first hospital in Broward County to receive certification from the Joint Commission for its joint replacement program.

Organization: **Firstsource Advantage LLC**
Location: Amherst, New York, USA
Team Name: Check-Return Rate Reduction Project
Benefits: The organization provides a service to credit card issuers in debt recovery, and there was a problem with a high rate of returned (bounced) checks. The team reduced the rate of returned checks by 30% and saved more than $400,000. The solution was then implemented across all sites (Jacobsen 2011a).

Organization: **Firstsource Solutions Limited**
Location: Mumbai, Maharashtra, India
Team Name: Improving TAT to Offer Compliance for Stores Channel
Benefits: For a major bank client, the team improved the rate of delivering its mortgages to its customers in 14 days or less from 69% of the time to 80%, without compromising lending standards. As a result, the bank realized additional revenue, and within Firstsource the project triggered many other initiatives across other client engagements (Jacobsen 2011b).

Organization: **Firstsource Solutions Limited—Healthcare Vertical**
Location: Chennai, TamilNadu, India
Team Name: Purchase Order Processing—Productivity Improvement
Benefits: The team improved productivity in the purchase order (PO) process from 56 to 100 POs per person. Profitability improved significantly, from −1.5 to +1.2, saving $93,883 USD per year. By providing 90% of the POs within a 30-minute turnaround time, it paved the way for Firstsource to get additional revenue from the client.

Organization: **Firstsource Solutions Limited**
Location: Navi Mumbai, Maharashtra, India
Team Name: Reduction in Repeat Call Percentage
Benefits: Repeat calls from customers for the same reason drive up cost and lead to customer dissatisfaction. The team reduced the repeat call rates from 15.8% to 10%, and the rate has continued at this lower level.

Organization: **Firstsource Advantage LLC**
Location: Amherst, New York, USA
Team Name: Reducing Nonproductive Working Time
Benefits: The goal of this team was to reduce nonproductive time for employees that work as collectors on delinquent credit card accounts for a variety of credit issuers. The process was operating at a .58 sigma level. The team improved the sigma level to 2.0, resulting in a 62% reduction in defects per million opportunities (DPMO). The financial benefit was approximately $250,000 (Jacobsen 2011a).

Organization: **Firstsource Solutions Limited**
Location: Chennai, Tamil Nadu, India
Team Name: EE CHP Quality Improvement
Benefits: This team confronted the problem of the organization failing to meet the accuracy level of 95% specified in its service level agreement for a particular client. This could have resulted in the client failing the state audit, with a potential penalty of $1 million and business risk. As a result of the solution, the accuracy levels improved to 98.34% in the customer audit and 96.76% in internal audits (Jacobsen 2010b).

Organization: **Praxair Mexico**
Location: Monterrey, Nuevo Leon, Mexico
Team Name: Praxair Mexico Team
Benefits: The company has 800 vehicles in its product distribution fleet. The vehicle accident rate (VAR) index measures the number of accidents per mission miles and percentage of vehicles with no

signal. By decreasing the percentage of vehicles that had no signal from 24% to 1%, the team reduced the VAR by 15%. Compliance with corporate policies was achieved, but more importantly, accidents were prevented and lives were saved.

Organization: **Allegheny Energy Incorporated**
Location: Greensburg, Pennsylvania, USA
Team Name: Supply Chain Order Fulfillment Team
Benefits: The purpose of the team was to improve supply chain order fulfillment as measured by *on time and in full* (OTIF). This measure is a leading indicator to getting all the material to the field workers so they can serve their end-user customers well. The solution improved OTIF from the baseline of 65% to greater than 93%. It also had a positive impact on responses to an item in the annual employee engagement survey, "Do employees have the material to do their job?" This team received the ITEA 2010 Silver Award.

Organization: **Ministry of Defence (MINDEF)**
Location: Singapore
Team Name: Hive
Benefits: A new method was devised for cleaning and inspecting gun barrel bores within a confined space. There was a 50% reduction in manpower and a 77.8% reduction in labor hours, resulting in savings of $241,173 USD per year. The turnaround time for equipment maintenance was reduced, and the equipment availability rate/equipment operational readiness for the customers was raised.

Organization: **Ministry of Defence, Singapore (Republic of Singapore Navy)**
Location: Singapore
Team Name: Rectifier
Benefits: The team met its overall objective, which was to enable ships to deploy further and for a longer duration. There was a 33% reduction in turnaround time for defective equipment. Reduction of equipment and manpower saved $221,200 USD per year.

Organization: **Humana, Inc.**
Location: Louisville, Kentucky, USA
Team Name: Print Less, Print Smart
Benefits: The team's focus was to reduce printing costs. They reduced ink toner usage by 40% and paper usage by more than 10%. This impacted the entire organization of 28,000 people, generating high savings. The solutions were simple and could be implemented in any organization that does printing.

34 *Chapter Two*

Organization: **Humana, Inc.**
Location: Louisville, Kentucky, USA
Team Name: Humana MarketPoint Protectors
Benefits: Defects in payments made to referral agents include payment discrepancies and cycle-time defects. The team increased the sigma level from 1.22 to 2.89 and reduced the defect rate by 86.56%. This resulted in major savings plus improved satisfaction on the part of the agent customers.

Organization: **Humana, Inc.**
Location: Louisville, Kentucky, USA
Team Name: Humana Quality Engineering 5S Showcase Team
Benefits: The training room used by the quality engineering team was redesigned by applying the 5S approach and eliminating waste. Education capacity tripled as a result. Because more lean projects were then generated, the impact went beyond to improve even more work processes in the organization. In addition, flexibility was created, expanding the types of training that were given. It became a showcase for how lean can be applied in an office setting.

Organization: **Humana, Inc.**
Location: Phoenix, Arizona, USA
Team Name: Packout Error Quality Improvement Project (QIP) Team
Benefits: As a mail-order pharmacy, the goal of this team was to reduce the number of times the wrong medication was sent to a customer because of errors made in the packing department. The team achieved almost 100% reduction in errors, resulting in an 85% cost reduction, improved customer safety and satisfaction, and increased employee morale in the packing department.

Organization: **Humana, Inc.**
Location: Louisville, Kentucky, USA
Team Name: Benefit Summary Automation Team
Benefits: This team transformed a manual 39-step process with a high rework rate and an aggravating history with all customers and stakeholders into an automated system. The new system produces benefit summaries in minutes instead of weeks without manual intervention, and with world-class quality.

Organization: **Movistar Argentina (A Division of The Telefonica Group)**
Location: Ciudad Autonoma de Buenos Aires, Buenos Aires, Argentina
Team Name: Less Is More
Benefits: Improved the means by which customers were served by

900 employees located in 53 offices around the country. The results were an improvement in the customer satisfaction index (CSI) from 7.6 to 8.0 and a cost savings of $3.46 million USD. This team received the ITEA 2011 Bronze Award.

Organization: **Movistar (A Division of The Telefonica Group)**
Location: Capital Federal, Buenos Aires, Argentina
Team Name: No Evil Lasts More Than 96 Hours
Benefits: The team was focused on improving the closing of invoices related to the sale of new mobile phones. The project impacted both effectiveness (through reduction of unpaid invoice and overdue invoice payments) and efficiency (through reduction of the effort involved in follow-up controls to detect "lost" payments). The improvements impacted the work of 900 employees in 92 sales offices. It saved $184,000 USD, reduced billing/collection process deficiencies by 55%, and lowered customer dissatisfaction levels (Schaar 2011).

Organization: **Telefonica Argentina (A Division of The Telefonica Group)**
Location: Ciudad Autonoma de Buenos Aires, Buenos Aires, Argentina
Team Name: Surfing Is Not So Complex
Benefits: The team improved the means by which complex broadband problems affecting customer cell phone service are detected, diagnosed, and solved. The goal was to implement solutions in less than 96 hours for 95% of the problems. The team exceeded this goal, achieving solutions in 48 hours or less in 100% of the cases. Savings were $400,000 USD. This team received the ITEA 2011 Gold Award.

Organization: **Telefonica (A Division of The Telefonica Group)**
Location: Capital Federal, Buenos Aires, Argentina
Team Name: Impossible Mission
Benefits: The team improved the company's ability to pay advertising placement invoices. The goals were to improve payment of media suppliers consistent with contract provisions and to reduce the number of transactions. On-time payments increased to 98%, and $3 million USD was saved (Schaar 2010b).

Organization: **Telefonica (A Division of The Telefonica Group)**
Location: Capital Federal, Buenos Aires, Argentina
Team Name: Cutting Cuts
Benefits: This project was focused on solving the transmission problems on mobile networks. The team was a collaborative effort

between Telefonica and Movistar. The solution reduced the number of breakdowns that took place at the base stations by 70% and reduced the intervention at the sites by 50%. It saved $4 million USD per year. It also improved the interaction between the two companies and synergized the processes of both companies. This team received the ITEA 2010 Gold Award.

Organization: **Lockheed Martin—Missiles and Fire Control**
Location: Grand Prairie, Texas, USA
Team Name: Shook PMT-GMLRS Radome Production Line
Benefits: The team increased production of this equipment by 106%, at the same time reducing risk, driving innovation, improving cost, schedule (100% on-time deliveries), and quality, and sustaining outstanding customer satisfaction. Internal company savings were $3.5 million.

Organization: **Ford Motor Company**
Location: Saarlouis, Saarland, Germany
Team Name: Base Coat Reduction Team VO Saarlouis
Benefits: The team achieved a savings of $2 million USD per year by reducing base coat consumption. At the same time it made a significant contribution to environmental protection by reducing volatile organic compounds by 70,000 kg per year.

Organization: **Ford Motor Company**
Location: Dearborn, Michigan, USA
Team Name: Team Ford—Body Engineering
Benefits: The company had a widely announced date for the launch of their Ford Fiesta model when it was found that the carpet supplier was having difficulty meeting Ford's required quality standards. The team, comprising Ford and carpet supplier employees, simultaneously optimized two responses for carpet quality (softness and brush marking). The project was completed in just two weeks, enabling an on-time launch of the Fiesta. It also healed and strengthened the company–supplier relationship.

Organization: **SGS**
Location: Lakefield, Ontario, Canada
Team Name: Environmental Services Lead Time Improvement Project
Benefits: The team's goal was to boost on-time delivery performance of an environment laboratory. They achieved sustainable, breakthrough on-time delivery success. They also reduced operating costs by $450,000 USD per year.

Organization: **CSX Transportation**
Location: Jacksonville, Florida, USA
Team Name: FRA Inspection Report Manager Team
Benefits: This team's purpose was to design and implement a company-wide system to track deficiencies across its entire 21,000-mile network within a 75-day implementation schedule. The system they developed set the standard for the rail industry. Benefits achieved included improving remediation of deficiencies within the time specification from 78% to 99%, standardized remediation procedures, and further improvement in the company's safety record.

Organization: **CSX Transportation**
Location: Jacksonville, Florida, USA
Team Name: Local Train Management Tool Team
Benefits: The team developed a new tool to manage local trains. The tool assisted the company in reducing local crew overtime by $10.6 million per year. It was also instrumental in allowing improvement in the Industrial Switching Excellence measure, which is the company's prime customer service measure.

Organization: **IGD**
Location: Bogatá, Cundinamarca, Columbia
Team Name: Sugar Cane Auditors
Benefits: Historically, the relationship between the sugar mills and the sugar cane workers has been difficult. One aspect is employee distrust in the payment process of the manual cut service process that the mills created to increase productivity in the sugar sector in Columbia. The team's solution built worker trust in the payment process. As a result, the relationship improved. There have been no more strikes since 2008, and cane grinding improved by 23% in 2009, benefiting the socioeconomic development of the region.

Organization: **The West Paces Hotel Group**
Location: Auburn, Alabama, USA
Team Name: The Hotel at Auburn University—Maximizing Customer Engagement
Benefits: This team focused on improving customer engagement so that customers would return often and tell everyone about the incredible service they received at the hotel. As a result of the project, the hotel achieved 95% customer satisfaction, increased its occupancy to 62%, and cut defects and the cost of poor quality in half. It enabled the hotel to become number one in its respective marketplace.

Organization: **CGI Federal**
Location: North Charleston, South Carolina, USA
Team Name: Material Request Process Improvement Team
Benefits: The team improved the material requisition process, mainly through standardization, and reduced the labor hours needed to complete a material requisition by 17.5%, generating $171,000 in annual savings and improving client confidence and support.

Organization: **CGI Federal**
Location: Fort Campbell, Kentucky, USA
Team Name: Left Behind Equipment Process Improvement Team
Benefits: The organization services and repairs equipment for its client while the client troops are deployed elsewhere. This is called *left behind equipment* (LBE), and the client's required cycle time was 180 days. The team reduced cycle time by 57%, exceeding the 180-day goal and completing the LBE mission in 120 days. It reduced costs for the client by $3.5 million. It achieved high quality at low cost with a high level of customer satisfaction.

Organization: **Ramaiah Institute of Management Studies**
Location: Bangalore, Karnataka, India
Team Name: Team RIMS
Benefits: The team's process improvements resulted in cost savings of $600,000 USD per year and RIMS becoming the only business school in India to have reduced the fee for the 2011–13 school years.

Organization: **Reliance Industries Limited**
Location: Surat, Gujarat, India
Team Name: RIL–Hazira Lean Six Sigma Team
Benefits: By eliminating non-value-added activities at their polyester plant, the team improved cycle time. Also, loading efficiency went from 95% to 99%, and a proposed capital expenditure of $225,000 USD was avoided.

Organization: **Reliance Industries Limited**
Location: Surat, Gujarat, India
Team Name: RIL–Hazira Team
Benefits: The team developed a convection coil cleaning methodology for furnaces. The annual thermal energy saved was 5851 ksm3 NG equivalent, and the annual GHG emission reduction achieved was 9800 tons in terms of CO_2. Even more importantly, the solution had huge replication potential.

Organization: **Parrish Medical Center**
Location: Titusville, Florida, USA

Team Name: Worst to First
Benefits: The team increased the center's ranking on its initial workforce culture and engagement survey results from the 0.0 percentile—the worst in a national comparative database—to above the 90th percentile in one year. This was recognized to be the first organization to improve so dramatically in one year. This cultural transformation also impacted the organization's ability to achieve all five of its strategic objectives. For example, core measure compliance for heart attacks increased 14%, for heart failure 17%, for pneumonia 38%, and 19% for surgical infection prevention..

Organization: **3M**
Location: Decatur, Alabama, USA
Team Name: Mini MSA Process and Testing Optimization Team
Benefits: The team successfully scaled an internally developed adhesive (Mini MSA) as a superior alternative to an externally sourced adhesive used in well-known 3M tape. It eliminated the long lead times associated with overseas sourcing, resulting in substantial cash (inventory turn) benefit. This adhesive needed no post-process time to cure on the tape, resulting in significant increase in capacity for the 3M site making the finished product.

Organization: **3M**
Location: Knoxville, Iowa, USA
Team Name: Flexographic Value Stream Transformation
Benefits: This team optimized one of 3M's high-impact supply chains. It significantly reduced the supply chain complexity and length, resulting in improved yield and customer satisfaction and reduced defective parts per million.

Organization: **3M**
Location: St. Paul, Minnesota, USA
Team Name: Abrasives Belt Fabrication Improvement Team
Benefits: Abrasive belt fabrication is a complex "make-to-order" operation with hundreds of products and belt sizes. This team has driven a step-change quality improvement every year for seven years. Defects have been reduced by 97%, and there have been hundreds of thousands of dollars in cost savings every year (Jacobsen 2010a).

Organization: **School District of Lee County**
Location: Fort Myers, Florida, USA
Team Name: Food and Nutrition Services Key Ingredients Team
Benefits: This team's focus was to ensure the goals of generating adequate profit and having a robust operating reserve. The profit was

$77,723 in 2004, and the projected trend was that the organization would start running a loss in 2005. As a result of the solution, by 2007–08 the profit was $384,145, and in 2008–09 it was $2,292,520. The operating reserve increased by $2,676,665 in a two-year period.

Organization: **Fabrinet Co. Ltd.**
Location: Lamlookka, Patum Thanee, Thailand
Team Name: DUC
Benefits: This team developed a solution to improve the transfer of files with higher security where problems from old approaches, such as production halts and shipment holds due to file transfer failures, can be prevented. The project saved $57,000 USD in the first year and continues to save money. Customer complaints went down 89%, and problems related to lack of data have been eliminated. Intangible benefits such as IP protection and data fraud prevention have been realized.

Organization: **Naval Surface Warfare Center—Crane Division**
Location: Crane, Indiana, USA
Team Name: Submarine Valve Regulated Lead Acid
Benefits: This team was based on a collaborative effort among customers and suppliers. It dealt with a capacity issue with newly installed and recently designed VRLA batteries on submarines. The result was the achievement of strong capability indicators relative to battery capacity specification and life cycle performance expectations. This ensured that the submarine operational specifications were robust, and it led to significant maintenance savings throughout the batteries' life cycle.

Organization: **Housing and Development Board**
Location: Singapore
Team Name: Vision Excel
Benefits: This organization plans and develops public housing towns that provide Singaporeans with quality homes and living environment. The team worked to improve the construction time for the Housing and Development Board rental flats in public housing towns. Their solution has saved three months of construction time as well as cost.

Organization: **The Boeing Company**
Location: Long Beach, California, USA
Team Name: Critical Path Tooling

Benefits: This team improved the process for ensuring availability of quality, cost-effective, and timely tooling to build the aircraft fuselage in a situation in which the supply chain for this equipment is unique and must be certified. A proposal for a high-risk $9 million solution had been made. The team developed a medium-risk solution costing $600,000. This solution avoided an $8.4 million cost, and saved $2.9 million. This team received the ITEA 2011 Silver Award.

Organization: **The Boeing Company**
Location: Long Beach, California, USA
Team Name: C-17 Supplier Management Lead Time Reduction Team
Benefits: The team's objective was to reduce the overall program cycle time of C-17 aircraft production. The result was an overall 10% cycle time reduction for the entire aircraft build cycle, and 19% reduction of lead time on major subcontract components. They mitigated millions of dollars in risk funding for the program, and established control methods to ensure that the reductions are sustained.

Organization: **The Boeing Company**
Location: Long Beach, California, USA
Team Name: C-17 Forward Fuselage Redesign Team
Benefits: The team addressed a problem with quality nonconformances that severely disrupted the assembly process of the forward fuselage. Their solution reduced assembly disruptions from 4 days to 1 day, forming-related defects by 80%, and part fabrication takt time by 40%. The company's commitment to ISO 14000 was substantiated by the elimination of heat treat.

Organization: **Bayer Health Care**
Location: Mexico City, D. F., Mexico
Team Name: Equipo Cipro
Benefits: This team increased the quantity of finished goods, decreased the waste, and instituted better process control. The team saved $108,498 USD and reduced the variation of process control.

Organization: **PMW 160 Tactical Networks**
Location: San Diego, California, USA
Team Name: Websites Improvement Team
Benefits: A total of 19 websites in 7 geographic locations was consolidated into 4 websites (79% reduction) and 2 locations (71% reduction). The organization also became more efficient in delivering web-based capabilities to customers and end users, resulting in improved customer satisfaction. Labor hours and infrastructure costs were reduced, saving $3.48 million.

Organization: **Barnes–Jewish Hospital**
Location: St. Louis, Missouri, USA
Team Name: Enhancing Quality in Patient Care by Embracing Lean
Benefits: The team deployed the use of lean through a training program coupled with traditional process improvement. The results include less waiting for patients, and improvements in safety, quality, service, employee engagement, and financial performance.

Organization: **Wipro BPO (a division of Wipro Limited)**
Location: Navi Mumbai, Maharashtra, India
Team Name: Improving Overall Claim Handling Accuracy
Benefits: In support of a leading healthcare organization, the team worked to reduce mis-paid insurance claim amounts. They improved the overall claim handling accuracy from 96.87% to 98%. They saved $6.1 million USD from reducing mis-paid amounts by 81% and reduced the rework equivalent to $600,000 USD.

Organization: **Pershing LLC**
Location: Jersey City, New Jersey, USA
Team Name: Pershing Quality Management Office
Benefits: The team achieved an 80% increase in satisfied customers, an 8% increase in customers who would definitely recommend the company to others, and a 10% increase in customers rating Pershing as much better than other providers. Service costs were saved, customer loyalty was increased, and customers became advocates.

Organization: **Nextel Argentina SRL**
Location: Ciudad Autonoma de Buenos Aires, Buenos Aires, Argentina
Team Name: Repair
Benefits: When customers return mobile phone equipment because of technical difficulties, it goes into the recycling or repair work flow, adding cost. The team reduced the amount of unnecessary incoming equipment, saving money in 25% of the branches in which it was implemented. It also helped improve the communication between stakeholders and created greater commitment to company goals.

Organization: **Southern California Edison**
Location: La Palma, California, USA
Team Name: SCE SmartConnect Supplier Improvement
Benefits: This team focused on the development, testing, and production operations of the company's advanced smart metering system, Edison Smart Connect (ESC). It did so by focusing on a key supplier of the system. As a result, the ESC program achieved the

planned results of installing approximately 1.8 million smart meters that remained below an aggressive field failure rate while remaining under the cost-per-meter goal. The design-and-build rigor and robustness reduced defects, increased the predictability of the production operations output, and exceeded initial reliability goals. SCE had never before adopted a quality management system with a continuous improvement methodology.

Organization: **Sterlite Industries India Ltd.**
Location: Tuticorin, Tamil Nadu, India
Team Name: Awesome
Benefits: Their effluent plant takes the bleed from the refinery and treats it by converting it into sludge. The sludge, which is sold, contains a certain amount of nickel, which is extracted and also sold. Customers of the sludge were dissatisfied with its moisture content. By changing the treatment process, the team significantly improved the amount of nickel extracted, resulting in more revenue, and also reduced the moisture level of the sludge to meet customer requirements.

Organization: **Sterlite Industries India Ltd.**
Location: Tuticorin, Tamil Nadu, India
Team Name: Sparklers
Benefits: Downtime of cranes due to breakdowns impacts production. The team successfully reduced the downtime of cranes by increasing their reliability from 56% to 94.54%. This, in turn, positively impacted production.

Organization: **Continental Guadalajara Services Mexico S.A. De C.V.**
Location: Tlajomulco de Zuñiga, Jalisco, Mexico
Team Name: Conti-Guad Pactan Conquest Pack
Benefits: The team's goal was to reduce chemical materials consumption used for manufacturing electronic assemblies. The project reduced waste by almost 1 ton, saving $300,000 USD. This also benefited the environment. It helped launch several other projects that have quadrupled the results obtained before. It also helped change the company culture by making chemical waste no longer acceptable. This team received the ITEA 2010 Bronze Award.

Organization: **Anheuser-Busch INBEV**
Location: Oklahoma City, Oklahoma, USA
Team Name: MCC-Oklahoma City ESPN Team

Benefits: In a plant that produces over 13 billion lids per year for the beverage industry, the team reduced maintenance expenses by almost 20%.

Organization: **Metal Container Corporation**
Location: Jacksonville, Florida, USA
Team Name: Front End Improvement Team
Benefits: In the beverage can production process, tear-offs cause the forming equipment to jam and can severely damage the tooling. The team reduced the tear-off rate by more than 50% in the plant. As a result, they improved equipment uptime and reduced tooling costs, resulting in several million additional cans of production.

Organization: **Wyndham Consumer Finance**
Location: Las Vegas, Nevada, USA
Team Name: SCAR
Benefits: The team improved the systems used by the company's call center agents by reducing defects and waste. Accuracy of adjustment requests was improved by 5%, processes were automated, the usability of their adjustment data set was improved, agent training was improved, storage costs were reduced by 50%, and $15,000 was saved.

Organization: **The Urology Group**
Location: Cincinnati, Ohio, USA
Team Name: The Urology Group
Benefits: The team's focus was on improving financial performance. They succeeded in reducing accounts receivable time from 90 days to 20 days. The project saved $750,000.

3
Team Excellence Criteria
How the Criteria Are Organized and Why

The TEF is a three-part framework comprising criteria, assessment methodology, and non-prescriptive feedback as described in Chapter 1, Figure 1.2. This chapter serves as an introduction to the TEF's criteria. We will describe the criteria and the rationale behind their organization. Because the criteria are non-prescriptive, they do not specify which CI techniques and tools a team should use for their particular project. The team must select the appropriate techniques and tools that fit the needs of that project. Therefore, the CI tool set is not part of the TEF. Fortunately, there is a very extensive body of knowledge on CI that offers a wide variety of tools that can handle almost every conceivable analytical need.

The ITEA Process provides two versions of these criteria, the "Criteria Summary" and the "Criteria." In this chapter we use the "Criteria Summary" because it provides all the items that are in the criteria. For those readers who are brand-new to the TEF, this information will provide most of what you need to know to get started using the criteria as a guide for your teams. In Chapter 5 we describe the "Criteria" because it gives more detail regarding what is expected by each item. That material is relevant to those who either already have experience with the TEF or have a sophisticated team-based CI approach in place.

The overall rationale behind these criteria is to codify the basis for best practice in team-based improvement projects. Figure 1.1 in Chapter 1 showed that the TEF is based on the intersection of bodies of knowledge on two subjects: CI and teamwork. The criteria provide a set of guideposts that enable teams to execute successful improvement projects. In the first section of this chapter we describe the criteria items themselves, including how they are organized. In the second section we explain the rationale behind them by covering each of the areas addressed by the TEF, namely, CI and teamwork.

The criteria were constructed with the recognition that there is no single cookie-cutter approach that guarantees success for every improvement project. The specific actions required for a team to successfully perform a particular project depend on many factors unique to the situation. As noted in Chapter 1, the TEF's approach is analogous to that of the U.S. Baldrige Performance Excellence Program. The Baldrige approach also recognizes that there is no one-size-fits-all approach to guarantee success in achieving organizational performance excellence. Examples of factors that make a difference in either individual projects or in entire organizations include: the competitive landscape, customer requirements and satisfaction levels, organizational culture, internal opportunities for operational efficiencies and cost reduction, the type of process, and process complexity. That is why the Team Excellence criteria are stated in a non-prescriptive manner. It is up to the team's management and members to decide what general CI model or approach they want to use and then which specific tools to apply to a particular project.

DESCRIPTION OF THE CRITERIA SUMMARY

The criteria are grouped into these five sections:

1. Project Selection and Purpose
2. Current Situation Analysis
3. Solution Development
4. Project Implementation and Results
5. Team Management and Project Presentation

The first four sections follow the sequence of activities that are performed during an improvement project. The last section covers additional elements necessary for successful teamwork and for a presentation that explains the completed project to others in a comprehensible manner. (See Figure 1.3 in Chapter 1 for the visual display of how the criteria are organized.)

Table 3.1 provides the 2011 version of the Criteria Summary. While the five sections have remained the same, occasionally the individual items are modified by ASQ as part of a systematic improvement cycle. The term "item" refers to the statements at the lowest level in each section. The scoring is done at the item level. For example, 1B states, "Explain how the

1. Project Selection and Purpose
   1A. Explain the methods used to choose the project. (Provide specific examples of techniques and data used.)
      a. Describe the types of data and quality tools used to select the project, and why they were used.
      b. Explain the reasons why the project was selected.
      c. Describe the involvement of potential stakeholders in project selection.
   1B. Explain how the project supports/aligns with the organization's goals, performance measures, and/or strategies.
      a. Identify the affected organizational goals, performance measures, and/or strategies.
      b. Identify the types of impact on each goal, performance measure, and/or strategy.
      c. Identify the degree of impact on each goal, performance measure, and/or strategy, and how this was determined.
   1C. Identify the potential stakeholders and explain how they may be impacted by the project.
      a. Identify potential internal and external stakeholders and explain how they were identified.
      b. Identify the types of potential impact on stakeholders and explain how these were determined.
      c. Identify the degree of potential impact on stakeholders and explain how this was determined.
2. Current Situation Analysis
   2A. Explain the approach/process the team used to identify the potential root causes/improvement opportunity(ies).
      a. Describe the methods and tools used to identify possible root causes/improvement opportunities.
      b. Describe the team's analysis of data to identify possible root causes/improvement opportunities.
      c. Describe how or if any of the stakeholders were involved in identifying the possible root causes/improvement opportunities.
   2B. Describe how the team analyzed information to identify the final root cause(s)/improvement opportunity(ies). (Include any appropriate validation.)
      a. Describe the methods and tools used to identify the final root cause(s)/improvement opportunity(ies).

Table 3.1 International Team Excellence Award (ITEA) criteria (2011).

- b. Describe the team's analysis of data to select the final root cause(s)/improvement opportunity(ies).
- c. Identify the root cause(s)/improvement opportunity(ies) and explain how the team validated the final root cause(s)/improvement opportunity(ies).

3. Solution Development

   3A. Explain the methods used to identify the possible solutions/improvement actions.
   - a. Describe the methods and tools used to develop possible solutions/improvement actions.
   - b. Describe the team's analysis of data to develop possible solutions/improvement actions.
   - c. Indicate the criteria the team decided to use in selecting the final solution(s)/improvement action(s).

   3B. Explain how the final solution(s)/improvement action(s) was/were determined.
   - a. Describe the methods and tools used by the team to select the final solution(s)/improvement action(s).
   - b. Describe the team's analysis of data to select the final solution(s)/improvement action(s).
   - c. Describe the involvement of stakeholders in the selection of the final solution(s)/improvement action(s).

   3C. Explain the final solution(s)/improvement action(s), validation, and the benefits expected to be realized by implementing the team's solution(s)/improvement action(s).
   - a. Describe the final solution(s)/improvement action(s) and explain how the team validated the final solution(s)/improvement action(s).
   - b. List the types of tangible and intangible benefits that are expected to be realized by implementing the team's solution(s)/improvement action(s).
   - c. Explain how the team used data to justify the implementation of the team's solution(s)/improvement action(s).

4. Project Implementation and Results

   4A. Explain how buy-in/agreement was achieved for implementation.
   - a. Indicate the types of internal and external (if applicable) stakeholder involvement in implementation.
   - b. Describe how various types of resistance were identified and addressed.

Table 3.1 *Continued.*

> c. Explain how stakeholder buy-in was ensured.
>
> 4B. Explain the approach used by the team to implement its solution(s)/improvement action(s) and to ensure the results.
>
>> a. Describe the plan developed by the team to implement its solution(s)/improvement action(s).
>>
>> b. Describe the procedure, system, or other changes that were made to implement the solution(s)/improvement action(s) and to sustain the results.
>>
>> c. Describe the creation and installation of a system for measuring and sustaining results.
>
> 4C. Describe the results achieved.
>
>> a. Identify the types of tangible and intangible results that were realized.
>>
>> b. Explain how the project's results link with the organization's goals, performance measures, and/or strategies.
>>
>> c. Describe how results were shared with stakeholders.
>
> 5. Team Management and Project Presentation
>
>> 5A. Explain how the team members were selected and how they were involved throughout the project.
>>
>> 5B. Explain how the team was prepared to work together in addressing the project.
>>
>> 5C. Explain how the team managed its performance to ensure it was effective as a team.
>>
>> 5D. The team will also be judged on the clarity and organization of its presentation.

Table 3.1 *Continued.*

project supports/aligns with the organization's goals, performance measures, and/or strategies." The items that are scored in this section are:

- *1Ba.* Identify the affected organizational goals, performance measures, and/or strategies.
- *1Bb.* Identify the types of impact on each goal, performance measure, and/or strategy.
- *1Bc.* Identify the degree of impact on each goal, performance measure, and/or strategy and how this was determined.

In order to score how well a team addressed each item in the Criteria Summary, assessors assign a rating to each item. They use a four-point rating scale to score each item, with the possible ratings being:

- Not covered—0
- Unclear—1
- Meets the criterion—2
- Exceeds the criterion—3

The details of how to apply this scoring scale are described in Chapter 4. The same scoring process would be used regardless of whether a team was being assessed by an external assessor group (for example, the International Team Excellence Award Process) or by one or more internal assessors. The information from either source is very valuable in helping the organization enhance how its teams perform improvement projects.

Section 1. Project Selection and Purpose

To what extent do your project teams always get assigned to work on the most important and promising improvement opportunities? In a typical organization the answer to that question is, "Sporadically." Every organization has numerous improvement opportunities; large organizations have thousands. So, making the optimal choices is not simple. The criteria remind management to explicitly make their choices based on alignment to organizational goals, measures, and/or strategy. The reasoning is that organizations can significantly enhance their performance by shaping their portfolio of projects to fulfill short- and long-term objectives (Benko and McFarlan 2003). This principle is often called "line of sight." These items also remind management and the team that taking the time to very clearly define the project is essential to its success.

As far as stakeholders are concerned, some items in this section remind the team and its champions that it is important to know from the outset exactly who the stakeholders are and what their potential influence might be. This knowledge helps avoid the pitfall of rushing forward into situation analysis without having concerned themselves with the potential impacts on stakeholders. Having this information early makes it much more likely that potential sources of resistance can be mollified and also that potential sources of stakeholder support can be marshaled for a high-impact improvement.

Within the CI body of knowledge there are numerous tools that are useful in project selection. One useful source of such tools is *The Memory Jogger Plus+* (Brassard 1996).

Section 2. Current Situation Analysis

Once the best project has been selected, how does the team understand the current situation with respect to the process at hand? What are the root causes of the problems, and what are the associated improvement opportunities? The Section 2 criteria require the team to address these issues. Among other things, the criteria show that driving to root cause is a three-stage undertaking. First, the team must identify possible root causes/improvement opportunities; next, narrow down those possibilities to a final list; and then validate that list. If the validation does not succeed, then the team must initiate the three-stage undertaking again. Validation of the root causes/improvement opportunities is a frequently skipped step by project teams. Also, the team is reminded to decide whether and how it is appropriate to involve the stakeholders in this phase.

Section 3. Solution Development

Now that the team understands the situation, how does the team go about picking the best solution? The Section 3 criteria require the team to address these issues. Similar to the logic embedded in Section 2, this is a three-step undertaking. First, they must identify possible solutions and associated improvement actions; next, pick a final solution set; and then validate it. If the validation does not support expectations, then the team must repeat the three-step undertaking. A similar point about validation that was described above in Section 2 also applies in Section 3. Validation of the final solution set is also a frequently skipped step in this stage of a project. Also, the team is reminded to decide how it is appropriate to involve the stakeholders in selection of the final solution set.

Section 4. Project Implementation and Results

Once the team has selected the solution set, how does the team go about implementing it, and what results did they obtain? The Section 4 criteria require the team to address these issues. Occasionally, even outstanding project recommendations wither on the vine due to lack of systematic and vigorous implementation. Here the criteria remind teams to consider the need to involve and communicate with stakeholders. In this section we also see the proverbial "bottom line." What impact did implementing the solution set have? This should be expressed in terms of both tangible and intangible results. While sometimes management has a tendency to focus on tangible results, intangible ones can be equally or even more meaningful. Avoiding loss of life, for example, by improving safety has some tangible benefits to the organization, but the biggest ones accrue to those who would have died if the process had not been improved. There is considerably more value to a human life than how it is rated in an actuarial life insurance table.

Section 5. Team Management and Project Presentation

How are the necessary interpersonal dynamics put into play to enable a group of people to engage in true teamwork? Logical and appropriate analysis is necessary but not sufficient for a team to achieve project success. Other conditions are necessary, and the first three items within Section 5 require management and the team to address them. The first of them, team staffing, is more a management responsibility because in most cases the team can not staff itself. Anyone who has ever been on a team recognizes the importance of placing the right people on the team, both in terms of the right skill mix and teamwork skills. If teamwork skills are not already present within the team, then part of the team preparation and ongoing team management must include development of these skills. The second criterion, team preparation, is a joint responsibility of management and the team. The third, team management, is more of a team responsibility, but management should oversee to make sure the team does not get "stuck" in its ability to more forward. There are two requirements embedded in team management. One is having the team work as a true team rather than simply as a group. The ability of a team to self-manage is related to its maturity. Applying the well-known *form–storm–norm–perform* model of team formation to facilitate the team's dynamics is one helpful way for a disparate group of people to evolve into a team. The other requirement is for the team to employ sound project management tools and techniques. Fortunately, there is also an extensive body of knowledge on the subject of project management. Among other places, it has been compiled as a formal body of knowledge (BOK) by the Project Management Institute (2008) and published as the *Project Management Body of Knowledge (PMBOK Guide)*. The last criterion in this section reminds the team that, as good as the project was, the team must be able to explain it coherently to others, especially management.

In the criteria there are two sets of linked terms that warrant further explanation:

- Root cause(s)/improvement opportunity(ies)
- Solution(s)/improvement action(s)

The reason behind this use of dual terminology is that improvement projects are of two general types: one is to fix a problem and the other is to take advantage of an opportunity. They represent two sides of the same improvement coin, and the distinction between them is not a hard-and-fast one. For instance, if a carpet cleaning company has a significant number of customer complaints about how their services were performed, this is usually characterized as a problem to be solved. On the other hand, if several more-efficient carpet cleaning technologies become available, the company can undertake a project to decide whether to take advantage of them, and if so, which one or what combination. Identification of "root causes" applies to solving problems, while "improvement opportunities" apply to capturing upside options. For many projects, it is not crucial to focus on drawing this distinction since the same challenge could sometimes be characterized as a problem or an opportunity. In the case of the carpet cleaning company, if their competition has higher complaint percentages, then their complaint rate is not necessarily a compelling problem. However, reducing the percentage of customer complaints below that of the competition could be considered an opportunity to gain market share. Similarly, if new carpet-cleaning technology might be adopted by the competition, then not having it could be considered a problem rather than an opportunity. The main point is simply for the team to ensure that the tools and techniques used are the ones most appropriate to the type of challenge embodied in the project.

An additional note about stakeholders is that most projects have multiple stakeholder groups, some internal to the organizational unit and some external. Not all of them have equal influence. So the team must decide which stakeholders to involve, how much, and at what stages in the project. The criteria remind the team to make these decisions explicitly at each project phase. It is one thing for a team to implicitly keep stakeholders in mind, but it requires a higher level of discipline to address each of these stakeholder items.

One last thing to note is that highly successful teams demonstrate integration across the items, especially across the first four categories. In other words, the assessors can follow a consistent story line throughout the project presentation. According to Barry Bickley (pers. comm.), a highly experienced ITEA judge, there are four specific areas in which teams should demonstrate integration in order to be operating at the highest level: (1) stakeholders, (2) tool usage, (3) data analysis, and (4) impact on company goals. To put it the opposite way, there should be no internal inconsistencies in the story line. For example, if the objectives of a project are to reduce cycle time and accidents, then the main tangible and intangible results reported in Section 4 should pertain to these two objectives. Those readers who are familiar with evaluation of Baldrige applications will recognize this same requirement: presentations that show internal consistency across the responses to the sections score higher on average than those that do not. More on the subject of integration is provided in Chapters 4 and 5.

RATIONALE FOR THE CRITERIA IN TERMS OF CONTINUOUS IMPROVEMENT MODELS AND APPROACHES, INCLUDING PDC/SA AND DMAIC

There are several generic models for achieving improvements in how any type of work is done. The development of these CI models has been one of the fundamental contributions of the quality revolution. As such, they are an integral part of the extensive knowledge base that has been developed on the subject of CI. It is very important to note that since the items are nonprescriptive, they accommodate the use of any of these well-known models or any other systematic approach.

By now, those readers familiar with CI will have recognized that the sequence of the first four categories follows the generic logic of all process improvement models. These models specify a phased order of activities required for executing improvement projects. Here we will cover some of the major models. The important point is that the criteria accommodate the use of all valid CI models. No matter which one a team uses, it fits directly within the criteria to meet the criteria's sequential logic. In fact, if you look at most of the award-winning presentations, you will see how the team fit the use of their model directly into the criteria.

The first of these models to be developed, and perhaps the most generic, is *plan–do–check–act*. It was first created by Walter Shewhart and became known as PDCA. Later, it was popularized by W. Edwards Deming, and its terminology was eventually modified to be *plan–do–study–act* (PDSA). It is variously called the *Shewhart cycle*, the *Deming cycle*, and the *cycle of continuous improvement*. Figure 3.1 displays this cycle.

The PDC/SA model is fundamental to the field of CI. In its essence, PDC/SA represents the systematic application of the scientific method to

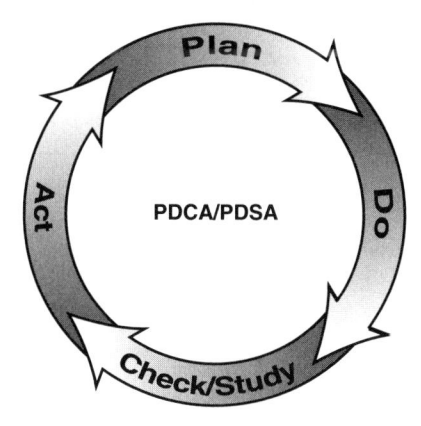

Figure 3.1 Cycle of continuous improvement—PDC/SA.

the practice of improving the way work is accomplished in organizations. There are other ways to decide how to change how work is done, including by hunch, power, trial and error, intuition, reaction, emotion, and whim. If a quick decision is needed, sometimes hunch or intuition are the only options. However, if there is time and the decision is important, the scientific method is far preferable. It is the one most likely to provide the best and lasting solution. The scientific method involves planning by generating hypotheses and experimenting to see if the facts do or do not support them. Two sets of hypotheses are generated. One is about what is causing the problem. The other is about what the best solutions are to the problem. Each set is tested for accuracy. That is why CI is often called a *fact-based approach* to management. Because it enables the team to avoid erroneous conclusions and poor solutions, risk is substantially reduced.

Another well-known CI model is *define–measure–analyze–improve–control* (DMAIC). This model was derived from the works of Shewhart, Deming, Juran, and Taguchi. Among their numerous contributions to the CI knowledge base, a major one was understanding the negative impact of *variation* on quality. Based on their understanding, these founders of the quality revolution also developed statistical tools to understand and improve processes. The initial manifestation was in the form of what was labeled *statistical process control* (SPC) tools. The basic SPC tool set includes graphical and mathematical tools to understand current process performance and then scientifically analyze how best to improve it. Gradually, the analytical tool set has been expanded well beyond the initial set. Use of these tools in a systematic sequence eventually became embodied in an approach labeled by Motorola as *Six Sigma*, and has since been widely popularized in CI circles (Brassard and Ritter, 2001). DMAIC is the sequential model used in the Six Sigma approach. Figure 3.2 displays this model.

At the same time, a related approach evolved from the work of Toyota Motor Corporation. This model was eventually labeled *lean*. It also became part of the foundation of the quality revolution and an integral part of the CI knowledge base. The emphasis in the lean approach is removal of non-value-added activity, also known as *waste*, or *muda*. Simplifying work by removing complexity is a hallmark of the lean approach. One CI model used in the lean approach is called 5S, which is a five-step sequence for simplifying work and workplaces. More recently, some have merged this approach with that of Six Sigma and labeled it *"Lean Six Sigma"* (LSS) (George, Rowlands, and Kastle 2004). DMAIC has remained the sequential model used by most LSS practitioners, although it is supplemented with other approaches such as 5S.

Several other CI models have been developed over the years. For example, in the popular book, *The Team Handbook*, two models are provided: a five-step model for problem solving and a seven-step model for process improvement. In addition, many organizations have developed their own models and require that improvement projects follow them. However, all the credible ones are based on the seminal logic of the original PDCA cycle.

Lastly, there are other, broader approaches to organizational improvement, such as *total quality management*, *theory of constraints*, and

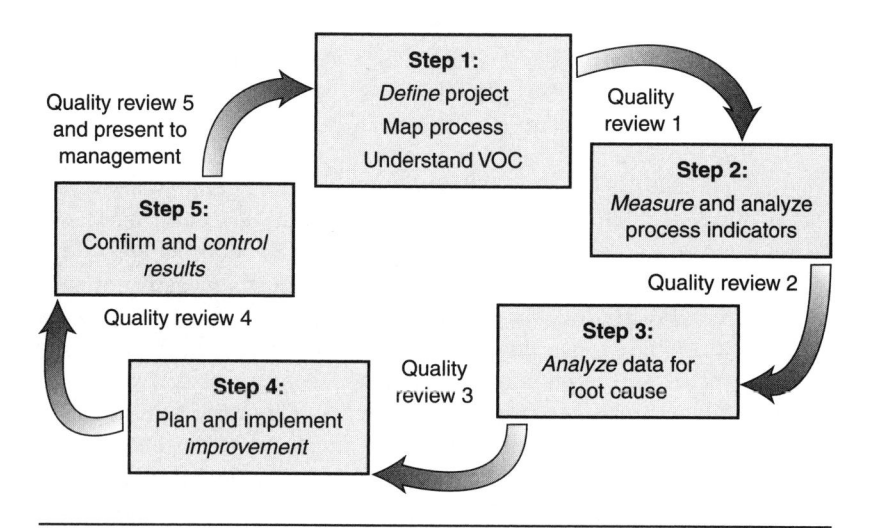

Figure 3.2 DMAIC model.

balanced scorecard. These approaches are of wider scope than just how to do individual improvement projects; they also address many of the root cause management issues that constrain organizations from achieving high performance. However, they all include an element that requires making improvements to specific work processes based on facts that are assembled using sound CI models and tools.

RATIONALE IN TERMS OF TEAMWORK AND COLLABORATION

We have now established that for a team to score well on the items, it must have used some systematic CI model and used analytic tools most appropriate to their particular project. However, the criteria also include two types of elements that are outside the analytic focus of CI models but are essential to successful projects:

- *Teamwork.* Behavior among the people on the team that demonstrates mutual respect, trust, responsibility, and accountability to each other and the team as a whole. As noted in Chapter 1, a group is not necessarily a team, and turning it into one for purposes of accomplishing a great improvement project is its own challenge. Teamwork might be considered the glue that turns a group into a team.

- *Collaboration.* Behavior between the team and others who have a vested interest in the impact of the improvement project (that is, stakeholders) that demonstrates recognition of the need for their buy-in and desire for win/win solutions. In today's interconnected world, most processes to be improved exist within a complex system of related processes and functions. Therefore, changing the process is likely to impact other activities and people outside those who are directly involved.

Achieving excellent teamwork and collaboration for any purpose is challenging. Consequently, a vast amount of literature exists regarding principles of teamwork and collaboration, scattered across many different disciplines. In his book, *The Five Dysfunctions of a Team,* Lencioni (2002) has provided a simple model of what must be overcome to create a team: (1) absence of trust, (2) fear of conflict, (3) lack of commitment, (4) avoidance of accountability, and (5) inattention to results. There are also many case study examples of successful teams from many fields of endeavor, such as sports, military and space exploration operations, major business projects, and civic projects.

Knowledge regarding the specific principles of teamwork and collaboration that apply to an improvement team using CI methodology, however, is considerably more limited. Figure 1.1 showed that the TEF's focus is on the intersection of these two activities. Tackling an important organizational issue is hard work for people working as an improvement team. The knowledge base on CI methods touches on a few of these principles, but its focus is on the mechanics of information collection and analysis. Relevant literature is also harder to ferret out because it is usually embedded in literature on other, related subjects. One notable exception is *The Team Handbook* (Scholtes, Joiner, and Streibel 2003), sometimes referred to by its many users as the "Team Bible." Another exception is *The Customer–Supplier Innovation Team Guidebook* (Norausky 2000). Also, part of the mission of ASQ's Team Excellence and Workplace Forum (TEWF) is to accumulate and make available this unique and important knowledge as a formalized BOK, along with knowledge on the broader topic of organizational culture that supports CI and organizational performance excellence. Arguably, teams more often fail to achieve the full potential of their projects for lack of excellent teamwork and collaboration than for lack of good CI methodology.

Three of the Team Excellence Criteria items specifically address the need for good teamwork. They are the first three items in Section 5. All the items related to stakeholder involvement address the need for broader collaboration. For purposes of our subject, the practical distinction between teamwork and collaboration is that *teamwork* requires developing a more intense set of interconnections, often colloquially called *bonding*. *Collaboration*, on the other hand, requires demonstrating a willingness to exchange views and a sincere intent to avoid win/lose outcomes. It is easy for a team to create a wonderful improvement that benefits their organizational unit but comes at the expense of other constituencies. As a rule of thumb, teamwork requires collaboration, but it also requires additional behaviors that create deeper positive relationships among the team members.

While it is possible to create an HPT within any organization, teaming really thrives when done within a culture of collaboration. Pfeffer (2005, 101) has provided a relevant observation:

> One important barrier to decentralizing decision making, using self-managed teams, and eliciting employee commitment and cooperation is the symbols that separate people from each other. Consequently, it is not surprising that many of the firms that are known for achieving competitive advantage through people have

various forms of symbolic egalitarianism—ways of signaling to both insiders and outsiders that there is comparative equality and it is not the case that some think and others do.

In *The Collaborative Work Systems Fieldbook* Beyerlein and Harris (2003, 33) provided the following ten critical success factors for team-based organizing:

1. Align the organization in multiple ways.
2. The work must be conducive to teams.
3. Teamwork must fit with and connect to the environment.
4. Craft a culture of collaboration and cooperation.
5. Structure the organization with an array of teams.
6. Reinforce cooperation and collaboration with organizational systems.
7. Create empowerment and authority at all levels.
8. Foster an atmosphere of entrepreneurship.
9. Increase the intangible resources of the organization.
10. Design an adaptable organization.

The Movistar/Telefonica organization has had a decade of sustained excellence by developing an innovative management model, and its cultural foundation is collaboration (Gadda-Thompson and Barrera 2010). See Box 3.1 for a description of its main elements.

BOX 3.1: AN INNOVATIVE QUALITY MANAGEMENT MODEL THAT HAS CREATED SUSTAINED EXCELLENCE

Movistar, part of Telefonica Group, has developed and implemented a model that is generating a growing stream of successful improvement projects (Gadda-Thompson and Barrera 2010). It consists of a trilogy for creating and sustaining results that they consider key practices for success:

- *Workshops.* These incorporate exchange of ideas between teams, different viewpoints, past experiences from different business units so mistakes are not repeated, and members' ideas to develop process improvements.

- *Quality improvement community.* This is a group of quality experts committed to actively participate in improvement initiatives in the company, including through giving training, developing people by facilitating workshops and encouraging them to tear down paradigms, mentoring people by providing support for Black Belts and Champions, and providing examples of best practice.

- *Inheritance stage.* The role of "heir" was formally established for each improvement team project. It is the person formally designated to sustain the team's results. The heir is an expert in the process and actively participates from the beginning of the project. The inheritance phase lasts one year, with quarterly reviews with the board of directors.

They incorporate formal awards and rewards to reinforce this model, such as belt certifications for successfully completed projects and monetary rewards for their belts and heirs. Awards are given out at celebrations attended by top leadership, sponsors, and team members. Most projects are cross-functional, and some are cross-company, including with suppliers.

Patti Trapp (pers. comm.), an experienced ITEA judge and ITEA committee member, has noted that one of the challenges organizations experience is how to involve all levels and all facets of the organization in CI. Often, the work of CI is done primarily by those who have been to formal training, selected staff from the quality or industrial engineering departments, those with relevant college degrees, and/or external consultants brought in to make improvements. Also, it is often focused on certain types of functions, such as production or service delivery, even though all functional areas could benefit from participating. Using the TEF allows everyone to be directly engaged by clarifying and simplifying what needs to be done and ensuring that their projects will have successful outcomes. It also is a very good means for encouraging labor–management collaboration. Trapp noted that all the teams from Boeing she has seen present projects have had both union and non-union people on them. Another critical point has been made by Daniel Munoz (pers. comm.), a participant in several improvement teams who has seen the change in culture from the perspective of the workforce. He said that there was initial workforce resistance due to fear over losing jobs. However, leadership relentlessly pursued this approach, along the way demonstrating to the workforce that they wanted them to get rid of waste, not people. The other cultural change he has observed is that employees can openly express concerns to management, whereas before they could not. See Box 3.2 for an example of top leadership's perspective regarding the importance and impact of employee engagement.

BOX 3.2: LEADERSHIP PERSPECTIVE ON EMPLOYEE ENGAGEMENT

In the Boeing Company, the program used to create employee engagement is called Employee Involvement (EI) (Rick Payne, pers. comm.). It has a number of formal elements, including teamwork training and self-assessment, to bring a group along a maturity continuum to eventually become a high-performance team. In several of their business units they have used a formal team maturity model that defines stages of team functioning. It enables the team to know their level of teamwork and what they must do to make it to the topmost level of team functioning. In their book, *The Making of a World-Class Organization,* David Spong and Debbie Collard (2009, 10) described how their use of EI contributed to two Baldrige Award wins, one for Service and one for Manufacturing, in two respective business units: Aerospace Support and C-17 (Airlift and Tanker Programs). "The achievement of EI is like magic or alchemy. The basic ingredients of developing the methodology, the training, and so on, seem to be very simple and maybe even unimpressive. The results, however, are incredible, not only in shaping the culture of the organization and the team behavior, but in the basic business results that directly relate to it." Moreover, in the case of the C-17 program, the United Auto Workers (UAW) represented most of the hourly workforce. "Our implementation and use of EI needed to be and only could be achieved with the support of the UAW leadership. While it did not happen overnight, the implementation of EI was a major help in establishing an excellent relationship with the UAW. During our years on the C-17 program in Long Beach the relationship between the company and the UAW leadership, 'Union Relationships' went from the worst we had ever experienced to the best. We went from an antagonistic, confrontational relationship to one of cooperation and trust" (42).

THE CRITERIA'S EMPHASIS ON METHODS THAT PRODUCE GOOD RESULTS

One last thing to understand about the criteria is that they are constructed on the principle that if a team uses the right set of methods to perform CI, teamwork, and collaboration, the best possible project outcome will result. Organizational functioning is measured by two types of indicators: lagging and leading. *Lagging indicators* are historical in nature. Once achieved, they can not be changed. *Leading indicators*, on the other hand, are the drivers of the lagging indicators. Put simply, what you get is a function of how you did it. This principle goes back to the work of W. Edwards Deming in the diagram that he provided as the logical foundation of his body of work. Its message was that productivity—broadly speaking—can be vastly enhanced by improving the quality of the processes by which outcomes are achieved.

The implication for the criteria is that they guide the team to be diligent and disciplined in selecting the methods, tools, and techniques appropriate for their particular project. The reason for the heavy emphasis on using good methodology is that the best methods will yield the best possible results. One of Dr. Deming's most famous questions was, "By what method?" meaning that the quality of facts is dependent on the methods used to derive them. Poor methods produce poor information. By the same token, the criteria also demand that the team present their actual achievements/outcomes, for example, improvements in customer satisfaction, cost, safety, or timeliness. So, the criteria balance the recognition of superior methodology (leading indicators) with the need for demonstrated results (lagging indicators).

In essence, a team that creates large tangible and intangible results for their organization but uses mediocre methodology would not score highly on the criteria because such results are a more matter of luck and not repeatable. Also, chances are that even more benefits could have been achieved using better methodology and that these additional benefits were left on the table. The other reason for the larger weight put on methodology is to normalize the scoring across a wide variety of teams. By this we mean that the absolute size of results is limited by the size of the enterprise. A business whose operating expenses are $50 thousand per year can not save the $100 thousand per year that a business with $1 million of annual operating expenses could accomplish. While normalization can partly be dealt with by using percentages, the nature of the base often differs among businesses, making percentages an apples-to-oranges comparison. The emphasis on good methodology also creates a level playing field for teams, which impacts motivation. Assigning people to a novice team with modest objectives should not limit the extent to which they can be recognized for excellent execution of their project if their methodology was very good and they did obtain the full possible benefits. So, the premise of the criteria is that good methodology will generate good results, and the best methodology will generate the best results. In Chapter 7 we discuss using the TEF as part of an organization's internal reward and recognition system. There are ways of supplementing recognition for good methodology with additional recognition for teams that also achieve benefits that are outstanding in absolute size.

The final set of information provided in this chapter is a summarized version of a project presentation from the 2010 Silver Award–winning team, Allegheny Energy Inc.'s Order Fulfillment Team. See Box 3.3 for this summary. It is provided so the reader can see an abbreviated example of how the team applied the criteria and accomplished a highly successful project. Their full presentation can be accessed from the ITEA website, http://wcqi.asq.org/team-competition/index.html, at the link "Winners' Presentations."

BOX 3.3: SUMMARY OF PROJECT PRESENTATION

Allegheny Energy, Inc. Order Fulfillment Team

This team was established to address material availability supporting its energy delivery business, a business that delivers power to commercial and residential customers. It used a DMAIC model of process improvement for its project.

Allegheny Energy, Inc. serves 1.5 million customers in three states. It has $3 billion in revenue.

Section 1. Project Selection and Purpose

1A. Explain the methods used to choose the project.

1Aa. Describe the types of data and quality tools used to select the project and why they were used.

The project selection process started with the company's vision, its high-performance work culture, and its balanced scorecard with six elements. Management used a *hoshin planning template* and applied four steps: Step 1—Gathering ideas and establishing a list of opportunities. Step 2—Prioritization and ranking. Steps 3 and 4—Identification of dependencies and external stakeholders. The project selected was to improve the fulfillment process for line item orders. Order fulfillment is a success if all the line items in an order are delivered in full and on time. If an order is not, then it is a failure. If any line item in the order is either short or late, the entire order is considered a failure.

1Ab. Explain the reasons the project was selected. Applying the hoshin process showed this project scoring significantly higher than all others. The need was further validated by results from the employee survey.

1Ac. Describe the involvement of potential stakeholders in project selection. A SIPOC diagram showed the stakeholders. The company's main external stakeholders, their customers, expect to have continuous power. A main component to customer service is having the necessary materials; it is the *supply chain*'s function to provide them. Internal stakeholders—company employees—were involved end-to-end from project selection to closeout. Additional "voice of the employee" involvement was achieved through breakfast meetings, executive visits, business unit representatives, and so on. A macro flow diagram illustrated where the order fulfillment process fits within the overall "end-to-end" material delivery process. The primary objective of the project was to improve order fulfillment, and the secondary objective was to decrease back order duration—the number of days to complete a failed request.

1B. Explain how the project supports/aligns with the organization's goals, performance measures, and/or strategies.

1Ba. Identify the affected organizational goals, performance measures, and/or strategies. The project supports three dimensions of the balanced scorecard. Each of these dimensions has goals set and performance measures associated with it. A chart shows the three affected dimensions and the goal set for each: operational excellence/order fulfillment of >95%, engaged employees/survey results +5% gain, and customer satisfaction/upper quartile of ACSI.

1Bb. Identify the types of impact on each goal, performance measure, and/or strategy. The same chart was expanded to show the impact in each area respectively, for example, operational excellence/ensure linemen have the materials available to do their job supporting service availability.

1Bc. Identify the degree of impact on each goal, performance measure, and/or strategy and how this was determined. A "degree of impact model" rating system was applied to determine the degree of impact of this project on each of the three goals. The result was that the degree of impact on operational excellence and employee engagement was rated as high; on customer service it was rated as critical.

1C. Identify the potential stakeholders and explain how they may be impacted by the project.

1Ca. Identify potential internal and external stakeholders and explain how they were identified. The hoshin process identified internal and external stakeholders, and a SIPOC diagram was used to confirm this list.

1Cb. Identify the types of potential impact on stakeholders and explain how these were determined. To identify the impacts and their interdependencies, the team created a chart, "Customer/Stakeholder Quality Requirements," which included the *critical to quality* (CTQ) requirements, such as business growth for suppliers and customer service for operations.

1Cc. Identify the degree of potential impact on stakeholders and explain how this was determined. The team added a column to the previous chart with the degree of each potential impact. The same degree of impact model that was used in 1Bc was applied to estimate the relative impacts. Of the eight impacts, one was rated low, two medium, four high, and one critical.

2. Current Situation Analysis

2A. Explain the approach/process the team used to identify the potential root causes/improvement opportunity(ies).

2Aa. Describe the methods and tools used to identify possible root causes/improvement opportunities. The team did interviews with employees and other stakeholders, asking what was causing the undesirable effect, and why. Then the team applied affinity diagrams, brainstorming, and data stratification.

2Ab. Describe the team's analysis of data to identify possible root causes/improvement opportunities. Affinity diagramming was done to sort the causes into categories. These categories were then ordered according to frequency with which they occurred. A chart was created displaying this information.

2Ac. Describe how or if any of the stakeholders were involved in identifying the possible root causes/improvement opportunities. Stakeholders were involved in several phases, from the initial brainstorming to verification of causes and prioritization of the impacts.

2B. Describe how the team analyzed information to identify the final root cause(s)/improvement opportunity(ies). (Include any appropriate validation.)

2Ba. Describe the methods and tools used to identify the final root cause(s)/improvement opportunity(ies). The team used the *5 whys* method to drill down to root cause for each of the eight impacts. They displayed an example of one in which it actually took 7 whys to get to the root cause.

2Bb. Describe the team's analysis of data to select the final root cause(s)/improvement opportunity(ies). The original causal data was further examined by deeper stratification levels to confirm root causes. Eight types of root causes were identified, such as exempt material, Service Center (SC) inventory accuracy, and SAP training.

2Bc. Identify the root cause(s)/improvement opportunity(ies) and explain how the team validated the final root cause(s)/improvement opportunity(ies). First an Ishikawa (fishbone) diagram was constructed using the eight root causes as the categories labeling the branches off the spine. The specific examples were added as smaller branches within the major branches. To validate the root causes, a solution matrix was created by collecting and analyzing data to verify the actual impact that resulted from each root cause category. The chart created showed, for each of these categories, the source of root cause verification. For example, SC Inventory Accuracy was validated by the Design Variance Report.

3. Solution Development

3A. Explain the methods used to identify the possible solutions/improvement actions.

3Aa. Describe the methods and tools used to develop possible solutions/improvement actions. Methods used included user/stakeholder input, brainstorming, benchmarking, economic analysis, and innovation.

3Ab. Describe the team's analysis of data to develop possible solutions/improvement actions. The team reviewed each root cause category and developed solutions it believed would create the most value for the company. It leveraged the database it had assembled for root cause analysis, which was a year's worth of order fulfillment data, to provide insight into solutions that would truly mitigate root causes of the problems.

3Ac. Indicate the criteria the team decided to use in selecting the final solution(s)/improvement action(s). The team used the solution's impact, its risk, and its cost as criteria.

3B. Explain how the final solution(s)/improvement action(s) was/were determined.

3Ba. Describe the methods and tools used by the team to select the final solution(s)/improvement action(s). The methods used were data confirmation, risk confirmation, cost confirmation, and resource mapping. Based on this, the team eliminated any solution that would impact the end-to-end process negatively. It then assigned clear accountability for each solution: that person had responsibility for collecting the data in the next step (3Bb).

3Bb. Describe the team's analysis of data to select the final solution(s)/improvement action(s). The team put together a solution matrix. In that chart, for each root cause the following information was assembled: when the solution could be implemented, cost–benefit, risks/barriers, success measures, and specific impacts. Each month, the team had analyzed each order that failed fulfillment and assigned a root cause. They used this information to help confirm the impact each solution would have.

3Bc. Describe the involvement of stakeholders in the selection of the final solution(s)/improvement action(s). Targeted stakeholders from the SIPOC were interviewed to see if the information in the solutions matrix tracked with their perceptions. These stakeholder types were listed by name, and included groups such as line engineering designers and retail delivery drivers. Then the final solutions were reviewed with the process owners and executives to gather their support. Stakeholders were involved in each stage of the DMAIC process throughout the project, including selecting the material for the pilot *kanban* program and developing the process to order and track the kanban material.

3C. Explain the final solution(s)/improvement action(s), validation, and the benefits expected to be realized by implementing the team's solution(s)/improvement action(s).

3Ca. Describe the final solution(s)/improvement action(s) and explain how the team validated the final solution(s)/improvement action(s). Eight final solutions emerged, such as kanban (a material-controlling signaling system that supports just-in-time inventory), first-pass accuracy (establish a goal to increase Service Center accuracy), and SAP configuration (implement system configurations properly aligned to business needs). The team validated these by data analysis and stakeholder confirmation. The team developed an improvement plan that estimated the impact of each solution over time. Each month, the team would ensure that the solution had the expected impact on performance.

3Cb. List the types of tangible and intangible benefits that are expected to be realized by implementing the team's solution(s)/improvement action(s). A chart was created containing four expected tangible benefits (for example, increased order fulfillment, lower inventory dollars) and three intangible benefits (for example, improved confidence and trust of the business units in the supply chain's ability to perform).

3Cc. Explain how the team used data to justify the implementation of the team's solution(s)/improvement action(s). For each solution a cost–benefit analysis was performed. These were presented to executive leadership for approval.

4. Project Implementation and Results

4A. Explain how buy-in/agreement was achieved for implementation.

4Aa. Indicate the types of internal and external (if applicable) stakeholder involvement in implementation. A chart was created showing each group of stakeholders and specifically what their involvement was in implementation of the solutions as well as in previous phases in the project. For example, the material analysts/buyers were involved in every phase of the project, extremely involved in implementation of the SAP solution, and facilitated the kanban implementation teams.

4Ab. Describe how various types of resistance were identified and addressed. The team categorized the resistance into two categories: (1) lack of employee willingness to change, (2) distrust of management. Then a more detailed chart was created with specific types of resistance and the actions needed to address each one. The team also referred back to the solutions matrix created during solution development for the "risks/barriers" identified there. Resistance was addressed and overcome by management actions to build trust and respect. They convinced the employees that improving organizational performance was in their best interests because it would provide them better job stability. In the case of kanban implementation, the project manager was carefully chosen for his ability to communicate well with the workforce.

4Ac. Explain how stakeholder buy-in was ensured. Buy-in was achieved by having had a representative from each stakeholder group involved in root cause analysis and solution development. For example, when developing the kanban solution, a regional representative from each of the states serviced was involved in a focus group that selected which material was to be included in that material handling process.

4B. Explain the approach used by the team to implement its solution(s)/improvement action(s) and to ensure the results.

4Ba. Describe the plan developed by the team to implement its solution(s)/improvement action(s). The project members reached outside the team to make sure a representative from every role that touches the retail delivery process was involved. Also, each distribution center has a very visible performance tracking board, and during the daily start-up meetings, the performance data are reviewed along with highlights of the coming day. A solution deployment Gantt chart was created. For each solution, it described the owner, the start and completion dates, and the main steps needed for implementation by month. The majority of solutions were implemented within six months. The kanban and distribution center (DC) inventory accuracy solutions took longer. A tracking chart was developed and used to monitor the resulting improvements in the overall order fulfillment rate.

4Bb. Describe the procedure, system, or other changes that were made to implement the solution(s)/improvement action(s) and to sustain the results. There were eight solutions implemented, and some were interdependent, requiring that certain ones be done before others. Moreover, some required a pilot program due to their magnitude and risk while others did not.

4Bc. Describe the creation and installation of a system for measuring and sustaining results. Daily control charts were implemented. They were used to track two types of order fulfillment failures: *DC process failures* and *material availability failures*. The DC managers are accountable for the former and the material analysts are accountable for the latter. In each case they are required to report on cause and take actions to mitigate the failures. This measurement system also created a change in culture, providing the employees with a greater sense of urgency to meet customer needs. Each month the consolidated data from these charts are reviewed by supply chain management. Another chart was created that is an aggregate gap analysis. Taken together, this information provides management the systemic knowledge they need to take necessary actions to sustain positive movement toward the overall goals. Lastly, several more documents were developed: (1) a *control plan* to create accountability that the solutions would remain in place, (2) a *process map* linked to the control plan in which each event has a person responsible, a process indicator, and an outcome measure, with this measure included in that person's performance review, (3) a *RACI chart* that documents for each solution who is to be responsible, accountable, consulted, and informed.

4C. Describe the results achieved.

4Ca. Identify the types of tangible and intangible results that were realized. The four tangible results presented were as follows: order fulfillment increased 38.4%, employee engagement as measured by the survey results on this particular issue increased 5%, inventory cost was reduced by $1.3 million, and customer satisfaction was in the upper quartile. An intangible result was an improvement in business unit confidence in the supply chain.

4Cb. Explain how the project's results link with the organization's goals, performance measures, and/or strategies. These results met the goals established at the beginning of the project.

4Cc. Describe how results were shared with stakeholders. A communications plan was developed and summarized in a chart presented by the team. The chart lists all the stakeholder groups. It includes three types of communication (BU leadership meeting, monthly dashboard, and daily reports) and specifies which types were used with which stakeholders. In addition, a Service Center Stratification Report was created. This enables supply chain employees to address customer service concerns at each of the 51 specific service center locations.

5. Team Management and Project Presentation

5A. Explain how the team members were selected and how they were involved throughout the project. Six criteria were used to select team members: problem-solving skills, people skills, communication ability, innovative thinking, customer focus, and providing representation from a stakeholder group. All team members were involved in all steps and aspects of the project.

5B. Explain how the team was prepared to work together in addressing the project. There were four aspects to team preparation: training session on problem solving and Six Sigma/DMAIC, a leader experienced with the *high-performance organization* approach as well as a Six Sigma Champion, use of structure (agenda, roles and responsibilities, action log), and checkpoints with senior leadership.

5C. Explain how the team managed its performance to ensure it was effective as a team. There were a number of elements used: project management tools such as a timeline, open team communications, mentoring, executive checkpoints, routine meetings, and recognition given at each milestone.

5D. The team will also be judged on the clarity and organization of its presentation.

CONCLUSION

The criteria embody a disciplined approach to improvement projects. They are generic enough to be relevant to all types of improvement projects, but they are sufficiently non-prescriptive to allow teams latitude in using the techniques and tools most appropriate to the project.

In Chapter 5 we will describe the criteria in more detail as well as provide guidance on how to select tools and techniques to address them.

First, we must cover how the project presentation is assessed relative to the items, how feedback comments from the assessment should be written, and how the organization and team can take best advantage of the feedback. These are the subjects of Chapter 4.

4

Team Excellence Assessment

How to Score the Criteria and Provide Useful Feedback

In Chapter 1 we explained that the TEF comprises three components: the Team Excellence Criteria, the method for assessing the extent to which the Criteria's items were met by the project team, and the method for writing and delivering feedback. This chapter is organized to accomplish three major purposes:

- To explain how to assess a project presentation.
- To explain how to write useful feedback.
- To describe how organizational management and teams can use the feedback to best advantage.

The audience for this chapter is both teams and those who assess their projects against the Team Excellence Criteria. One of our goals is to increase the number of qualified assessors to support more teams using the criteria as a guide to doing their projects. As assessors better understand these criteria, they will score more accurately and provide better feedback. Also, when the teams better understand how projects are assessed, they will produce better results.

This chapter is organized to meet its threefold purpose. In the first section we discuss how to assess a project presentation. In other words, we cover how to score the items in the Criteria and explain the rationale for doing so. In the second section we explain the "3 wide 3 deep" dimensions of the criteria (see Figure 4.1) and how to write actionable feedback that is useful for teams and their management sponsors. In the third section we describe ways in which to use the feedback to improve the performance of your improvement teams.

Team materials can be found at the ITEA website at http://wcqi.asq.org/team-competition/criteria-scoring.html and other websites noted in

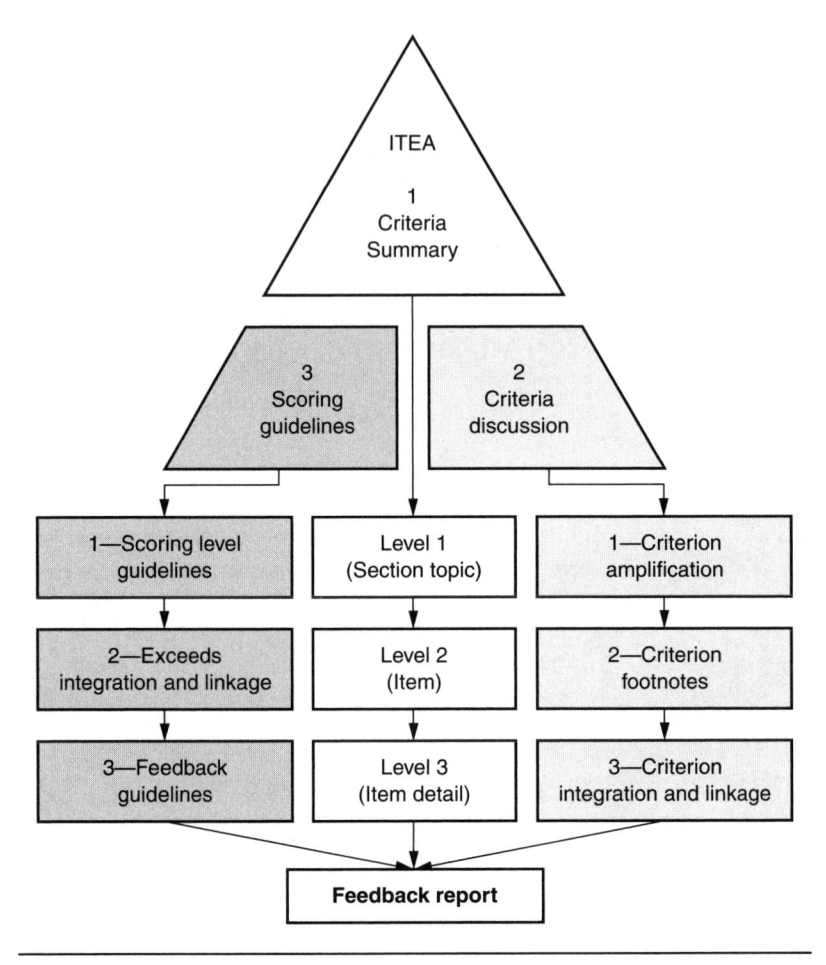

Figure 4.1 Criteria 3×3 dimension tree.

this chapter. Who should be selected to assess project presentations? A prerequisite for people being chosen to score project presentations and write feedback is that they must have an adequate understanding of both CI and teamwork. The more they know about both these subjects, the better they can be at the task. Then they must learn the assessment methodology of the TEF. Experience has shown that most people with these prerequisites can learn how to score presentations and write feedback fairly quickly. Not surprisingly, there is a continuum between being a novice and an expert at scoring. The most highly qualified TEF assessors (who are called "judges" in the ITEA recognition process) have years of experience, and these are the people who serve as judges in the final round of the ITEA (described in Chapter 7). The point here is that your organization does not need world-class assessors to do a credible job at scoring and writing feedback. Someone with the prerequisite qualifications can learn this skill at a basic level in six to eight hours. Also, there are different ways for people to learn this skill, including online, in classroom, through coaching by a lead assessor, or a combination of these.

In this chapter we explain how to score and write feedback, and readers can glean much of what one needs to know on this subject. If you are experienced doing other forms of assessment, such as Baldrige examinations or quality audits, you will find this skill even easier to learn. However, it can be advantageous to supplement this explanation with some form of training, especially if you have not had any type of assessment experience. Chapter 7 describes opportunities for training through the ITEA Process and associated Showcase programs in other countries and states. Another option is offered by the California Team Excellence Award (CTEA) program (described in Table 7.1). CTEA, a unit of the California Council for Excellence, is an authorized State Showcase of ITEA's recognition process. CTEA offers a free comprehensive set of online materials to assist teams and assessors located anywhere. One is an effective online training package required of all those who serve as judges in their Showcase team presentations. CTEA makes this training available online to anyone who wants to take it, so this is another training option. To access this training package, visit their website at: http://www.calexcellence.org/ctea.html. A helpful hint to make your teams more successful in producing results is to train some team members, facilitators, and champions to be assessors. Becoming an assessor is a very useful means of learning how to meet and exceed the requirements in each item of the criteria.

A last thing to consider when using assessors is how many you want to use for a given project presentation. In an external formal recognition process such as ITEA, a panel of three to five is used, and there is a consensus procedure that enables them to agree on a single set of scores. However, there are circumstances when one assessor will suffice, including: (1) when you are using the TEF for internal purposes of improving project success rather than for formally recognizing team accomplishments, (2) when your organization is just getting started with using the TEF and can not dedicate too many people to improvement teams and their assessment.

HOW TO ASSESS PROJECT PRESENTATIONS

The Basic Elements of Scoring Project Presentations

The basic elements of scoring are straightforward. Assessment simply involves making a judgment about the extent to which the presentation addresses each Criteria item requirement. There are only three things an assessor needs: (1) the Criteria, (2) the team's presentation, and (3) the scoring scale and guidelines.

- *The Criteria.* Use the Criteria at the level of detail that the team used. In other words, match the precision of assessment to the maturity of the team/organization in terms of its CI and teamwork sophistication. There are three overall options: If the team used the Criteria (amplified), then assess them at that level. If the team used the Criteria Summary, then assess them accordingly. If the team used only the higher level of the Criteria, for example, 1A, 1B, 1C, 2A, 2B, then apply that level of assessment.

- *"Two-part" Criteria questions.* When looking closer at the criteria detail, one will notice that at the level 3 criteria detail, many of the criteria questions are two-part questions. These two-part questions are found in 1Aa, 1Bc, 1Ca, 1Cb, 1Cc, 2Bc, 3Ca, 3Cb, 4Ab, 4Bb, 4Bc, 4Ca, and 5A. Here, when scoring at the level 3 criteria detail, the team must address both criteria questions to be considered for scoring at the "Meets" level. If the team is missing one of the two-part criteria questions, then the team response is unclear, thus warranting only an "Unclear" level score.

- *The presentation.* This can be in the form of a live team presentation, a video of a team presentation, or in the form of a hard/soft copy of the slides accompanied by speaker notes, which should be the same verbiage as what the team would have said if they had presented it.

- *Option scores and scoring guidelines.* The assessors evaluate the extent to which each item in the Criteria is addressed in the presentation and assign one of the four possible scores (level 0 score—Not covered, level 1 score—Unclear, level 2 score—Meets criteria, or level 3 score—Exceeds criteria). In order to render each judgment, they use the scoring guidelines to help them pick the most accurate score for each item. See Table 4.2, Table 4.3, and Figure 4.4.

If the scoring and feedback are being used primarily to drive internal improvement, especially by organizations relatively new to the TEF, the level of effort put into the details of scoring should be tailored to the level of sophistication of the teams. For example, if an organization is not sophisticated about why and how to select projects that are aligned to organizational goals, then general scoring that informs them about where they did well and where they fell short is simple but very valuable information. The point here is to match the level of precision of your scoring to the level at which the team and organization can assimilate the information. Providing a novice team or organization with large amounts of detailed scoring and associated feedback can be overwhelming and discouraging. Make the feedback information value-added, meaning that the team and its management can absorb it and will find it motivating to participate in future improvements.

In the remainder of this section we cover all the elements of full-blown scoring that should be used for team presentations in an organization with mature team-based CI programs and/or presentations being submitted to a recognition process. Recognition programs must be highly credible and detailed so that they are viewed as fair and technically professional by the teams who are participating. This is true for both external recognition programs and ones that are internal to organizations.

Understanding the Various Dimensions of the Criteria

The first step is to understand the multiple dimensions of the criteria and how they are used to provide an objective assessment and non-prescriptive feedback on a team project. The Team Excellence Criteria have *three dimensions*: (1) *Criteria Summary*, (2) *Criteria Discussion*, and (3) *Criteria Scoring Guidelines*. The objective of the *"Criteria 3×3 Dimension Tree"* is to provide a best practice framework for a systematic approach to guide team assessment, scoring, and actionable feedback.

To graphically present these three dimensions, we developed a model called the "Criteria 3×3 Dimension Tree" as shown in Figure 4.1.

The Team Excellence Criteria Three Dimensions and Dimension Detail

The Criteria consists of five sections and three dimensions (levels) of detail. They form a systematic, sequential step-by-step approach for a team to self-assess or qualified evaluator to perform an assessment of an improvement project. An example of Section 1 is shown in Table 4.1, which presents the

> **Level 1 (Dimension 1 of the Criteria Summary)**
>
> 1. Project selection and Purpose (9 items @ 3 points = 27 points possible)
>
>   **Level 2 (Dimension 2 of the Criteria Summary)**
>
>   1A. Explain the methods used to choose the project. (Provide specific examples of techniques and data used.)
>
>   **Level 3 (Dimension 3 of the Criteria Summary)**
>
>   a. Describe the types of data and/or quality tools used to select the project, and why they were used.
>
>   b. Explain the reasons why the project was selected.
>
>   c. Describe the involvement of potential stakeholders in project selection.

Table 4.1 Criteria Summary example.

three dimensions of the criteria in the *Criteria Summary*, *Criteria Discussion* (amplification), and *footnotes* to clarify the intent of the criteria.

Criteria Summary Dimension (1)

Figure 4.2 identifies the criteria process flow for each section, items and scoring points, and number of item requirements to address.

Note that Table 4.1 is based on Figure 4.2, which was obtained from Whisman and Levenhagen (2011). Figure 4.2 also includes the information about the scoring point distribution.

Criteria Discussion Dimension (2)

Level 1

1. Project selection and purpose focus on both why and how a project was selected, including explaining the importance of the project as it relates both to the organization sponsoring the project and to potential project stakeholders.

Level 2

1A. Explain the methods used to choose the project. Provide specific examples of techniques and data used. The project may be selected by the team or assigned by management, but the process used to select the project must be clear and well stated.

Level 3

1Aa. *Describe* how data and/or tools were used to support the selection, even if the project is assigned to the team. Explain the tools and/or data the organization used and why they used them.

Systematic approach for team projects

1. Project selection and purpose	2. Current situation analysis	3. Solution development	4. Project implementation and results
(3 items, 27 points)	(2 items, 27 points)	(3 items, 27 points)	(3 items, 27 points)
(9 item requirements)	(6 item requirements)	(9 item requirements)	(9 item requirements)

→ Project logical flow and timeline →

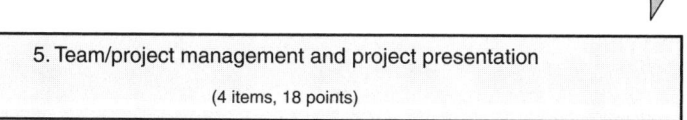

5. Team/project management and project presentation
(4 items, 18 points)

Figure 4.2 Criteria process flow.

Note: 1Aa addresses the tools and data used. The emphasis in this item is on the decisions made as a result of the tool usage/data analysis in 1Aa.

1Ab. *Explain* how and why the project was selected—what discerned gap or observed opportunity led to the launching of this project?

1Ac. *Describe* the potential stakeholders for the project and how they participated in the selection process. If the stakeholders were not directly involved, then *describe* how their interests were known and taken into account.

Note: This is intended to be a historical presentation, and the actual/final stakeholders may be different from the potential stakeholders at the time the project was being defined. The goal here is to be sure that the project was not selected in a vacuum without an understanding of the organizational environment.

Also, there are four descriptors (*describe*, *explain*, *identify*, and *indicate*) used in each criteria to show the level of information being requested. Each is further defined as follows:

- *Describe* looks for sufficient information such that the object or methodology being described would be recognizable to another.

- *Explain* goes a step further by giving sufficient information such that an observer would at least be able to understand the usage and implications of what is explained, if not actually be able to use or apply it themselves.

- *Identify* means that a simple list is all that is necessary to meet the requirements.

- *Indicate* means that something needs to have attention drawn to it, such as in a list or possibly by a statement about a single item.

The model in Figure 4.3 further demonstrates the progressive structure in the application of the criteria. The *section* level is the overarching subject matter, the *item* level is the general question on the subject matter, and the *item requirements* are the multiple questions to be addressed on the item-level general question.

Criteria Discussion Dimension (3)

Criteria amplification, Criteria footnotes, and Criteria integration and cross-linkage.

1. *Criteria amplification (Dimension 1 on the Criteria Discussion).* Each *criteria summary* section has three dimensions of criteria question detail, except for Section 5, which has two dimensions. This is reflected here in the criteria hierarchy as shown in Figure 4.1, Criteria Summary, and the Criteria Discussion. You will note this by looking at each of the criteria sections in both the Criteria Summary and the Criteria Discussion.

Example: Section 1 Project Selection and Purpose is the (Level 1)—subject matter to be addressed, 1A is the (Level 2)—core subject matter question (*describe, explain, identify,* and *indicate*) to be answered, and *1Aa* is the (Level 3)—detail subject matter question to be answered. The three dimensions of the criteria also correlate with the three levels of scoring in the Scoring Guidelines.

The team must have a balanced focus on all sections and levels of detail to score well on an assessment. In addition, there are three key factors in a team presentation: (1) scripted speaker notes that address all criteria in

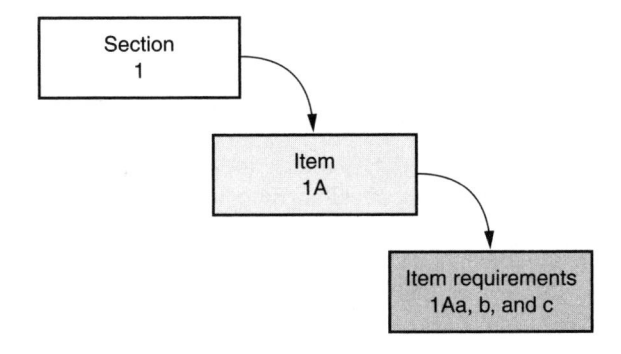

Figure 4.3 Criteria progressive structure.

each section and dimensions of the criteria in support of the slides, (2) clear PowerPoint slide text and graphics along with speaker notes that support the Criteria items, (3) Criteria Sections 1 through 4 represent a four-phase timeline of the team project or process improvement event and should unfold like the story line in a four-act play.

    2. *Footnotes (Dimension 2 on the Criteria Discussion).* Throughout the criteria you will find numerous footnotes. The footnotes provide an added level of amplification to bring further clarity to the criteria.

    3. *Integration and cross-linkage (Dimension 3 on the Criteria Discussion).* Both the Criteria Discussion Notes and Scoring Guidelines "Exceed" column draws attention to where an item detail has a connection (cross-linkages) to other criteria item(s). The objective is to identify to the criteria user that addressing a criteria item detail in one area has an impact on one or more other criteria areas. How the team addresses these cross-linkages indicates the degree of integration within the team project, stakeholder, and organization direction. This is a significant factor for a team to score at the "Exceeds" level. This is discussed further next in the Scoring Guidelines dimension.

Criteria Scoring Guidelines—Dimension (3)

Here we will discuss:

- The four levels of scoring
- Guidelines for scoring each level
- Methods for reaching consensus
- How to write effective feedback comments
- How teams can best use the feedback.

Table 4.2 shows the four scoring levels (Not covered, Unclear, Meets, Exceeds) that an assessor can assign to each of the criteria items. These scoring levels are intended as a high-level guideline for determining a first impression score and not a method for the final score for all or any items. To arrive at an appropriate score, an assessor must understand the item requirements, measure them against the evidence presented, and then use the Scoring Guidelines as shown in Table 4.2. Even here the scoring level may not be black and white. A seasoned assessor's tip! When you know it's not the lower scoring level but uncertain if it meets the requirements for the higher level, give the team the benefit of the doubt and assign the higher scoring level. If you are serving on an assessment panel, don't be too concerned about this indecision at the independent scoring step because this

Assessor option	Score
Not covered	**(Level 0 score) 0**—Totally missing. **(No approach evident)**
Unclear	**(Level 1 score) 1 (1.5) points**—Touched on, but not clear. Not enough information is provided to determine if the team's approach met, or could meet, the criterion requirements. **(Approach evident)**
Meets criteria	**(Level 2 score) 2 (or 3) points**—Sufficient information is provided to determine that the team's approach met the criterion requirements. **(Approach applied with results evident)**
Exceeds criteria	**(Level 3 score) 3 (or 4.5) points**—The team's approach goes beyond meeting the criterion and provides additional clarity indicating increased accuracy in the team's analysis, actions, and/or conclusions. *Integration* with other criterion items is apparent and enhances the team's overall results. A "best practice" or "role model" approach. **(Approach broadly integrated and evident)**
Example of integration: Many criteria questions reference other criteria items of the criteria. An example of this integration is, in 1Aa which tie to your response in 2Aa. This indicates there must be evidence here of this linkage to justify an Exceeds level score. Also, it should be evident that key approaches and CI tools are broadly used by the team as a "Best Practice or Role Model throughout the project or CI event.	

Table 4.2 Assessment option score for item requirements.

can be addressed in the consensus scoring process. See the material below, under The Method for Reaching Consensus.

Although Figure 4.4 defines the requirements for each scoring level in Table 4.2, we suggest for internal assessments you may want to consider a simpler method, shown in Table 4.3.

Exceeds Criteria—Scoring Integration and Cross-Linkage

Throughout the Criteria Sections 1 through 4 you will find that some items will reference another item within the same or another section. For example, there is an "Integration" requirement cross-linked to different stakeholder groups that is important to address in 2Aa and 4Ab. Integration with other criteria items, if apparent, can enhance the team's overall results. To

Assessment Worksheet						
Section/item	Section/item description	Not covered	Unclear	Meets criteria	Exceeds criteria	Score
1	**Project selection and purpose (9 item requirements at 3 points each = 27 possible)**					
1Aa	Describe the types of data and quality tools used to select the project, and why.	0	1	2	3	0
Strengths						
OFIs						
1Ab	Explain the reasons why the project was selected.	0	1	2	3	
Strengths						
OFIs						
1Ac	Describe the involvement of potential stakeholders in project selection.	0	1	2	3	
Strengths						
OFIs						
Scoring guidelines >>	No approach evident >	X	^	^	^	
	Approach evident >		X	^	^	
	Approach applied with results evident >			X	^	
	Approach broadly integrated evident >				X	
	Progressive maturity score > > > >					

Figure 4.4 Assessment notes and scoresheet.

score at the "Exceeds" level the team must effectively demonstrate it has addressed this and provide evidence of this in their presentation.

Example in criterion 1Cb amplification: 1Cb. Identify the types of potential impacts on stakeholders and explain how these were determined.

> - Totally missing = No approach is evident
> - Unclear = Approach evident (an approach to the item requirement question is evident)
> - Meets criteria = Approach is applied with result evident
> - Exceeds criteria = Approach is broadly integrated

Table 4.3 Alternate scoring method.

Stakeholders may be impacted in many different ways by the project, from quality to timeliness. Demonstrating that the team understands how the project may have different impacts on the different stakeholder groups is important. As with 1Bb (type of goal impact), the impact is implied to be directional. *Note: This section could later tie to 4Ab, as correctly predicting potential negative impacts early in the project can help the team prepare to overcome resistance later.* (See Appendix A, "International Team Excellence Award Process—Criteria," for all criteria cross-linkages and integration requirements.)

The cross-linkage in 1Cb with 1Bb and 4Ab, if addressed per the criteria, would indicate there is a degree of *integration* in the team's approach across the project and/or organization.

Teams who take the time to understand the *cross-linkage* and *integration factor* and use it during the team project will achieve greater results in cost, quality, and cycle time reduction, as well as in stakeholder involvement and satisfaction.

Assessor's Assessment Notes and Scoresheet

Figure 4.4 shows the Assessment Worksheet. It is used to record first impressions on Dimension 3, which we call the "item requirements" (1Aa, b, and c) level of the criteria scoring, and comments as to *strengths* and *opportunities for improvement* (OFIs) as they relate to the criteria. Feedback guidelines for writing strengths and opportunities for improvement comments will be covered later in this chapter.

The Method for Reaching Consensus—Applicable Only to Assessment Panels

The next step in the scoring process is the assessment panel's *consensus scoring* session. As mentioned above, using more than one assessor is not necessary in all circumstances. However, in some circumstances it is desirable, and in other circumstances it is necessary. An example of the latter is when presentations are being assessed for a recognition process.

The process of reaching consensus should be well defined in advance of the session, and all the recognition programs use a fairly similar process. In essence it is as follows: A member of the assessment panel collects and posts all scores to the Consensus Scoresheet (Figure 4.5). If there is more than one scoring level deviation (see example on line 1Bb, 3–2–2–1, in Figure 4.5), the assessment panel must come to a consensus score within one deviation. As you can see, through this consensus process the assessors

	Assessment Panel Consensus Scoresheet					
Section/ item	Section/item description	Assessor 1	Assessor 2	Assessor 3	Assessor 4	Average score
1	Project selection and purpose (9 item requirements at 3 points each = 27 possible)					
1Aa	Describe the types of data and quality tools used to select the project, and why.	2	2	1	1	1.5
1Ab	Explain the reasons why the project was selected.	2	3	2	1	2.0
1Ac	Describe the involvement of potential stakeholders in project selection.	1	2	1	2	1.5
1Ba	Identify the affected organizational goals, performance measures, and/or strategies.	3	3	2	3	2.8
1Bb	Identify the types of impact on each goal, performance measure, and/or strategy.	3	2	2	1	2.0
1Bc	Identify the affected organizational goals, performance measures, and/or strategies.	2	2	2	2	2.0
1Ca	Identify potential internal and external stakeholders and explain how they were identified.	3	3	2	3	2.8
1Cb	Identify the types of potential impact on stakeholders and explain how determined.	2	3	1	2	2.0
1Cc	Identify the degree of potential impact on stakeholders and explain how determined.	2	2	1	2	1.8
	Section consensus score					2.0

Figure 4.5 Assessment panel consensus scoresheet.

are able to arrive at an accurate score for the team presentation. This step is also is a contributing factor in crafting the feedback report comments discussed later in this chapter.

How to Write Effective Non-Prescriptive Actionable Feedback Reports (Dimension 3 of the Scoring Guidelines)

The Feedback Report contains two types of information. One is the scores, and putting them into the Feedback Report is simply a matter of transferring them from the assessor scoresheet. The other type is the feedback comments. This section covers how to write feedback comments.

From the assessor's individual Assessment Worksheet comments the assessor(s) develop a clear statement for each *strength* and *opportunity for improvement* (OFI) using the Comment and Style Guidelines below. In the case of an assessment panel, they also have to agree on all the comments written.

According to Jim Bianchetta (pers. comm.), a long-time ITEA judge, there are several important characteristics of good feedback comments:

1. What to include in each comment: (a) the number of the Criteria item, (b) the number on the presentation slide(s) that the comment addresses, (c) the language of the Criteria item in the form of a brief quote or paraphrase from the item, (d) the language of the team in the form of a brief quote or paraphrase from the relevant slide(s).

2. What the qualities of a good comment are: (a) accurate, (b) specific, (c) non-prescriptive, (d) actionable, (e) complete sentences, (d) criteria-based, meaning it makes an explicit connection of the comment to the content of the Criteria item.

His advice on how to select the items for comment is as follows: The highest-scoring items should be the ones selected for strength comments, and the lowest-scoring items should be selected for OFI comments. Comments on integration should only be written if they show up on the scoring sheet as exceeds criteria.

Comment Guidelines

Do:

- Address comments to the basic, overall, or multiple-criteria requirements that are most important to the team—keep the feedback to what was presented.

- Write a unified, coherent, well-developed comment to provide value to the team. Include a topic sentence to express the main point of the comment, followed by concisely written evidence that develops the main idea in greater detail. *(Hint: Reach a conclusion and write it first, moving from generalization to support.)*

- Include factual supporting detail. Ask, "What examples can be provided from the team's response to clarify the strength or improvement?" Include slide numbers in comments, as appropriate. Do not, however, construct an exhaustive list of every method described by the team that is related to your conclusion.

- Use the scoring guidelines (not covered, unclear, meets requirements, and exceeds criteria) levels approach to clearly articulate the areas of strength or to provide insights that will help the team improve overall effectiveness and capabilities. Where appropriate for the "exceeds" level, draw linkages across items or between items that show evidence of integration.

- Ensure that the comment does not contradict other comments in the same item or other items.

Do not:

- Go beyond the requirements of the criteria or assert your personal opinions.

- Be prescriptive by using "could," "should," or "would."

- Be judgmental by using terms such as "good," "bad," or "inadequate."

- Comment on the team's style of presentation or data and graphics presentation, except for item 5D.

Style Guidelines

Do:

- Use a polite, professional, and positive tone.

- Use active voice (for example, "completes" rather than "is completed") and present tense.

- Use vocabulary/phraseology from the criteria and the scoring guidelines.

- Describe what is missing if something "is unclear."
- Use "the team" and generic terms to avoid repetition in comments.
- Use the team's terminology when appropriate.

Do not:

- "Parrot" the team or the criteria. Provide only enough language to add clarity—seek to add value rather than restate information.
- Use jargon or acronyms unless they are used by the team.

Examples of Good Comments on Strengths and Opportunities for Improvement

1. Project Selection and Purpose

Strengths:

- Excellent information was provided explaining why this project was selected (slide 3) (1Ab). Six Sigma tools were used to justify the project selection and were clearly explained and illustrated in slides 6–9. Additionally, the use of data to substantiate this project's selection was highly informative.
- The team adequately aligned their project choice with the organizational goals and provided clear and concise details on the data used to show linkage. The team exceeded expectation by using underlying customer satisfaction–based issues to further justify project alignment with overall global organizational goals (slide 11) (1Ba).
- The presentation effectively identified the internal and external stakeholders and clearly assigned rated measures to show how much they will be impacted by the project (slide 17) (1Cb).

Opportunities for improvement:

- While the team showed how they used Six Sigma tools DMADV and SIPOC to identify potential stakeholders, there was no evidence provided to describe how these potential stakeholders were involved in the selection of the project (slide 10) (1Ac).
- While the team described the assignment of measurable factors of the impact of the project on organizational goals, it was not evident "*how*" the team arrived at this determination (slide 10) (1Bb).

- The team clearly explained the types of impact and the degree of impact of the project on both internal and external stakeholders; however, in order to strengthen this item the judges were searching for information on "*how the scores and measurable data were obtained*" (slides 17–18) (1Cb and 1Cc).

A final thought on learning the skill of writing good feedback comments is taken from the following observation by Jim Bianchetta (pers.comm.): "All judges should be required to write good feedback because it forces them to better understand the intent of the criteria. Usually this takes several cycles of experience." This observation ties back to the benefits for individuals and their organizations to develop selected people into good team excellence assessors.

HOW ORGANIZATIONS AND TEAMS CAN BEST USE THE FEEDBACK

The purpose of feedback is to help organizations increase their success rate with team-based improvement projects. This section provides suggestions to management and teams on how to do this. The capacity to improve by using feedback is the essence of an adaptable, learning organization.

Customers for the Feedback

There are two customers for the feedback report: the team and management. The first actually consists of all those associated with the team, for example, members, facilitators, leaders, champions, and sponsors. They should each individually read and reflect on the feedback, thinking about what they learned from it. Then they should convene and discuss it. Lastly, they should develop a written list of things they learned that can (a) help them do a better job on improvement projects in the future, and (b) could help others in the organization do the same. These latter lessons learned should be provided to the second audience. If the team thinks that any of the lessons learned warrant changes that go beyond their specific project, then they should also make recommendations to management about the organization's approach to team-based improvement projects.

The second audience is the management structure and staff responsible for CI in the organization. This includes both line management and CI/quality staff. They should independently review the feedback and draw their own conclusions. Then they should also get the lessons learned report of the team:

> Lessons learned, also called "after action reviews," "sunset reviews," and "postmortems," bring project stakeholders together to discuss what went well, and not so well, during the course of the project. It's an important step that is often lost to competing interests as the project team, clients, and sponsors rejoice in the successful close of the project.... Project leaders... gather feedback ... about what went well and what could improve.... Second, they invest in the team members who did the heavy lifting on the project. By engaging these team members and asking for their feedback, project leaders nurture strong relationships that help ensure successful projects in the future. (Passion and Gotsill 2010, 58)

The lessons learned have implications related to how the organization does CI projects and how it creates and uses teams to do so. This information can improve policies, procedures, employee development, and team staffing. For example, if feedback suggests an issue with the way the team was selected, this suggests that management is doing it ad hoc and is in need of a sound procedure. If this same feedback is received for several different teams, it is a strong sign that this issue needs attention. In another example, if management gets feedback on a series of projects that they meet the criteria on root cause analysis items but never exceed them, then to get to the next level, management needs to improve their toolbox and tool training in order to achieve the highest level of team excellence in this area. By the same token, if their teams consistently receive high scores accompanied by strength comments in the area of root cause analysis, management knows that their efforts should be put into beefing up other CI capabilities that did not score as high.

Sources of Feedback

There are two sources of feedback: (1) from internal assessors and (2) from assessors (judges) in an external recognition program, such as ITEA or other regional Showcase programs described in Chapter 7. In either case, the two types of feedback should be aligned since the same general approach should be used to write it. There are only two important differences. One is that internal assessors can match the level of detail in the feedback to the maturity level of their organization and/or team. The other is that the teams might be able to solicit additional clarification from their internal assessors, something they can not do with external assessors. In either case, you should understand that the feedback report is not meant to be a detailed evaluation. It is designed to provide you with effective knowledge that helps you learn how to improve future team projects.

Understanding and Applying the Feedback Report

Lack of Clarity

Both the team and other receivers of the feedback report must be aware that the feedback report is based on the team presentation, which includes the slides and speaker statements or written speaker notes. Therefore, both the slides and the accompanying statements from the team must be clear to the assessor. And, understand that if the assessor is external to your organization, he/she is likely unfamiliar with your industry. Therefore, it is possible for some scores to be impacted simply because the presentation did not adequately communicate all the good work that was done. Your score on item 5D, pertaining to "the clarity and organization of its presentation," will give you a general indication of how much this issue affected the scores. Another indication is when an item has been scored as "unclear." There are two reasons this can happen. One is that it was not explained clearly by the team. The other is that the method or data used were clearly explained, but were not up to the task required by the item. If you see an item scored as "unclear" but you are sure that the team at least met the item criteria or perhaps even exceeded it with good methodology and/or data, then you can conclude it was not communicated properly. The obvious take-away is that teams need to work on their presentation clarity. Specific helpful hints include: presentations should be done in plain language, each slide should be labeled with the item that is being addressed, and be sure to explain any acronyms or technical terms unless you are positive everyone in the audience knows them. While in one way it may seem unfair that good work got low scores for lack of clarity, in the big picture this is perfectly reasonable. There are countless examples of excellent improvement projects that did not get adopted for lack of the team being able to articulate their case to their own management. Getting your message across is not sufficient, but it most certainly is necessary.

Substantive Issues

For items where communication clarity has been discounted as an issue, then the feedback communicates the substance of how well the project was done. The feedback report scores are indicators for each item, but the most valuable part of the feedback report is the feedback comments. Because these are written to be actionable, they are meant to be straightforward. Taken together, they are intended to provide both the team and its organization with the means for improving the success rate of improvement teams.

The two categories, *strengths* and *OFIs*, each provide useful information. The usefulness of OFI information is more obvious because it informs management and teams about the specific areas in which to change their approaches and tools for team-based improvement. However, the use of strengths information is equally useful but sometimes overlooked. Principles of employee engagement show that leaders should use more positive feedback than negative feedback for most employees. (The exception is employees whose behavior requires disciplinary measures.) Yet many managers often neglect to acknowledge employees when they perform tasks well. The feedback report gives management a great opportunity to compliment the team on all the specific strengths documented in the comments as well as the items in which they scored as "meets" or "exceeds." One of the principles of good feedback is that it helps to be specific, and the Team Excellence feedback report is very specific.

CONCLUSION

In conclusion, this chapter on assessment provided information on how to score presentations, how to provide useful feedback comments, and how organizations and their teams can best use the feedback scores and comments to continuously improve. In addition, it gave insight into the professional means used by the ITEA Process to provide a quality assessment and feedback report for the project team and their organization. Having qualified assessors who use an objective, accurate, and consistent method is crucial to the credibility of the assessment and recognition process. However, the most important point is that you can employ the same assessment and feedback process inside your organization and tailor its level of detail to the needs of your organization.

The material in this chapter is useful to both assessors and to those associated with the improvement teams themselves. In Chapter 5 we present information that is particularly useful to teams and everyone in the organization who supports them. There we provide information on how to apply models, tools, and techniques to improve project success, using the Team Excellence Criteria as a guide. We supplement this information with examples from validated success stories.

5
Application of the Criteria and Related Tools
How to Successfully Apply the Criteria

The purpose of this chapter is to provide more-detailed information on how to use the Team Excellence Criteria to have more successful team-based improvement projects. Throughout this book we emphasize the benefits of applying it as a guide in planning and executing your projects. This chapter is directed at teams who are starting new improvement projects, including the sponsors, champions, leaders, technical support staff, and members. We want to help you and your organization have the most beneficial project possible. The information is also useful to anyone who is putting together a presentation to submit to the ITEA recognition process or its affiliated regional Showcase programs described in Chapter 7.

The Criteria has four distinct groups: (1) Section 1 is the *"Whys"* and *"Whats"* the project is about, (2) Sections 2 and 3 are the *"Hows"* of the project analysis and problem resolution, (3) Section 4 is all about the *"Outcomes,"* and (4) Section 5 is focused on *"Team and Project Management."*

For example, when the criteria are used by teams as a checklist, it significantly improves the approach, deployment, and outcomes of the project and boosts team performance. Another example would be when the criteria are used on a process improvement event or project that has been completed, and it is just a matter of answering the criteria requirements, creating the graphics for the PowerPoint slides, and writing the script (speaker notes) for a project presentation.

This chapter covers material in the following five categories:

1. How to use the criteria as a project checklist

2. Techniques and tools to meet and exceed the criteria

3. Best practice examples of using tools to exceed the criteria
4. Must-do's for an effective project presentation
5. Advice from experienced assessors

HOW TO USE THE CRITERIA AS A PROJECT CHECKLIST

Table 5.1 represents our suggestion for how to use the Criteria as a project planning and management checklist. Our thinking is, before a team starts a project, one should first start with Section 5, "Team Project Management and Project Presentation." We say this because Section 5 defines the four core requirements for a team and its management sponsors to successfully handle the management of the team dynamics and the execution of the project. So, we highly recommend that organizations use the Criteria as a project planning tool. Much of what is required by Section 5 must be done by management, both general management and the team sponsors, champions, and/or leaders. Some of it must be done by the team itself in its ongoing self-management to learn and practice effective teamwork. And the other four sections should be used as a project management checklist to assure desired project outcomes.

TECHNIQUES AND TOOLS TO MEET AND EXCEED THE CRITERIA

The value-add from using the Team Excellence Criteria is the positive impact on business results when it starts being used as a best practice coupled with the use of CI/quality tools across the organization. Improvement teams are a great way to begin to integrate CI across an organization. The best part about the improvement team approach is that it is like working with a focus group. You zero in on the targeted area using a systematic improvement model, for example, PDC/SA or DMAIC-V approach as mentioned in Chapter 3, and supplement these models with a toolbox of CI/quality tools such as the Table 5.2 ASQ quality tool kit. This would be a step in the right direction in addressing the ITEA criteria. The ASQ quality tools web page can be found at: http://asq.org/learn-about-quality/quality-tools.html. Many of these tools are listed in Table 5.3, "DMAIC-V methodology," and

Application of the Criteria and Related Tools 95

1. (Criteria Section 5) Team and Project Management and Project Reporting

    5A. How will the team members be selected and how will they be involved throughout the project?

    5B. How will the team be prepared to work together in addressing the project?

    5C. How will the team be managed in its performance to ensure it is effective as a team?

    5D. How often and how will the team prepare for project progress reporting intervals?

2. (Criteria Section 1) Project Selection and Purpose

    1A. What methods will be used to choose the project?

    1B. How will the project support/align with the organization's goals, performance measures, and/or strategies?

    1C. Who are the potential internal and external stakeholders and how might they be impacted by the project?

3. (Criteria Section 2) Current Situation Analysis

    2A. What approach/process will the team use to identify the potential root causes and improvement opportunities?

    2B. How will the team analyze information to identify the final root causes and improvement opportunities, including any appropriate validation?

4. (Criteria Section 3) Solution Development

    3A. What methods will be used to identify the possible solutions/improvement actions?

    3B. How will the final solutions and improvement actions be determined?

    3C. What final solutions, improvement actions, validation, and expected benefits will be realized by implementing the team's solution?

5. (Criteria Section 4) Project Implementation and Results

    4A. How will the team get buy-in/agreement to achieve the solution's implementation?

    4B. What approaches will be used by the team to implement its solutions and improvement actions, and to ensure the results?

    4C. What results are expected to be achieved?

Table 5.1 Team Excellence Criteria as a project planning and management checklist.

Use of the ASQ quality tools by application.

Cause analysis tools
- Fishbone (Ishikawa) diagram
- Pareto diagram
- Scatter diagram

Data collection and analysis tools
- Check sheet
- Control chart
- Design of experiments
- Histogram
- Scatter diagram
- Stratification
- Survey

Evaluation and Decision-Making Tools
- Decision matrix
- Multi-voting

Idea Creation Tools
- Affinity diagram
- Benchmarking
- Nominal group technique

Process Analysis Tools
- Flowchart
- Failure modes and effects analysis
- Mistake-proofing

Project Management Tools
- Gantt chart
- PDCA cycle (plan–do–check–act)

Seven Basic Quality Tools
- Cause-and-effect diagram (fishbone diagram)
- Check sheet
- Control chart
- Histogram
- Pareto chart
- Scatter diagram
- Stratification

Seven New Management and Planning Tools
- Affinity diagram
- Relationship diagram
- Tree diagram
- Matrix diagram
- Matrix data analysis
- Arrow diagram
- Process decision program chart

Table 5.2 ASQ quality tool kit.
Source: ASQ Quality Tools at http://www.asq.org/learn-about-quality/quality-tools.html.

the ASQ quality tools website provides a brief description and application on each tool to help choose the right one to suit the task. Plus, add the Table 5.4 lean tools and it makes a nice foursome for the team's toolbox. And remember, in Table 5.1 the Team Excellence Criteria adaption provides you with a project checklist for developing a team project or process improvement

Lean Six Sigma uses a modern problem-solving method called DMAIC. The model was presented in Chapter 3 and illustrated in Figure 3.2. A subsequent enhancement to it is *DMAIC-V*, which stands for *define–measure–analyze–improve–control–validate*.

- DMAIC-V has proven itself to be one of the most effective problem-solving methods ever used because *teams* use data to . . .
  - Confirm the nature and extent of the problem
  - Identify true causes of problems
  - Find solutions that evidence shows are linked to the causes
  - Establish procedures for maintaining the solutions even after the project is done

Note: The letter in parentheses is the item being addressed. Example: (D) is define, etc.

(D)MAIC-V

- The purpose of the first phase of the DMAIC process is for a team to agree on what the project is. Items that should be accomplished during the *define* phase include:
  - Discussing the project charter as a team.
  - Getting customer data.
  - Reviewing existing data about the process or problem.
  - Drafting a high-level map of the process.
  - *Process maps* are one type of improvement tool used often in DMAIC.

  In the define phase these help establish project boundaries, setting up a plan and guidelines for the team.

- The tools most commonly used in the *define* phase are:
  - Project charter
  - Process and value stream mapping and analysis
  - Voice of the customer
  - Stakeholder analysis
  - Suppliers, inputs, processes, outputs, and customers (SIPOC) process map
  - Affinity diagram
  - Kano model
  - Critical-to-quality (CTQ) tree

Table 5.3 DMAIC-V methodology and aligned quality tools.
Source: Standardized DMAIC-V available on the Internet.

D(M)AIC-V

- *Measure* is the heart of what makes Lean Six Sigma work when other approaches haven't.
- In the *measure* phase, teams will evaluate the existing measurement system, observe the process, gather data, and map the process in more depth.
- The tools most commonly used in the *measure* phase are:
  - Prioritization matrix
  - Process cycle efficiency
  - Time value analysis
  - Pareto charts
  - Control charts
  - Run charts
  - Failure modes and effects analysis (FMEA)

DM(A)IC-V

- The purpose of the *analyze* phase is to make sense of all the information and data collected in *measure*, and to use that data to confirm the source of delays, waste, and poor quality.
  - In the *analyze* phase teams develop theories of root causes, confirm the theories with data, and finally identify the root cause(s) of the problem.
  - The verified cause(s) will then form the basis for solutions in the *improve* phase.
- The tools most commonly used in the *analyze* phase are:
  - 5 whys analysis
  - Brainstorming
  - Cause-and-effect diagram
  - Affinity diagrams
  - Control charts
  - Flow diagram
  - Pareto charts
  - Regression analysis
  - Scatter plots

Table 5.3 *Continued.*

DMA(I)C-V

- The sole purpose of the *improve* phase is to make changes in a process that eliminate defects, waste, cost, and so on, which are linked to the customer need identified in the *define* phase.
- In the *improve* phase teams will:
  - Identify a range of possible solutions
  - Review existing *best practices* to see if any can be adapted to the situation
  - Develop criteria for selecting the solution and pilot the chosen solution
  - Plan for full-scale implementation
- The tools most commonly used in the *improve* phase are:
  - 7 wastes + 1 (*Underutilization of the human mind*)
  - Brainstorming
  - Flowcharting
  - Failure modes and effects analysis (FMEA)
  - Stakeholder analysis
  - Setup reduction
  - Queuing methods for reducing congestion and delays
  - 5S + 1 method—sort, set in order, shine, standardize, and sustain + *safety*
  - Kaizen

DMAI(C)-V

- The purpose of the *control* phase is to make sure that any gains a team makes last. That means creating procedures and work aids that help people do their jobs better:
  - The team must transfer what they learned to the process owner and ensure that everyone working on the process is trained appropriately.
  - During the *control* phase, teams will document the new, improved process, train everyone, set up procedures for tracking key "vital signs," hand off ongoing management to the process owner, and complete project documentation.
- The tools most commonly used in the *control* phase are:
  - Control charts
  - Flow diagrams

Table 5.3 *Continued.*

– Charts to compare before and after, such as Pareto charts

– Quality control process charts standardization

DMAIC-(V) Recently added to DMAIC

A sequential, five-step DMAIC improvement process with the addition of a sixth step, "validation," in which project benefits are subjected to an after-the-fact validation/verification process.

Table 5.3 *Continued.*

Although there are many lean tools available today, the following are among the ones most commonly used.

- 5S + 1 (Work organization + Safety)
- 7 hidden wastes
- Buffer and safety stock
- Building quality in
- Cellular layout
- Continuous flow
- Cycle time
- DMAIC-V
- Just-in-time (JIT)
- Kanban (pull system)
- Line balancing
- Load leveling
- Mistake-proofing
- Plan–do–check–act (PDCA)
- Quick changeovers
- Rapid improvement process (RIP)
- Sequencing
- Single-piece flow
- Six Sigma
- Standard operating procedures (SOPs)
- Takt time
- Total productive maintenance (TPM)
- Value stream mapping
- Visual controls

Table 5.4 Lean tools.
Source: The Lean Pocket Guide (Tapping 2003).

event that helps to keep the task on track. PDC/SA, DMAIC-V, ASQ quality tools, and lean tools are a great four-part package because information on all of them is virtually free to anyone. As described in Chapter 1, anyone can access the information on the TEF from ASQ's ITEA website. With respect to the models (such as PDC/SA and DMAIC-V) and CI/quality tool set, there are numerous places (websites, books, articles, and so on) where they can be found. Some of these websites are open and free to everyone through the Internet. The ASQ tool set is available to all members and is included in the cost of annual membership. In addition, many other professional associations, such as in manufacturing, engineering, or healthcare, offer information on CI models and tools, or links to this information, on their websites. These resources are frequently tailored to the types of tools typically used by that profession. Also, most large organizations with established CI programs have their preferred models and tools on their intranet, along with information on how to use them.

As mentioned in Chapter 3, the PDC/SA (plan–do–check/study–act) model traces back primarily to the process control and improvement techniques developed by Dr. Walter Shewhart and later expanded on by Dr. W. Edwards Deming and other gurus of the quality revolution. It also forms part of the foundation for the approach developed by Dr. Eliyahu Goldratt called the *theory of constraints*. PDC/SA is an excellent CI model to use along with the ASQ quality tools when you have relatively little experience with improvement teams because it is not as daunting as DMAIC-V. Therefore, it might be all you need to get started. Also, some organizations have expanded how they use their PDC/SA model to include the steps of DMAIC-V.

However, if an organization can handle the DMAIC-V model and it adds to their CI capabilities, it can have the following benefits:

1. The organization does not have to make the transition from PDC/SA to DMAIC-V and therefore does not have to retrain the workforce.

2. DMAIC-V explicitly carries you two steps farther in the CI cycle with the *control* and *validate* steps.

3. CI/quality tools are well linked to the two additional steps of DMAIC-V.

4. DMAIC-V is well linked to lean and Six Sigma. Also, Lean Six Sigma methodology has integrated both lean and Six Sigma into a less complex CI methodology.

All that being said, the following combination of the DMAIC-V model, CI/quality tools, and lean tools provides a team with an excellent package for successfully meeting the Team Excellence Criteria requirements.

Data and Metrics

Accurate and timely data for improvement teams are critical to make fact-based and timely decisions. But there is a broader consideration here that the user of the criteria needs to consider. That is, some of the criteria in Sections 1, 2, 3, and 4 ask the team to *describe* and *explain* data/metrics, analysis, and methods used to meet the criteria. Here also there must be consideration for data and metrics on possible impact on internal and external stakeholders. Therefore, understanding of data sources and metrics as well as multiple levels of data applications, such as data points, performance metrics, key performance indicators, balanced scorecards, dashboards, tools, and analysis methods, is important to the success of the team in addressing the criteria requirements. Also see the section in Chapter 6 on metrology.

Project Management

The Criteria is also a great project planning and management tool in addition to being an assessment tool. It serves as an excellent check sheet in planning many of the higher-level aspects of a project as well as ongoing project management elements and performance metrics.

Starting New Teams

If you are thinking of starting improvement teams or are in the early stages of developing teams, you may want to consider taking a less aggressive approach in the application of the criteria. This may also be a good way to jump-start a team program at your organization. The approach is to use only the level 2 criteria, for example, 1A, 1B, 1C, 2A, 2B, 2C, and so on. This approach would reduce the number of criteria items from 37 to 15, making it a much less daunting approach and more applicable to less experienced teams and/or smaller projects.

BEST PRACTICE EXAMPLES OF USING TOOLS TO EXCEED THE CRITERIA

The presentations and case studies based on successful team projects provide a rich source of information on best practices in the use of tools and techniques to address the requirements of the criteria. It must be reemphasized that the team should select the appropriate tools and techniques for their problem or opportunity and the business context. Having said that, it is likely that learning what successful teams have done will expand your understanding and skill in using the tools and techniques of CI and of teamwork. Boxes 5.1 and 5.2 provide examples of tools used by excellent teams along with the references to case studies that offer more information on how they applied tools to accomplish their projects.

BOX 5.1: AN EXAMPLE OF TOOLS AND TECHNIQUES USED BY ONE SUCCESSFUL IMPROVEMENT TEAM THROUGHOUT THEIR ENTIRE PROJECT

Healthways, Inc. provides programs to health plans, employers, and healthcare providers. This project team won the ITEA Silver Award in 2008. This is a high-level summary of the tools and techniques used. For more detail on this project, see the case study (Daniels 2009) and the project presentation itself. Both are available from the ITEA website.

Section 1. Project Selection and Purpose

Healthways' customer satisfaction data showed that the area of member contact was an opportunity for improvement. In the *define* phase the house of quality tool was used, and it identified improving the member contact rate while supporting the company's business model and objectives as an opportunity. These are phone contacts made by "clinicians" who are registered nurses and other professionals. The project was submitted to the quality committee for final approval. The committee uses an impact and effort project scoring system to screen and select projects that are best aligned to company goals.

A charter was used to define the project, including success metrics: increased member contacts that decrease healthcare spending for their members, and a cost avoidance of $3 million.

A supplier–input–process–output–customer (SIPOC) analysis was used to identify potential stakeholders.

A stakeholder analysis identified types of potential stakeholder impacts, the amount of project impact, and the influence strategy on each key stakeholder.

Section 2. Current Situation Analysis

To analyze the root causes, the team used measurement system and stability analyses, normality test, and muda (waste) walk.

Many stakeholders helped identify potential root causes.

An overall process effectiveness test showed that the biggest impact could be made by focusing on the calls per clinician per hour. The team found that only 7.7% of the clinicians exceeded the standard set by Healthways, meaning that the process was not capable of producing a contact rate that meets either internal standards or customer expectations.

A fishbone diagram identified factors impacting call rate.

To validate root causes, the team used the house of quality tool and also discussed them with stakeholders.

Section 3. Solution Development

To identify potential solutions, the team benchmarked other successful internal productivity improvement projects, conducted interviews and brainstorming sessions with stakeholders, and used the 5 whys tool to provide insight into improvement actions.

To select final solutions they evaluated potential solutions relative to their likely impact on their key success metrics. They selected solutions with the highest scores.

A capability analysis verified that the implemented solutions improve key metrics.

Based on their subject matter expertise, stakeholder team members validated the final solutions by assessing the impact of each solution on the project's success metrics.

Section 4. Project Implementation and Results

The tangible results were a 67% increase in median calls per hour along with an improvement or maintenance of all call-quality indicators. Intangible results included a significant improvement in colleague opinion survey results, lower employee turnover rate, and encouragement for future employee-led improvement projects at Healthways.

Implementation included creation of new key processes for streamlined standard call flows, transformation of supervisors to coaches, and use of standard reporting templates and analysis processes.

Section 5. Team Management and Project Presentation

Using the SIPOC and stakeholder analysis, a cross-functional team was selected that included members from each key process area. Criteria for member selection included multi-skill and multitasking capability, effective communication and people skills, and ability to think outside the box.

The team met regularly throughout the project to ensure that timelines were met. Team members provided constant updates and received productive recommendations throughout the project.

Process Excellence Training supported the methods outlined in the Healthways to Excellence approach to process improvement. Healthways Basic Training focused on team skills, meeting skills, consensus decision-making techniques, and financial and outcomes aspects.

The team used a standardized agenda and minutes template to record weekly meeting results and decisions. Team progress reports were posted on the Process Excellence intranet site and updated as progress occurred. The champion, process owners, and team members received a Project Status report. The champion met with the project sponsor on a monthly and as-needed basis to review project status and surface any barriers.

BOX 5.2: SAMPLE TOOLS AND TECHNIQUES USED BY SUCCESSFUL TEAMS TO ADDRESS EACH SECTION OF THE CRITERIA

The information presented here provides selected summary information. All teams have been finalists in the ITEA recognition process. In each case a reference is given to a case study providing much more detail about the tools used in the entire project. Also, some of the actual project presentations are posted on the ITEA website.

Section 1. Project Selection and Purpose

Pershing LLC is a global provider of clearing and financial business solutions. To make the best project selection, it had focus groups brainstorm improvement opportunities for key performance measures. The result was 20 opportunities, and these were taken to focus groups to rate on a five-point scale. Results were put into a scatter plot to identify the opportunities with the biggest return. A decision matrix was then used to narrow down the choice. The team tackled customer service problems and developed two service-level management tools as a solution (Bronze Award recipient, 2009) (Adrian 2010).

Singapore's Housing and Development Board's (HDB) mission is to provide affordable housing of quality and value, supporting active and cohesive communities. More than 80% of the population lives in HDB housing. To select a project that best supports the organization's mission, the *lotus blossom technique* was used to identify four possible projects. It requires that potential solutions be identified for each of the four problems. The problem with the most potential solutions would likely be the easiest to solve. To validate the choice, a *paired comparison analysis technique* (PCAT) was used to compare the four problems using the criteria of time saved, improved work process, impact of solution, and cost savings. This analysis validated the results of the lotus blossom method. The project became one to reduce the time spent measuring the gradients of ramps that provide accessibility to housing for the elderly and disabled. The team solved the problem by designing a new method rather than improving on the existing method (Brush 2009b).

The Aldine Independent School District has earned many honors for helping children of poverty and minority students reach high levels of academic performance. The means by which they identified a major improvement opportunity was a gap identified by feedback from two external sources. As a winner of the state's Baldrige Award (Texas Award for Performance Excellence), they received feedback from the examiners. They also received an analysis from the Broad Urban Award. Both pointed to gaps in deploying key initiatives throughout the district, particularly in sharing and documenting its practices. The resulting project created a peer review process to identify, document, and spread best practices in instructional strategies (Jacobsen 2009e).

Littelfuse manufacturing company produces automotive fuses and products that protect consumer electronic devices. The team's purpose was to reduce the number of loose caps in square nano fuses. The team used a SIPOC diagram to identify key internal and external stakeholders (Silver Award recipient 2009) (Ellifson 2010).

Boeing's Support Services Center (BSS) found its relationship with its U.S. Air Force customer threatened by cost overruns and late deliveries associated with maintenance and modification of aircraft. The team that tackled that problem used a value stream map to identify potential stakeholders (Bronze Award recipient, 2009) (Krzykowski 2010).

Fidelity Wide Processing provides communications to Fidelity Investments customers. The team's goal was to improve the productivity and unit costs of the bulk shipping process and reduce dissatisfaction due to increased overtime and shipping costs. Stakeholders were identified and put into a matrix displaying them, the type of impact, and the degree of impact (Gold Award recipient, 2006) (Nourse and Hays 2004).

Section 2. Current Situation Analysis

Kaiser Permanente Colorado is part of one of the largest integrated healthcare delivery systems in America. They were losing over $100,000 USD a month in revenue by missing Medicaid filing deadlines. The team utilized a highly detailed value stream map to identify possible areas of waste. They then used SIPOC diagrams to identify the outputs and inputs for each step. For each output, two cause-and-effect diagrams were created, one positive and one negative, to understand why the desired outcomes were not being achieved. Drilling down, the team did micro–value stream maps identifying waste. Using the 5 whys analysis tool, six final root causes were identified (Jacobsen 2009a).

At the U.S. Naval Ship Repair Facility and Japan Regional Maintenance Center, Yokosuka, Japanese and U.S. military and civilian personnel work together on a common mission. The Yokosuka Calibration Laboratory had to increase its efficiency and timeliness in anticipation of increased workload from an incoming aircraft carrier. When the team found that 40% of the test equipment calibrated in the shop was customer micrometers, they focused on finding the root causes for delays in servicing this equipment. They compared their own processes with standard operating procedures for their specific type of work. They also employed data analysis, failure modes and effects analysis (FMEA), and the 5 whys. Results were a reduction of 3000 labor hours annually, a 70% reduction of travel distance, 68% reduction in lead time, and 11.25% increase in productivity (Chircop 2009).

Boeing's C-17 aircraft contains an On-Board Inert Gas Generating System (OBIGGS) that prevents fuel tanks from exploding if struck by gunfire. While it successfully protected the fuel tanks, its low reliability caused high repair costs, required many labor hours, and resulted in aircraft held out of use. The team used an FMEA to search for a final root cause. The results led the team to the conclusion that the system was too complex to fix and that a complete systems redesign was the necessary solution (Silver Award recipient, 2007) (Adrian 2007).

MEDRAD, Inc. designs and manufactures products used in medical diagnostic imaging. Its packaging team was working many hours of overtime plus using temporary workers. To analyze the current situation, brainstorming was first used to answer a simple question, "What stops us from packaging more units?" From these responses an affinity diagram was constructed. Then time studies were used to analyze process steps and identify waste. The team constructed a fishbone diagram to help zero in on root causes (Schaar 2010a).

CSX Corporation's rail and intermodal businesses provide rail-based transportation services including traditional rail service and the transport of intermodal containers and trailers. A team learned that the company was paying more than $9.5 million annually on arbitrary or extra pay claims to its train and engine employees. To identify root causes the team first mapped the process for approving or denying arbitrary payments using a swim lane process map. They used a modified 5S procedure to review claims that fell into the "miscellaneous" arbitrary code category. They analyzed data from one pilot division and discovered clusters of geographic and type-of-claims data. They then used process maps, data review, customer insights, and a 5 whys exercise that narrowed down the results to two primary root causes. The outcome was a savings of $5.1 million USD (Jacobsen 2008a).

Section 3. Solution Development

For Singapore's Housing and Development Board (HDB), water seepage was the most frequently reported defect during the first year of occupancy. However, there was no standardized procedure for testing watertightness. Individual contractors proposed their own testing methodologies, and HDB gave final approval. To generate ideas for solutions, the PCAT tool was used to determine the most important dimensions of any watertightness testing procedure. To generate ideas about what other features a solution should have, a random entry method was used in brainstorming. For example, using the words "washing machine," team members thought about how these features could be applied to a solution for watertightness testing. Combining the features generated by both methods into a tree diagram, the team determined which features best aligned with project goals. This information was the blueprint for a preliminary solution (Brush 2009c).

Siemens VDO is a leading international supplier of automotive electronics and mechatronics. It created a team to decrease the high number of soldering defects at the electric indicators station in the final assembly of Mack Trucks. To determine the final solution the team performed hypothesis tests, regression analysis, and analysis of variance (ANOVA). After the critical factors were discovered, the next step was using a design of experiments (DOE) to optimize the process (Bronze Award recipient, 2006) (Perez and Vasquez 2007).

A hand-drilling process was used for placing fasteners into the fuselage of Boeing's C-17 aircraft. It was effective but inefficient, requiring a lot of labor and creating injuries and ailments among mechanics. A team was formed to improve the process, and it ultimately developed a machine that automated the process. The team used several methods to develop potential solutions, including brainstorming and lessons learned from other benchmarked automated systems, including the flex rails used in Boeing's 787 aircraft program. They then used value stream mapping to assess the impact of the various possible solutions (Gold Award recipient, 2008) (Edmund 2009).

Caseworkers at the SunCoast Region of the Florida Department of Children and Families generated more than 1.5 million paper documents annually. It formed a team whose goal was to redesign its paper-based document filing and retrieval system. Their solution was an electronic system that eliminated all paper files, allowed instant access, reduced cycle time, and saved money. In order to validate their prototype, the team got user feedback, did comparisons with industry standards, and predesigned audit processes. QA staff did daily audits to ensure compliance with requirements for accuracy and efficiency (Silver Award recipient, 2007) (Daniels 2007).

Bayer MaterialScience is a global manufacturer of polymers used as raw materials for products such as CDs and automotive finishes. Shipping costs are a significant component of total costs, and it was found that 83% of jobs were shipped suboptimally. For its situation analysis the team had used FMEA to identify root causes, so it followed up in this phase by using the tool of design FMEA, which entailed developing a potential improvement or corrective action for each of the 50 failure modes identified by the first FMEA. The other key tool in solution development was organization process mapping. A new process flow eliminated non-value-added steps, and added missing steps based on what had been learned during root cause analysis. Results included a savings in shipping costs of $1 million USD per year (Bronze Award recipient, 2008) (Adrian 2009).

R. L. Polk & Co. provides automotive information and marketing solutions to automotive industry organizations. It launched a project to improve its customer issue resolution process. The potential solution was to enhance its existing paper-based customer relationship management system by automating it. To validate this solution, a pilot study was conducted using the automated system (Schroeder 2009).

Section 4. Project Implementation and Results

A problem with unsafe conditions while installing the tailcone of Boeing's C-17 aircraft generated this improvement project. The team involved the stakeholders in implementation. Mechanics helped support personnel with a new build sequence and manpower usage. Supplier management issued contracts and mitigated supplier issues. Stakeholders verified contractual compliance; they installed the tailcone and made recommendations for change. They attended daily meetings to discuss successes and issues. Sources of stakeholder resistance were identified in meetings, surveys, and interviews. Concerns included possible loss of jobs, learning new processes, and not being listened to. Their concerns were addressed by the team during interviews, and statistical data regarding manpower were provided to allay concerns. The solution eliminated safety hazards and reduced labor hours by more than 300% (Gold Award recipient, 2007) (Adrian 2008a).

A team formed by the Singapore Housing Development Board was formed to find new ways to motivate staff at its 29 service centers to improve customer service. It focused on improving its service huddles, which are the supervisors' morning talks that prepare the staff for each day's delivery of customer service. Since the effectiveness of the huddles depends on each supervisor's facilitation skills, the solution was a M.A.G.I.C Huddles Handbook that addressed the root causes of supervisor deficiencies in performing effective huddles. The handbook reduced supervisor preparation time by 75%, saving 7200 labor hours and improving service delivery. To sustain the implementation, the team performs quarterly surveys of supervisors and customer service officers to gather feedback about their use of the handbook, collects feedback at any time through their staff suggestion scheme and service portal, and updates the handbook annually (Brush 2009a).

At CSX a team found that idling locomotives wasted 30 million gallons of diesel per year, with additional negative impacts on the environment. Their solution saved $28 million over three years. The team recognized that successful implementation required buy-in from its 6000 operators. The team brainstormed potential sources of stakeholder resistance and the team's response. It developed a specific strategy and an explicit action plan. They recognized that a rule change would not be sufficient, that it had to be accompanied by an education and communications campaign. Also, large, obvious indicators were built at locomotive shops to reinforce when to shut the locomotive down and when to leave it running. A daily report was created that was a score card of "Previous 24 Hours Percent Shutdown" (Bronze Award recipient, 2007) (Adrian 2008b).

MEDRAD, Inc. found that up to 20% of all in-process device history record (DHR) packets contained an error even though employees were double- and triple-checking this required paperwork. To support its implemented solution, 70 quality system documents were revised, which required training. The company also produced a DHR database, which provides the measurement system necessary to monitor performance. Trend and Pareto data are reviewed during monthly quality council meetings and quarterly management review sessions (Jacobsen 2009c).

In a project at New Breed Logistics, a third party that helps companies design and operate efficient supply chains, a team addressed a problem with a key client, Boeing. Their order volumes and packaging needs surpassed the contractual requirement, causing New Breed a 23% decrease in on-time packaging. The solution was a new layout that created space in an existing facility that maximized flow and improved lighting. Throughput increased from 167 to 240 orders per day with an increase in shipping accuracy. To sustain the gains, measurement systems were put in place, including a training database, a document control database, and customer service level summaries (Jacobsen 2009a).

Section 5. Team Management and Project Presentation

A team was formed in Boeing's C-17 Program to address employee safety concerns and rising workers' compensation costs. The solution was implementation of the Integrated Safety Management System, which resulted in significant cost savings and injury rate reduction. The team credits its success to use of team training guides that gave them the skills needed for working together effectively and identifying indicators of team dysfunction. They also credit their self-management style and effective communication through routine project interactions for keeping the project on track (Silver Award recipient, 2007) (Adrian 2008a).

At Barnes–Jewish Hospital traditional performance improvement efforts had had pockets of success but were rarely sustained. Then the hospital leadership pulled together a team of management engineers using a foundation in lean or Six Sigma techniques, which made improvements by implementing value streams. The result has been sustained improvements. The team has guided its own project work through a focus on value stream activities, at the same time disseminating lean thinking to all employees (Kincade and Wolf 2010).

MUST-DO'S FOR AN EFFECTIVE PROJECT PRESENTATION

Unless you are part of an external recognition program, there is no externally imposed time constraint on your team presentation time length. However, it is good discipline to be able to condense your story to something you can explain to management in approximately half an hour. If they want more detail, they can ask questions at the end. The same holds true if management or an assessor is reading your presentation in the form of the PowerPoint presentation with embedded speaker notes.

Telling your success story can be a challenge when you are addressing so many items. The reason that a half-hour time limit was imposed by the ITEA Process was based on many years of program experience. It is long enough to cover every item but prevents the presenters from getting bogged down in details. This is the level at which most managers prefer to be briefed. It is a very good skill for team members to learn.

To effectively do this, you will need to put some serious thought into the approach and delivery process. When your presentation is over, you want the audience to know that you have covered all the criteria items, clearly told your story, and that the slides support the story. To do that, there are six areas winning teams always address, and do so well. They are: the appropriate (1) *number of slides*, (2) *slide heading*, (3) *slide layout*, (4) *graphics and metrics*, (5) *speaker notes* (your script), and (6) cross-linking criteria items and slide graphics. All this is to be done within a presentation application such as MS PowerPoint with speaker notes (see Figure 5.1 example).

All teams are still encouraged to be as creative and as innovative as possible in sharing their stories. Let us address each of these areas [(1) *number of slides*, (2) *slide heading*, (3) *slide layout*, (4) *graphics and metrics*, (5) *speaker notes* (your script), and (6) cross-linking criteria items and slide graphics] individually.

Application of the Criteria and Related Tools 113

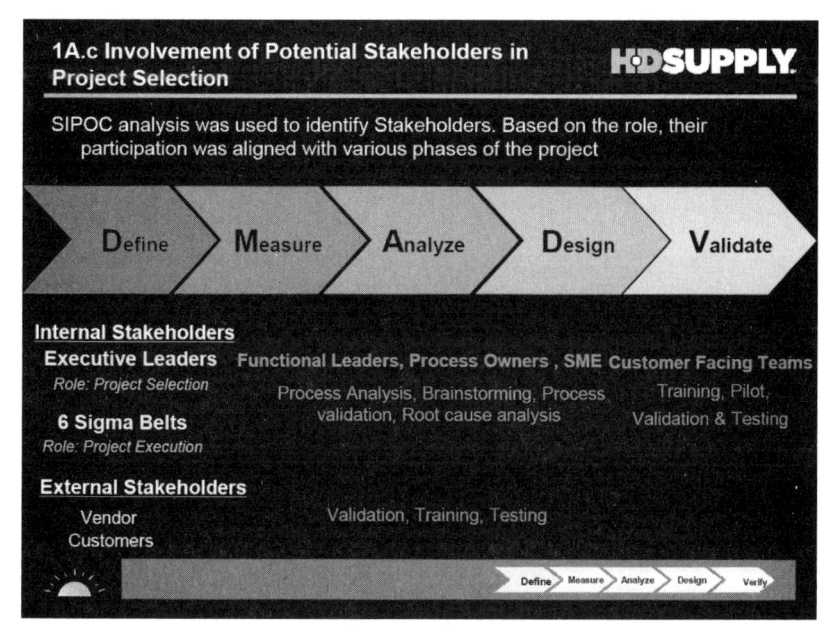

Figure 5.1 PowerPoint slide example.

1. *Number of slides.* You must consider your team's ability to deliver the presentation. You will need to match this to the number and content (data and graphics) of the slides. Scale the number of slides to the maturity of the project, team members, and the organization. If the team is in the early stages of development, slides that only address each of the five sections at the criteria level 1 or 2 (See Figure 4.3, Chapter 4) may suffice. If you are at the intermediate level, you should address all 37 items in the Criteria Summary, but may choose not to include all the nuances provided in the Criteria. This is also true if your presentation is primarily for the purpose of convincing your management of the project's worth. However, if you are also submitting it for internal assessment, you may want to develop a more detailed version. If you are entering an external recognition process, the judges tend to see 60 to 80 slides for high-scoring teams, but always do what makes best sense in getting your message across. Also, the number of slides should be in proportion to the time available.

2. *Slide headings.* Title each slide with the related item number and letter and deliver your presentation in the same sequence

as the Criteria Summary. An example of a slide heading is: "1Ab Explain the reason why the project was selected." A slide heading serves two purposes: (1) it aligns the progression of your presentation to the sequential logic of the Criteria, and (2) it allows the audience to clearly see which item you are addressing at any given moment.

3. *Slide layout.* Keep it clean and simple with:

   a. Criteria item number and question on top

   b. Black text on white background (best) or a reverse as in the slide example shown in Figure 5.1.

   c. Avoid watermark backgrounds; a small logo is OK in a corner.

   d. Whether you are delivering your presentation internally or externally, be clear in your speaker notes and slides.

4. *Graphics and metrics.* Keep them clean and readable:

   a. You want graphics that will talk to management and the assessment panel and say more than your team has time to say.

   b. Don't use pop-up graphics on slides because they will not show on the slide when you print a hard copy. Make the pop-up a new slide.

   c. Make the graphic meaningful; flashy fluff graphics may not tell your story and they won't get you scoring points.

   d. Use complementary (one color goes with another) color schemes that help express the graphics. Colors should be used to help separate/highlight the graphic or metric.

   e. Metrics are very important in *meeting* or *exceeding* the criteria requirements in Sections 2, "Current Situation Analysis," 3, "Solution Development," and 4, "Project Implementation and Results." Do your homework on metrics and present fact-based *tangible* and plausible *intangible* results. Most teams project a good image of their project but will fall short in *meeting* or *exceeding* the requirements due to the absence of positive performance metrics. (See Chapter 6 for more on the subject of *metrology.*)

5. *Speaker notes*—tell your story with enthusiasm.

   a. Script your presentation slide by slide just like a child's storybook.

b. Write your script in complete sentences and read the script verbatim.

c. Put it in plain language.

6. *Cross-linking criteria items and slide graphics.* Gain valuable time to tell your story:

    a. Make sure you understand the cross-linked criteria. Example: 3Ac has a linkage to 3Aa and 3Ab and 3Aa is linked to 2B.

    b. Decrease the number of slides and increase your presentation scope by presenting your graphics once and referencing them as needed later where there is a cross-linkage requirement. This gives you more space and time to tell your story. At least shrink the graphic and reference it, and the assessor can go back and see the referenced slide.

    c. If you want to use information you previously stated in another slide, don't waste the time on another slide. Make a reference on this slide where you had previously addressed it and then speak to it as needed.

7. Other

    a. Address all criteria items and pay attention to the actions (describe, explain, identify, and indicate).

    b. If you skip a criteria detail requirement, you should explain why you skipped it.

    c. If you are delivering the presentation in person (versus submitting a copy to be read or a video), the slides should be readable to anyone in the audience (viewable from at least 15–20 feet away).

ADVICE FROM EXPERIENCED ASSESSORS

The TEF documents are designed to help clarify each criteria requirement, identify related situations, give generalized examples, and provide expected outcomes. Also, the Criteria draws attention to where the criteria items are cross-linked to other areas of the Criteria. Without the team looking at the Criteria in amplification, they could miss the intent of the criteria items.

The criteria and item requirements in and of themselves do not disclose the full scope of what one must be thinking to effectively assess and score the presentation and provide effective non-prescriptive actionable feedback comments. Although the project is usually localized within the organization, there is an organization-wide relationship to many of the criteria requirements. The assessor's expectation is that the team knows the criteria requirements and process. This is not always the case, though, and the assessor must try his or her best to understand the team's intent and where it fits in the criteria. To be able to exceed the requirements, the team's presentation also must demonstrate integration. To overcome many of these issues, the TEF also provides the user with the Criteria Summary and Discussion (amplification), footnotes, Assessor's Scoring Option, and Scoring Guidelines to help clarify the criteria and what an assessor or assessment panel should be looking for.

CONCLUSION

In most cases the team's score appropriately reflects the strength of the presentation relative to the criteria. The exception is when the team had content but didn't express it clearly. What most experienced assessors are concerned about is giving fair and accurate feedback that is valuable. Also, refer back to the section in Chapter 4, "How to Write Effective Non-Prescriptive Actionable Feedback Reports."

This chapter has provided teams and their management with information about appropriate models and tools to increase the likelihood of project success. As organizations become more sophisticated in using the TEF, they will fine-tune their capabilities in team-based CI.

Next, Chapter 6 covers how to incorporate use of the TEF into an organization that has one or more organization-wide performance excellence initiatives. When integrated well, the TEF can provide useful synergy to such other initiatives.

6

Relationship of the TEF to Broader Performance Excellence Programs

How Organizations Can Integrate It

The purpose of this chapter is to show how using the TEF, which requires a fact-based management approach, can positively interconnect with other broader initiatives your organization may have under way. The ones we choose to cover are: (1) the Baldrige Performance Excellence Criteria for *organizational management*, (2) Shingo model and ISO 9001:2008 quality management system for *operations and process management*, (3) enterprise systems/enterprise resource planning (ERP) for *information and knowledge management*, and (4) using metrics, key performance indicators (KPIs), balanced scorecards, and dashboards for *performance management*. Each of these initiatives, if applied well, can be best practices in their own right. Using one of more of them in concert with Team Excellence can result in world-class performance. The correlation we want to draw here is the importance of the *enterprise organizational system* to the consistent success of team improvement projects as well as the overall success of the organization.

The issue addressed in this chapter is how to use the TEF in a way that it is integrated with these other, broader, organizational initiatives so that synergy is created. To put it the opposite way, how do you avoid introducing it as a separate, stand-alone program? The TEF is a natural complement to selected aspects of each of these four elements: *organizational management, operations management, information and knowledge management,* and *performance management*.

When a team does an improvement project in a structured manner, it is sometimes referred to as *continuous process improvement*. The word *process* implies that whatever the team is working on may have a broader impact beyond the issue on which the team is directly working. The process change often has impact not only on the direct process and its output but also on other internal and external processes and stakeholders. As described in Chapter 3, four of the five Team Excellence Criteria sections require addressing stakeholder involvement. Addressing these requirements will guide the team to identify and understand where interrelated process activities occur and important related data sources within the activity for key performance metrics. (See the last section of this chapter, "Integrating the Framework's Use with Metrics, Key Performance Indicators, Balanced Scorecards, and Dashboards.") In essence, it requires the team to understand the broader systems in which their targeted process operates. Other parts of the Criteria require the team to address alignment to organizational goals, performance measures, and/or strategies. When these are unclear to the team, it is an indicator of a lack of an integrated enterprise system and/or their understanding of it.

Globalization and enterprise/ERP systems have put products and services in the hands of the user in ever shorter time cycles of the supply chain. As a result, organizations have become more connected with their suppliers, stakeholders, and end users. Teams whose organization has one or more elements of an integrated enterprise system are in an especially strong position for current and future organizational successes and long-term sustainability. In order to explain how to integrate use of the TEF with one or more of these four enterprise programs, we must first cover what an integrated enterprise system looks like.

This chapter is organized into six major sections. The first is an overarching look at what comprises an integrated enterprise system. The second is how to integrate the TEF into an organization that has a Baldrige-based initiative. The third is how to integrate it with a Shingo-based initiative. The fourth is how to integrate it with ISO 9001:2008. The fifth is how to integrate it with integrated enterprise management system software. The sixth and last is how to integrate it with use of metrics.

AN INTEGRATED ENTERPRISE SYSTEM OF BEST PRACTICES FOR ORGANIZATIONAL SUSTAINABILITY AND TEAM EXCELLENCE

The following are the key elements of an integrated enterprise system of best practices for organizational *sustainability* and *team excellence*.

1. Enterprise *architecture for sustainability*
2. Enterprise *strategy for sustainability*
3. Value creation chain framework for *enterprise sustainability*

4. Best practices *for sustainability*
   - 4.1 Baldrige Criteria for *enterprise management*
   - 4.2 Shingo Prize model for *operations management*
   - 4.3 ISO 9001:2008 standard for *quality and process management*
   - 4.4 Enterprise system software/ERP for *information and knowledge management*
   - 4.5 Metrology—data, metrics, key performance indicators (KPIs), balanced scorecards, and dashboards for *performance management*

Enterprise Architecture for Sustainability

Enterprise Strategy and Vision

- Organizational pillars (see Figure 6.1)
  - Process alignment and process agility

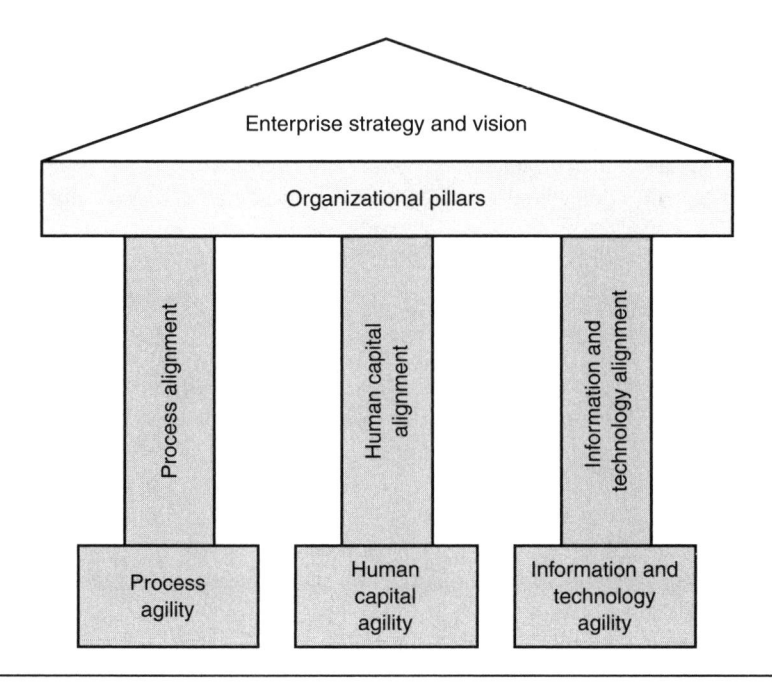

Figure 6.1 Enterprise architecture for sustainability.

– Human capital alignment and human capital agility

– Technology alignment and technology agility

The organization's strategies, goals, mission, vision, and values are important overarching key factors in the Team Excellence Criteria 1B items. These key factors should drive why projects are selected and align team efforts to the organizational direction.

Using the Baldrige Organizational Profile criterion and category 1.1 and 2.1 criteria will help give a broader scope for meeting the criterion in ITEA Section 1, Project Selection and Purpose. (See the chapter section "Enterprise Strategy for Sustainability" for more information.)

Even if your organization has an *enterprise architecture for sustainability* that includes strategies, goals, mission, vision, and values, we suggest you consider benchmarking to the Baldrige Criteria for Performance Excellence Organizational Profile section as a SWOT analysis tool, Category 1.1, Senior Leadership, for your vision, values, and mission, and Category 2.1, Strategy Development, for strategic planning and objectives to develop your enterprise strategy and vision.

Additionally, the three *organizational pillars* of process, human capital, and informational and technology alignment are aligned with Baldrige Categories 6, Operations Focus; 5, Workforce Focus; and 4, Measurement, Analysis, and Knowledge Management.

The Baldrige Business/Nonprofit Criteria can be found at http://www.nist.gov/baldrige/publications/business_nonprofit_criteria.cfm. Also see the Healthcare and Education Criteria at http://www.nist.gov/baldrige/publications/hc_criteria.cfm and http://www.nist.gov/baldrige/publications/education_criteria.cfm, respectively. Also, see below in this chapter for an overview of the Baldrige Criteria for Performance Excellence.

Enterprise Strategy for Sustainability

Figure 6.2 relates closely to the Baldrige criteria (Figure 6.5) in the following way. *Enterprise management* ties to the Baldrige (Preface) Organizational Profile categories (1) Leadership, (2) Strategic Planning, and (3) Customer Focus. *Operations and process management* ties to categories (5) Workforce Focus and (6) Operations Focus. *Information and knowledge management* ties to category (4) Measurement, Analysis, and Knowledge Management. And *performance management* relates to Category 7, Results, of the Baldrige Criteria.

In Figure 6.2, the second, third, and fourth circles have a *value creation chain and direct support functions/operations focus*, which is further developed in Figure 6.3, "Enterprise Sustainability Tree."

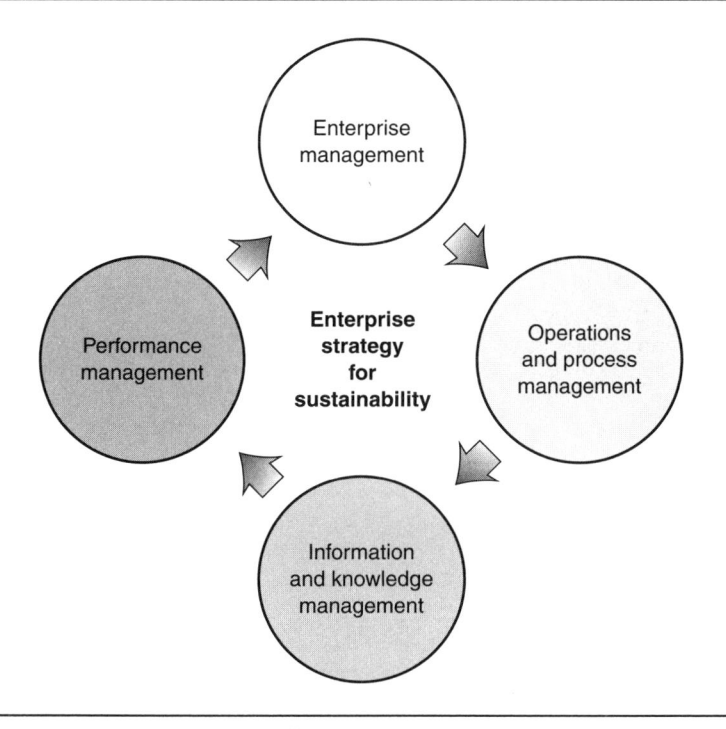

Relationship of the TEF to Broader Performance Excellence Programs 121

Figure 6.2 Enterprise strategy for sustainability.

The objective here is to put a greater focus on the organization's *value creation chain* and *direct support functions*. Together these are often referred to as the "operations" side of the organization. The operations are often where the most fertile ground is found for organizational improvement and present great opportunities for TEF-based teams. We're not saying there aren't benefits in the indirect areas as well; it's just that the value creating chain and direct support areas and their stakeholders generally have the greatest impact on the organization's tangible benefits.

Although there are many different industries and many best practice frameworks for each, there are just too many to address in this book. Our objective, then, is to identify a basic and generic infrastructure that is time-proven and cost-effective. For example, although at the higher end, SAP's enterprise system/ERP for *information and knowledge management* is considered a best practice software system for larger applications; for mid-sized and small organizations there are many cost-effective mid-range and PC-based enterprise/ERP systems to fit any size organization's needs and industry. That being said, we will limit our discussion to those that are considered time-proven best practice applications, approaches, and/or tools, presented in the next section.

Value Creation Chain Framework for Enterprise Sustainability

The "enterprise sustainability tree," Figure 6.3, addresses the product/service value creation chain key processes and their management. The objective of the tree is to focus on the organization's key product and/or service processes using best practice methods that support the four strategies in Figure 6.2.

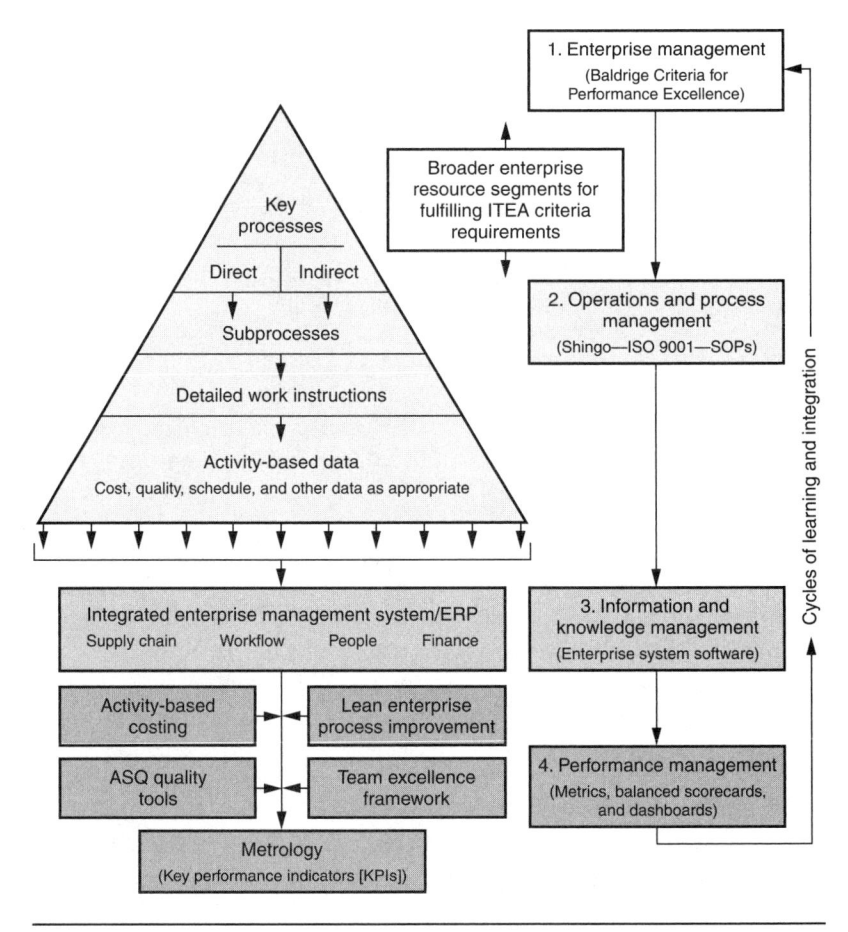

Figure 6.3 Enterprise sustainability tree.

The most important segment in this model is number 2, *operations and process management* of key processes. This is where cost, quality, schedule, and other data streams flow down into number 3, *information and knowledge management*, and then out to populate number 4, *performance management* into metrics, key performance indicators (KPIs), balanced scorecards, and dashboards on key processes for project team metrics and departments, and finally up to number 1, *enterprise management*, broader segments of the organizational structure.

In our experience, improvement teams give the greatest ROI in the value creation chain key processes. The second best ROI is from the key support processes. These key process activities are the rich data streams on which teams rely for historical and current data for analysis, possible solutions, final solution selection, and solution validation steps. But all too often, teams underachieve when there is a breakdown in one or more of the four segments of the framework for enterprise sustainability. And it is here where leadership must put forth their best effort to pave the way and remove hurdles for project teams to fully succeed.

On the right side of the *enterprise sustainability tree* are the four broader segments identified in Figure 6.3. In each of the four boxes there are one or more *best practice* approaches for organizational sustainability.

Best Practices for Sustainability

For the four enterprise segments identified in Figure 6.2—(1) enterprise management, (2) operations and process management, (3) information and knowledge management, and (4) performance management—we have chosen what we consider to be a time-proven set of best practice approaches and tools that support high-performance process improvement and project teams, drive organizational sustainability, and are aligned to the TEF criteria. These best practices are presented below and in Figure 6.4.

Enterprise Management. An overarching framework for organizational performance excellence.

- *Baldrige Criteria for Performance Excellence* at http://www.nist.gov/baldrige/publications/business_nonprofit_criteria.cfm.

Operations and Process Management. Value creation chain frameworks for direct and direct support processes.

- *Shingo Prize for Operational Excellence* at http://www.shingoprize.org/
- *ISO 9001:2008 Quality management system* at http://www.iso.org/iso/home.htm

```
┌─────────────────────────────────────────────┐
│ • Baldrige Criteria for Performance Excellence │   **Enterprise**
└─────────────────────────────────────────────┘   **management**

    ┌─────────────────────────────────────────────┐
    │ • Shingo Prize for Operations Excellence     │   **Operations**
    │ • ISO 9001 quality management system         │   **and process**
    │ • Standardized processes (SOPs)              │   **management**
    └─────────────────────────────────────────────┘

        ┌─────────────────────────────────────────────┐
        │ • Integrated enterprise system software/ERP  │   **Information and**
        │                                              │   **knowledge**
        └─────────────────────────────────────────────┘   **management**

            ┌─────────────────────────────────────────────┐
            │ • Activity-based costing                     │
            │ • Lean enterprise process improvement tools  │
            │ • ASQ quality tools                          │   **Performance**
            │ • Team Excellence Framework                  │   **management**
            │ • Performance metrics                        │
            └─────────────────────────────────────────────┘
```

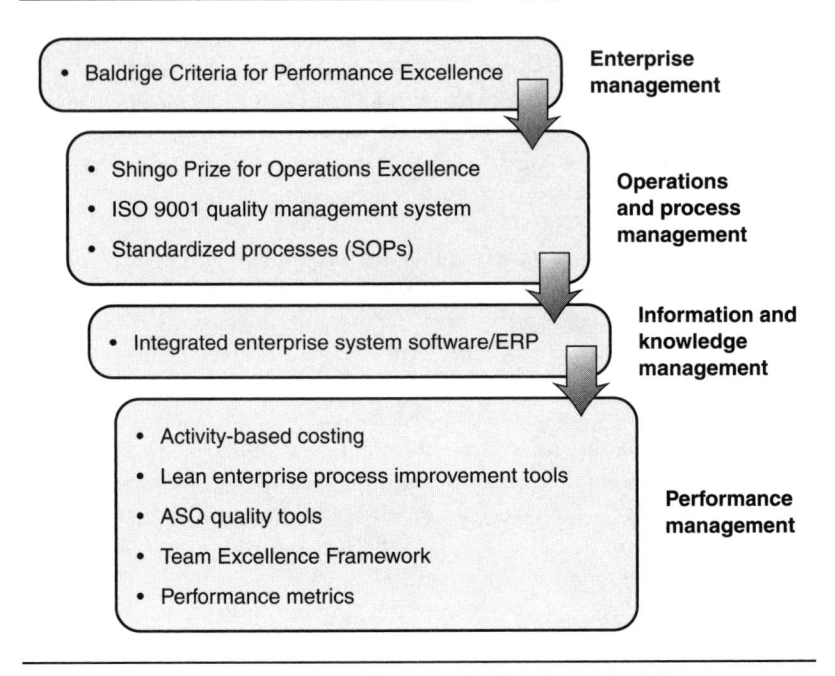

Figure 6.4 Best practice systems for organizational sustainability.

- *Standardized processes* (SOP's)—Search Web for multiple approaches

Information and Knowledge Management. Integrated software that facilitates the flow of information between all the main processes of a business.

- *Integrated enterprise system (ERP) software*

Performance Management. Lean-based performance improvement of the organization, departments, workforce, and key processes.

- *Activity-based costing* (Kaplan and Anderson 2007). This is further addressed in the last section of this chapter.
- *Lean enterprise tools—The Lean Enterprise Memory Jogger* at http://www.goalqpc.com/shop_products_detail.cfm?PID=43
- *ASQ quality tools*
- *Team Excellence Framework* (TEF)
- *Metrology (performance metrics)*—See the last section in this chapter.

INTEGRATING THE FRAMEWORK'S USE WITH USE OF THE BALDRIGE CRITERIA

Most organizations that are on a path of performance excellence use teams along with systematic CI methodology to improve, and many do achieve a measure of results. But those organizations using Baldrige along with the TEF will get better tangible and intangible results and will do so quicker. The reason is that the three-way synergy of Baldrige, CI methodology, and teamwork inspires and leverages the organization's people through involvement and engagement.

Note: The Baldrige Criteria are available in three different versions: Business/Nonprofit, Health Care, and Education. All the versions are similar, but for our purposes we will refer to the Business/Nonprofit version.

The requirements are embodied in seven categories, as follows: (1) Leadership, (2) Strategic Planning, (3) Customer Focus, (4) Measurement, Analysis, and Knowledge Management, (5) Workforce Focus, (6) Operations Focus, and (7) Results.

Figure 6.5 provides the model connecting and integrating the categories. From top to bottom, it has the following basic elements.

Organizational Profile

The *organizational profile* sets the context for the way an organization operates. Your organization's environment, key working relationships, and

Figure 6.5 Baldrige framework.
Source: Baldrige Performance Excellence Program, 2011, NIST.

strategic situation—including competitive environment, strategic challenges and advantages, and performance improvement system—serve as an overarching guide for your organizational performance management system.

Performance System

The performance system is composed of the six Baldrige categories in the center of the figure that define processes and the results.

Leadership, *strategic planning*, and *customer focus* comprise the leadership triad. This triad emphasizes the importance of a leadership focus on strategy and customers. *Workforce focus*, *operations focus*, and *results* comprise the results triad. An organization's workforce and key operational processes accomplish the work that yields overall performance results. All actions point toward *results*—a composite of product and process outcomes, customer-focused outcomes, workforce-focused outcomes, leadership and governance outcomes, and financial and market outcomes.

The horizontal arrow in the center links the leadership triad to the results triad. It indicates the central relationship between *leadership* (category 1) and *results* (category 7). The two-headed arrows indicate the importance of feedback in an effective performance management system.

System Foundation

Measurement, *analysis*, and *knowledge management* are critical to a fact-based, knowledge-driven system. Therefore, measurement, analysis, and knowledge management serve as a foundation for an effective performance management system.

Criterion Structure

The seven Criteria categories shown in the figure are subdivided into items and areas to address (see Table 6.1).

Items
There are seventeen process and results items, each focusing on a major requirement. Item titles and point values are given on page 3 of the Baldrige Criteria (2011–2012) manual. The item format is shown on page 29.

Areas to Address
Items consist of one or more areas to address (areas). Organizations should address their responses to the specific requirements of these areas.

Preface: Organizational Profile
 P.1 Organizational Description
 P.2 Organizational Situation

Categories and Items
1. Leadership
    1.1 Senior Leadership
    1.2 Governance and Societal Responsibilities
2. Strategic Planning
    2.1 Strategy Development
    2.2 Strategy Implementation
3. Customer Focus
    3.1 Voice of the Customer
    3.2 Customer Engagement
4. Measurement, Analysis, and Knowledge Management
    4.1 Measurement, Analysis, and Improvement of Organizational Performance
    4.2 Management of Information, Knowledge, and Information Technology
5. Workforce Focus
    5.1 Workforce Environment
    5.2 Workforce Engagement
6. Operations Focus
    6.1 Work Systems
    6.2 Work Processes
7. Results
    7.1 Product and Process Outcomes
    7.2 Customer-Focused Outcomes
    7.3 Workforce-Focused Outcomes
    7.4 Leadership and Governance Outcomes
    7.5 Financial and Market Outcomes

Table 6.1 Baldrige categories and items.

Implications for Integrating the TEF into an Organization Using the Baldrige Criteria

Put simply, effective use of the TEF will improve the success of improvement teams. This will boost the organization's scores on quite a few of the Baldrige criteria. Areas in which it will especially help are (1) Leadership, (2) Strategic Planning, (5) Workforce Focus, (6) Operations Focus, and (7) Results. Lindborg (2011) has pointed out that section 5.2 of the 2011–12 Baldrige Criteria explicitly covers employee engagement. It asks, "How do you engage your workforce to achieve organizational and personal success?" Box 6.1 gives a case example of how an organization steeped in the use of the Baldrige Criteria used the TEF to enhance its performance excellence according to the Baldrige model. The most important take-away is that successful improvement teams deliver outstanding results for the organization, far more so than most organizations can achieve without relying on the power of teamwork combined with CI methodology. Use of the TEF is a powerful engine for delivering outstanding business results.

BOX 6.1: HOW THE TEAM EXCELLENCE FRAMEWORK SUPPORTS BALDRIGE-BASED PERFORMANCE EXCELLENCE IN BOEING'S C-17 PROGRAM

The Boeing C-17 organization is an excellent example of the synergistic support that the TEF provides to pursuing ever higher levels of organization-wide performance excellence. For more than 20 years the organization's approach to achieving overall performance excellence has been through the use of the Baldrige criteria. The leadership adopted this approach more than a decade before they began using the TEF. They achieved external recognition for performance excellence both at the state level (California Award for Performance Excellence program) and the national level (Malcolm Baldrige National Quality Award). Internalizing these criteria as a way of doing business assisted them in establishing a strong culture of CI and employee engagement through teamwork. Because CI and teamwork are the two elements directly supported by the TEF (as shown in Figure 1.1), management decided that applying the framework would provide a powerful enhancement to achieving better organizational results. They see several significant points of synergy between Baldrige and Team Excellence (Howard Chambers, pers. comm.; Rick Payne, pers. comm.).

Leadership and strategic planning. According to the Baldrige criteria, leadership must set the vision, develop goals, and translate them into a strategic plan, which gets deployed to the entire workforce. According to the TEF, managers should use tools to select projects that best directly support organizational goals. Doing so avoids at least two common problems with project selection. One is that the project is simply fire-fighting or someone's pet interest. The other is that the team members lack clear line-of-sight to how their project will impact the overall business in an important way.

Operations management. According to Baldrige, operations must be continuously and significantly improved. Getting cost out of the process was the main customer requirement during the tenure of Howard Chambers as the C-17 leader (see Box 1.1). He found the TEF to be a powerful driver to ensure that all improvement projects were aligned to support that primary organizational goal.

Workforce focus. According to Baldrige, a necessary component of performance excellence is an excellent workforce. While this point is obvious, the ways to pursue it are not so obvious. The TEF provides a means in one specific area of this domain. It is a way to improve the workforce in their capacity as improvement team members. In the case of the C-17 organization, it bolstered their preexisting employee involvement program, which was transforming the entire organization from a traditional command-and-control, functionally stovepiped organization to a team-based organization with strong capacity to work cross-functionally and collaboratively. According to Ron Gill (pers. comm.), one aspect of their workforce transformation was that all their employees learned how to impact the business. Rick Payne (pers. comm.) put it succinctly, saying, "Everyone in the organization is now a stakeholder."

INTEGRATING THE FRAMEWORK'S USE WITH THE SHINGO PRIZE MODEL

The Shingo model is based on the lean management approach and model taught by Dr. Shigeo Shingo. Shingo, a management consultant and a practicing engineer, recognized vital management philosophies and shared them through his many books. (Shingo and Dillon 1989; Shingo et al. 2007; Shingo et al. 2009). His teachings describe three levels of business improvement, which we refer to as levels of transformation: *principles*, *systems*, and *tools and techniques*. Shingo grasped that true innovation is not achieved by superficial imitation or the isolated or random use of tools and techniques and systems ("know how"), but instead requires the "know why," that is, an understanding of underlying principles (Shingo Prize 2011).

The Shingo Prize model (Figure 6.6) is an engine for transformation that speeds an organization through the challenges toward the real prize—exceptional business results and customer satisfaction. Managers can use the model to assess lean understanding throughout their organization's business processes and to drive lean transformation. The application of the model—like real transformation—is not a sequential, well-cadenced progression throughout a company. The dimensions are not meant as separate and successive achievements of progression.

For example, the Shingo levels of transformation can vary within a dimension or business process, and, further still, some aspects of a business

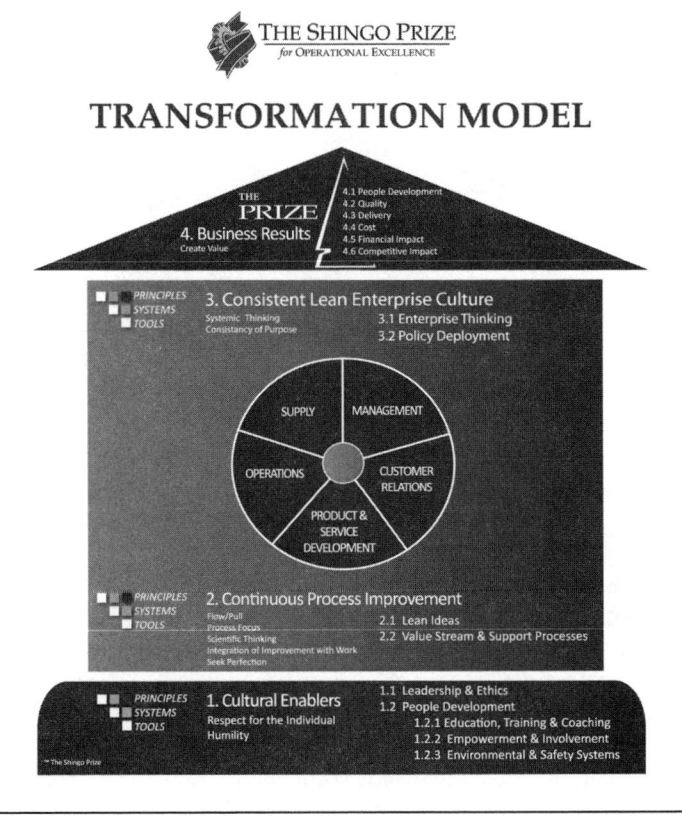

Figure 6.6 Shingo Prize model.

process might be developed to an *enabler* dimension while others operate at a more advanced *process-focused improvement* dimension as shown in Table 6.2. Similarly, business processes will move through dimensions at varying rates (for example, in manufacturing companies it's not unusual to see Operations leading the lean charge, well ahead of other nonproduction functions). And while we attempt to place specific practices and concepts within the dimensions, there is obviously some overlap in their use and applicability throughout dimensions (for example, scientific thinking).

While progress for companies working through the Shingo Prize model varies, the ultimate goal is clear: integration of lean philosophy across the enterprise and its value streams to create a complete, systemic view, leading to consistent achievement of business results. Consequently, a Shingo Prize recipient is expected to have applied most aspects of lean principles—the highest level—in all of its business processes: product/service development, customer relations, operations, supply, and management.

The Shingo Prize model is meant to be flexible so that it can be applied to all types of organizations As a result, some aspects of the model may be more applicable to an organization than others. For example, a plant without on-site product development processes will assess the practices and performances of this function differently than would an entire company complete with research and development and new-product development activities.

Implications for Integrating the TEF into an Organization Using the Shingo Model

The Shingo model supports an ideal organizational environment in which improvement teams can meet and exceed the Team Excellence Criteria and consistently get great results. Because it fosters the use of lean principles and tools, it enables improvement teams to remove large amounts of waste (non-value-added activity), thereby saving time and money, increasing product/service quality, and improving employee and customer satisfaction.

INTEGRATING THE FRAMEWORK'S USE WITH ISO 9001:2008 FOR QUALITY AND STANDARDIZED PROCESSES

Although ISO 9001:2008 is called a "quality management system," it is much more than that. Yes, it is about quality but equally important is about process management and meeting customer requirements in a continuous improvement environment. To maximize the continuous improvement

1. Cultural Enablers
   1.1 Leadership and Ethics
   1.2 People Development
       1.2.1 Education, Training, and Coaching
       1.2.2 Empowerment and Involvement
       1.2.3 Environmental and Safety Systems
2. Continuous Process Improvement
   2.1 Lean Principles
   2.2 Value Streams
       2.2.1 Customer Relations
       2.2.2 Product/Service Development
       2.2.3 Operations
       2.2.4 Supply
       2.2.5 Management
3. Consistent Lean Enterprise Culture
   3.1 Enterprise Thinking
   3.2 Policy Deployment
4. Business Results
   4.1 People Development
   4.2 Quality
   4.3 Delivery
   4.4 Cost
   4.5 Financial Impact
   4.6 Competitive Impact

Table 6.2 Shingo Prize criteria categories and items.

effort, the Team Excellence Criteria as it relates to stakeholders ensures where and how the customer and their requirements are considered.

ISO 9001:2008 Quality Management System

ISO 9001:2008 is an international standard broadly used as a framework for managing and improvement of organizations' direct and indirect (overhead) processes.

The ISO 9001:2008 international standard promotes the adoption of a process approach when developing, implementing, and improving the effectiveness of a quality management system to enhance customer satisfaction by meeting customer requirements.

For an organization to function effectively, it has to determine and manage numerous linked activities. An activity or set of activities using resources, and managed in order to enable the transformation of inputs into outputs, can be considered as a *process*. Often, the output from one process directly forms the input to the next.

The application of a system of processes within an organization, together with the identification and interactions of these processes, and their management to produce the desired outcome, can be referred to as the *process approach*.

An advantage of the process approach is the ongoing control that it provides over the linkage between the individual processes within the system of processes, as well as over their combination and interaction.

When used within a quality management system, such an approach emphasizes the importance of:

- Understanding and meeting requirements
- The need to consider processes in terms of added value
- Obtaining results of process performance and effectiveness
- Continual improvement of processes based on objective measurement

The model of a process-based quality management system shown in Figure 6.7 illustrates the process linkages presented in ISO 9001:2008 clauses 4 to 8. This figure shows that customers play a significant role in defining requirements as inputs. Monitoring of customer satisfaction requires the evaluation of information relating to customer perception as to whether the organization has met the customer requirements. The model shown covers all the requirements of the international standard, but does not show processes at a detailed level (International Organization for Standardization 2011).

ISO 9001:2008 Clauses

The clauses are divided into two sections: *General requirements* and *Quality management system (QMS) requirements*. The general clauses include 1) Scope, 2) Normative reference, and 3) Terms and definitions. And the QMS requirements are 4) Quality management system, 5) Management responsibility, 6) Resource management, 7) Product realization (development), and 8) Measurement, analysis and improvement. (See Figure 6.7, "ISO 9001:2008 framework").

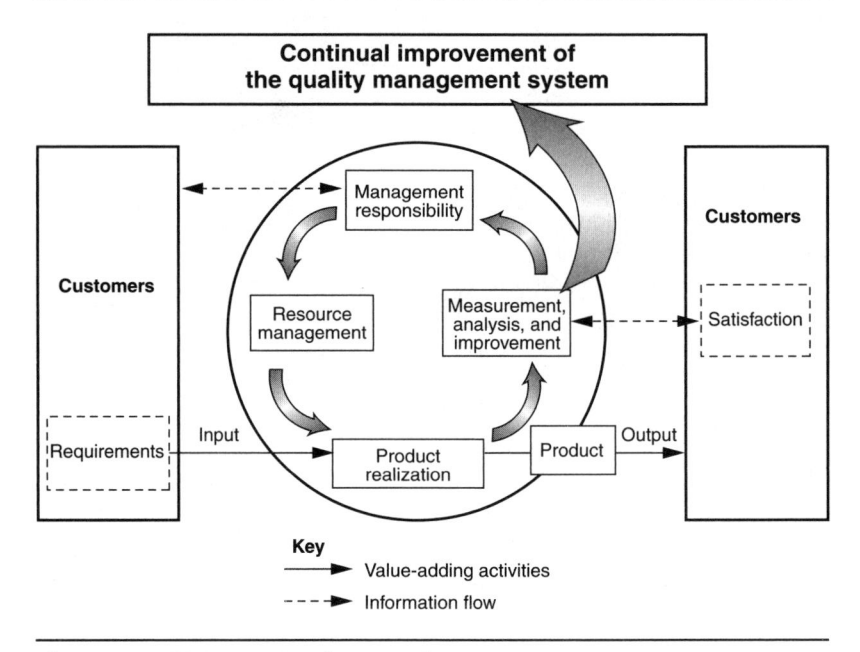

Figure 6.7 ISO 9001:2008 framework.

Implications for Integrating the TEF into an Organization Using ISO 9001:2008

As noted, these initiatives are focused on the importance of having excellent processes to get excellent results. Use of the TEF enables improvement of any type of process and also includes the requirement of controlling the process once it is in its improved state.

INTEGRATING THE FRAMEWORK'S USE WITH INFORMATION AND KNOWLEDGE MANAGEMENT USING INTEGRATED ENTERPRISE MANAGEMENT SYSTEM SOFTWARE

Accessible, accurate, and timely data are critical to any successful improvement project. Often, such data are difficult for teams to acquire. The reason is that these data lie in many and not necessarily connected locations. Today, *enterprise system software*, commonly known as *enterprise*

Enterprise system application modules

```
                    Sales and distribution    Financial accounting
   Value         Material management                Controlling
 creation        Production planning   Enterprise   Asset management         Finance
   chain        Quality management    system        Project system
                                      client server
                       Plant maintenance            Work flow            Process flow
      People        Human resources                 Industry solutions   Industry specific
                              Web applications
```

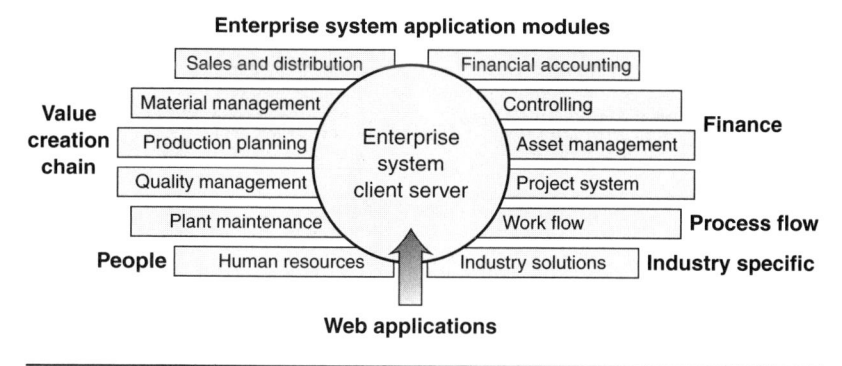

Figure 6.8 Enterprise system framework.

resource planning (ERP) systems can collect, integrate, and disperse information/data and knowledge in user-friendly formats. These systems are available for all sizes of organizations, are cost-effective, and can greatly enhance process improvement activities in support of ITEA-based teams.

ERP integrates internal and external management information across an entire organization, embracing finance/accounting, manufacturing, sales and service, customer relations management (CRM), and so on. ERP systems automate this activity with an integrated software application (see Figure 6.8, "Enterprise system framework"). Its purpose is to facilitate the flow of information between all business functions inside the boundaries of the organization and manage the connections to outside stakeholders.

Enterprise software (also known as ERP software) is integrated to facilitate the flow of information between all the main processes of a business. It provides a holistic view of a business within single information system technology architecture. All the processes of an organization's supply chain and value chain activities are included (Hayen 2006).

Implications for Integrating the TEF into an Organization Using Enterprise Resource Planning Systems

An important benefit to using the TEF in this environment is that it helps to understand how the various improvement projects can work together and build on each other. That is because the connections across the organization are more clearly understood and much better managed. It feeds into the holistic approach. Also, making a positive improvement one place can, through such integrated information technology, also benefit other areas without having to redo or create specialized IT applications.

INTEGRATING THE FRAMEWORK'S USE WITH METRICS, KEY PERFORMANCE INDICATORS, BALANCED SCORECARDS, AND DASHBOARDS

Metrology consists of the parameters or measures of quantitative assessment used for measurement, comparison, or to track performance. A core concept in metrology is (metrological) *traceability*, defined as "the property of the result of a measurement or the value of a standard whereby it can be related to stated references, usually national or international standards, through an unbroken chain of comparisons, all having stated uncertainties." An example of this is *Six Sigma quality level*, which means reducing defects to a level of no more than 3.4 per million of possible defects in a process or product.

Data and analysis are major requirements in the Team Excellence Criteria to ensure that the teams are making fact-based decisions. This is especially true in Sections 2, "Current Situation Analysis," 3, "Solution Development," and 4, "Project Implementation and Results."

The enterprise sustainability tree (Figure 6.3) identifies process activity data flowing into the *information and knowledge management system* (IKMS, also known as just KM) or more commonly known as the *enterprise resource planning* (ERP) system. From the IKMS process performance data, metrics are provided as required to manage process standards/requirements and report to both internal and external stakeholders as appropriate. This process is what makes performance management possible. The following will give you a brief description of performance data and metrics, key performance indicators, balanced scorecards, and dashboards.

Activity-Based Costing

Activity-based costing (ABC) is a special costing model that identifies activities in an organization and assigns the cost of each activity with resources to all products and services according to the actual consumption by each. This model allocates more *indirect costs* (overhead) to *direct costs* compared to conventional costing models. This is an important model to consider in team projects and CI in that it provides a more accurate way to address the real costs when considering Criteria Sections 3, "Solution Development" and 4, "Project Implementation and Results."

Performance Data

Performance data, or *raw data*, is a term for data collected at the source of a process that has not been subjected to processing or any other manipulation. It is also known as *primary data*. Raw data can be input to a computer program or used in manual analysis procedures such as gathering statistics from a survey or a process step.

Performance Metrics

Organizational performance metrics should support a broad range of activities, considering both internal and external stakeholder requirements. Generally, internal metrics focus mostly on cost, quality, and schedules while external metrics should focus on supplier performance and meeting customer requirements. Performance metrics should not just reflect past and current data, but should be trended and compared to targeted goals or established requirements. These performance metrics tend to be used mostly to manage performance at the process activity level rather than the management level. (For a comprehensive overview of quality for metrics, visit the ASQ website at http://asq.org/learn-about-quality/quality-tools.html.)

Key Performance Indicators

At the mid-management and above level performance measurement should give a higher-level picture. Detailed metrics are grouped together to represent larger natural segments of process performance or end results. At this point they become key performance indicators, or KPIs. These KPIs should also be shared with the process owners and with other appropriate internal and external stakeholders.

Balanced Scorecard

The first balanced scorecard gained prominence in the 1990s, mostly as a result of publications (Kaplan and Norton 2007). Since that time there have been many iterations of the balanced scorecard approach. One in particular is *Beyond the Balanced Scorecard: Improving Business Intelligence with Analytics* by Mark Graham Brown (2007).

Today, when an organization uses a balanced scorecard, one key factor still remains: the scorecard at any level has to be aligned with the organization's key strategic goals and objectives and its vision, mission, and values.

Most of the purveyors of the balanced scorecard suggest that the following areas be considered as key elements of a balanced scorecard:

- *Financial.* Measures that indicate the financial health of the organization or a key process and external stakeholders.

- *Internal processes.* Measures that focus on cost (application of lean as it relates to the 7 wastes), quality (meeting or exceeding customer requirements all the time), and schedule (cycle time reduction).

- *Customer.* Measures that relate to both the customer and organizational requirements.

- *Supplier.* Measures related to quality, accuracy, and on-time delivery.

- *Stakeholders.* Measures related to both internal and external stakeholders.

- *Cycles of learning and growth.* Evidence of regular cycles of analysis, solutions, and action plans.

Dashboard

The dashboard is designed to reflect the real-time status of the key processes and/or health indicators of the organization. That is, if all is going well, there are no action indicators that you need to attend to. But if an action indicator should appear, the system allows you to drill down to the source of the issue and take quick corrective action.

The term *dashboard* originates from the automobile dashboard where the driver can monitor the key functions at a glance. Although you can't see them, there are many microprocessors that are monitoring hundreds of functioning areas of the vehicle. Yet you aren't aware of these unless something is functioning outside its parameters. At that time the system will advise you of the issue, and you will need to take the appropriate action.

Today, through the information and knowledge management system, a digital dashboard is possible. The digital dashboard is driven by the internal and external activities of the organization's enterprise system software, that is, an integrated enterprise management system or an enterprise resource planning system.

Implications for Integrating the TEF into an Organization Using Various Metrics

Use of the TEF reinforces fact-based management. The Team Excellence Criteria requires good collection and analysis of metrics. It drives teams to both use appropriate analytical methodology and to clearly present the results of those analyses. The more members of the workforce who participate in team-based improvement projects, the higher the level of workforce sophistication rises in this regard. When an organization has a critical mass of its workforce who appreciate the importance of metrics and understand how to produce them and make decisions based on them, it turns a corner in its effectiveness.

CONCLUSION

In conclusion, this chapter has explained how using the TEF can provide synergy to any and all of these other initiatives that your organization may have under way. If you have such initiatives, there is no reason to treat the TEF as a stand-alone initiative. The information in this chapter has provided you with the rationale of how the TEF fits in a synergistic way.

Up to this point we have focused on the usefulness of the TEF for significantly improving your organization's results. However, many organizations have also found it to be a useful tool for giving internal and external recognition to its improvement teams. Therefore, the next chapter is dedicated to explaining how to use it as a motivational tool to recognize good team performance, both in terms of good project results and also in demonstrating true teamwork.

7
The ITEA Process
How to Participate and Obtain External Recognition for Your Teams' Achievements

We have emphasized throughout this book how useful the Team Excellence Framework is apart from having your teams enter an external award and recognition process. However, many organizations do also find it useful to have their teams participate in external recognition. The ITEA Process is a program of major professional stature that provides teams with external evaluation, feedback, and formal recognition. Its scope and influence have grown over the years in the numbers of participating organizations, teams that participate, and international mix. It attracts teams from around the world.

This chapter provides summary information for those interested in participating in the ITEA Process, either as team members or as individuals wanting to support it. It depends on the active support of many dedicated volunteers. First, we present a brief history of the ITEA Process. Then we describe the structure within which teams can participate, including the procedures and the types of recognition given. We describe how some organizations have also linked their internal team recognition programs to the ITEA based on the TEF. Finally, we explain how you and your colleagues can participate as individuals.

ASQ provides detailed information for those who are interested in getting involved. Information can be found at http://wcqi.asq.org/team-competition. This website is directly accessible to the general public. The ITEA Program staff is also an excellent source of information. There is an ITEA Committee comprising long-time volunteers who work with the ITEA Program staff to help guide and continuously improve the program. The committee members come from a diversity of business sectors and positions and have in-depth experience with team-based improvement projects. Most of them have also served as ITEA judges. They employ an annual learning and improvement cycle based on CI methodology to assure that the quality of the criteria, judging, and procedures meets current and future needs of customer organizations. Given the program's long history, the criteria themselves are mature, and changes are now rarely made to them. However, if a team wants to participate, it should download the latest version of the criteria. They are kept up-to-date on the website.

HISTORY

The ITEA Process has existed for over a quarter of a century, being established in 1985. Its roots were in the employee participation dimension of the quality movement. Quality assurance and CI are difficult to achieve without active involvement of employees. The Association of Quality and Participation (AQP) was formed to focus on this aspect of quality, starting with the successes of *quality circles*, first in Japan and then, as this approach was being imported into the Western world, taking forms such as General Electric's Work-Out methodology (Ulrich, Kerr, and Ashkenas 2002). ASQ became the sponsor of this program in 2005 when ASQ acquired AQP. Since that time ASQ has provided dedicated stewardship to what has evolved into the International Team Excellence Award Program.

WHY ENTER AN ITEA-SPONSORED EVENT?

Entering your teams in an external assessment and recognition process is not appropriate in all cases, but it is very useful in some circumstances. All people are motivated by recognition for a job well done, and all organizations should provide continuous learning for their members. We described the power of recognizing and celebrating successful improvement teams in Chapter 3. Ideally, organizations already provide internal recognition for their successful teams.

- *External recognition.* Participating in an ITEA-sponsored activity represents external recognition based on validated best practice using trained judges. Therefore, the scoring is not influenced by organizational idiosyncrasies or office politics. It is fair and transparent since each team is judged by the same criteria according to the same standards. Every competing team receives formal recognition for simply participating since that is worthy of being honored. The topmost-scoring teams get additional recognition for achieving the high levels that make them true benchmarks. Management usually places certificates and trophies received in public spaces used to recognize employee achievements. Organizations also do press releases. The information is good news plus an achievement recognized by an external, professional, non-biased program that exists to encourage and validate business successes. Box 7.1 shows excerpts from the press release issued by HD Supply Facilities Maintenance when they won the 2009 Gold Award. This is the best kind of business press!

- *Celebration.* This is the time to have fun. Celebration is related to recognition but goes beyond it. All the teams and their management sponsors celebrate in many ways, some of which are very creative. Invariably, lots of pictures and videos are taken, both official ones of the teams accepting their awards and many personal ones. These end up in many places in addition to public organizational spaces, including personal work spaces, team spaces, and, perhaps most importantly, in homes. Family members can often attend the presentations and/or award ceremonies. As described in Chapter 3, one of the most powerful employee motivators is to show their families that you recognize and appreciate their competence and hard work along with the support that the families themselves have contributed. Many types of celebration parties are hosted by team sponsors and organizational management. The combination of recognition and celebration is something that employees never forget, and sometimes represents the most memorable experience of their professional lives.

- *Continuous learning.* Each participating team receives a feedback report from their judging panel describing strengths and opportunities for improvement. Also, teams and their management sponsors have the chance to observe other teams give their presentations and have off-line discussions with them about their projects. This provides excellent exposure to a variety of approaches and new ideas. Moreover, it exposes teams to other business sectors outside their own. Such knowledge expands employee horizons and enhances their creativity. It is very valuable in raising expectations for how future teams should conduct their projects. This information is useful not only to the teams but especially to project champions, sponsors, organization leadership, and the staff who have responsibility for CI in their organizations.

- *Benchmarking.* The discipline of benchmarking has shown that the best ideas for breakthrough improvements often come from organizational sectors other than your own (Camp 2006; Brown 2007). Teams often have the opportunity to observe best-in-class projects. They have opportunities to network real-time with other teams as well as establish professional contacts for future discussions.

BOX 7.1: EXCERPTS FROM PRESS RELEASE

HD Supply Facilities Maintenance Wins Team Excellence Award from American Society for Quality

San Diego, Calif.—May 27, 2009—HD Supply Facilities Maintenance earned top honors by capturing the Gold Award at the 24th International Team Excellence Awards Process at the 2009 American Society for Quality Conference on Quality and Improvement. HD Supply won the Gold Award in a competition featuring 26 other companies from around the world.

"We are honored and pleased to earn the Gold Award from the American Society for Quality," said Anesa Chaibi, President, HD Supply Facilities Maintenance.

HD Supply's "Voice of the Customer" Captains Team won the Gold Award for the development of an innovative approach that used voice of the customer data to drive customer loyalty, continuous improvement, and operational excellence. The company realized benefits that included creation of a cross-functional team tasked with executing the company strategy while providing foresight into setting operational goals. Additional tangible benefits included an impact in customer loyalty via a six percent increase in the company's Net Promoter Score (which rates whether a current customer would recommend HD Supply to another customer) along with a 22 percent improvement in the top 10 customer defects. This process resulted in $3 million in savings for the company.

"We have a culture that is passionate about service and flawless execution on behalf of our customers," added Kaye Stambaugh, Vice President, Customer Care, HD Supply Facilities Maintenance. "The Gold Award is an excellent endorsement of our practices, and we are extremely proud to have been honored against such top competition."

WHY ATTEND AN ITEA-SPONSORED EVENT?

These events also provide a showcase for successful teams. Attending them provides an opportunity to witness the work of excellent teams from other organizations. It provides you exposure to other types of organizations and best practice use of tools. It offers an inside look at how projects have been done within a company that otherwise would be invisible to outsiders.

> These . . . teams all help to prove the power of teamwork. In today's work environment, we all hear about teamwork, and many of us have even led or participated in team problem-solving activities, but rarely do we get to see the power of what happens when groups of people come together from companies worldwide to showcase their methods and achievements. Each team used different tools and ideas, but they were all united in the quest to better their organizations. The World Conference provides a unique opportunity to observe these teams in action and learn from their struggles and successes. (Peotter 2009, 36)

DESCRIPTION OF THE STRUCTURE

How do teams participate? Any team can participate provided their project has been completed in the last two years. A team must submit its project presentation showing how it addressed each of the team excellence criteria. All presentations are scored by expert judges trained in use of the criteria, and the judges provide a feedback report to each team. The details of scoring are covered in Chapter 4. The ITEA judges come from these same trenches of managing and doing team-based improvement projects. They have assessment and other relevant skills acquired from a broad range of industries and positions. The team judge selection and training process brings the best of the best to the table to assure that the program provides a fair assessment and actionable feedback for all team presentations.

The ITEA Process sponsors two sets of award and recognition processes:

1. *International-wide process.* Any team can directly participate as long as they meet the requirements. Over the past five years (2007–2011) 176 teams have been involved.

2. *Regional Showcase programs in various geographic locations.* These are similar to the ITEA Process but are operated within countries outside the United States and within U.S. states and

municipalities. The teams are required to apply the same or similar criteria and are judged similarly.

The International-Wide Process

This has a two-step procedure:

- The *preliminary round* in the fall of each year requires that you submit a PowerPoint presentation describing how your completed project addressed each of the team excellence criteria. Speaker notes must accompany each slide. These notes must be able to be read aloud by someone else within a 30-minute time period. Each presentation is given to a trained judging panel that scores it. An actionable feedback report, along with your point scores, is later provided by the panel that judged your presentation. The highest-scoring teams are selected to go to the *final round* event. These teams have the opportunity to use their feedback to improve their presentations before moving to the final round.

- The *final round* in mid-May involves your team giving a live presentation at ASQ's World Conference on Quality and Improvement. Again, the presentation should show how the project addressed each of the team excellence criteria and should include speaker notes for each slide. The presentation must be delivered by the team members themselves within a 30-minute time period in front of a panel of trained judges. The presentation is scored. An actionable feedback report, along with your point scores, is later provided by your judging panel.

Major steps an organization takes to participate are as follows:

Step 1—Identify successfully completed projects. Identify projects completed in the last two years that achieved measurable results. Do not submit projects submitted previously; they are not eligible.

Step 2—Select which projects to enter into the event. You may submit up to five entries from any participating site or location.

Step 3—Create a PowerPoint presentation describing the project. Ensure that it is aligned with ASQ's Team Excellence criteria. Check the program's website to make sure that you have the current version of the criteria. See how past winners aligned their presentations to the award criteria. Occasionally, a team decides to enter the event with a completed project before it knows about the existence of the criteria. If the team used a systematic improvement process, it is possible to recast it in terms of the criteria so it is not precluded from participating. Teams have successfully done this. However, using the criteria from the outset of the project is far preferable and will result in even better outcomes for future teams.

Step 4—Complete the online entry form and submit payment of the entry fee.

Regional Showcase Recognition Programs

Regional Showcases have sponsored arrangements with the ITEA Process. Each of these regional Showcases bestows its own recognition awards. These programs are a useful adjunct to the international-level events for several reasons. They allow much broader participation in the team excellence events and receipt of outside recognition. Many teams and their organizations are in earlier stages of maturity. They feel they can not participate on the world stage, so a local event is a good place for them to start. Through continued feedback plus learning from observing fellow teams give presentations, an organization's teams gradually improve. Because many organizations can not afford to send their teams long distances to the ASQ World Conference, local events are a way to expose them to this experience and gain the outside recognition they deserve. Throughout the whole award structure from international to regional there is an emphasis on recognizing team performance regardless of their scores. No matter what the level of proficiency, every team member who uses the TEF, even as beginners, has accomplished something worthwhile and achieved some respectable business outcomes. In addition, they have all learned something; many of them have learned a great deal. Similar to the Olympics, regional events serve as a developmental platform for organizations who want to build proficiency in team-based continuous improvement.

An equally important point is that regional Showcase programs have also promoted development and recognition of world-class teams. In most cases, their top-scoring teams can directly qualify as finalists in the ITEA event since the same scoring standards are applied. In other words, it is the score of the team that enables them to qualify as an ITEA finalist, not its relative standing in the local event. Numerous of the ITEA Gold, Silver, and Bronze Award winners have first come through these regional Showcases, such as teams from Telefonica, Boeing, and HD Supply.

The mechanics of each event depend on the regional Showcase. Table 7.1 provides information on each regional program, with contact information if you want to learn more. ASQ is open to adding more Showcase programs from various localities provided certain conditions are met. If you are interested, contact the ITEA program office.

Location: Argentina

Program name: Competencia Nacional de Equipos "Torneo Estrellas de la Excelencia" (National Team Competition "Excellence Stars")

Description: This program has been in existence since 2008 and is open to any team in the country of Argentina. It is sponsored by ASQ and uses the ITEA Criteria. Its main purpose is to foster teamwork by motivating and recognizing it, and provide benchmarking opportunities. There are two judging rounds. In the preliminary round, PowerPoint presentations are submitted and scored by appointed judges, first individually and then by consensus. Best teams are awarded finalist status. Then there is a one-day final round (open to the public) in which the finalist teams present their projects live before a panel of judges who ask questions of the teams and adjust their scores. By the end of the day, formal awards are given to best projects and presentations. All teams, no matter whether they were finalists or not, receive feedback from judges. Gold, Silver, and Bronze winners are invited to attend and participate in the ITEA. As evidence of the quality of competing teams and the judging process, one of the 2009 winners in Argentina won the ITEA Gold Award in 2010, and two of the 2010 winners in Argentina won the Gold and Bronze ITEA Awards in 2011.

Sources for more information:
Technical director: Raúl Molteni (raul@molteniconsulting.com);
Administrative director: Mario Casellini (m_casellini@fundece.org.ar);
http://equipos.ipace.org.ar/ipace/equipos/index.html

Location: California, USA

Program name: California Team Excellence Award (CTEA) Program

Description: The CTEA program has been in existence since 1998. There are two levels of participation: Gold Nugget and Gold Rush. In the Gold Nugget process the judging is held in several state locations with live team presentations and video presentations for those teams that can not come to the event. The Gold Rush process is intended to encourage less-experienced teams to participate and learn. They are required to submit a PowerPoint presentation that only addresses 15 items from the Criteria Summary document. These are the top-level items in the hierarchy, that is, 1A, 1B, 1C, 2A, and so on. A team can submit their presentation any time during the year and get scoring and feedback. Awards and recognition for all teams are provided at a later date during the annual ceremony hosted by CTEA's parent organization, the California Council for Excellence (CCE) (www.calexcellence.org) which also runs the state's Baldrige Award program. The objective is to formally recognize each team's achievements. Therefore, the team's award level is based on its point scores, and all teams receive at least an honorable mention. The program has had numerous of its high-scoring teams move on to win Gold, Silver, and Bronze ITEA Awards at the international-level events.

Sources for more information:
http://www.calexcellence.org/ctea.html; 858-486-0400.

Table 7.1 Summary of Showcases: feeder programs in the ITEA Process.

Location: Florida, USA

Program name: Florida Sterling Council Team Showcase

Description: The Team Showcase has been in existence since 1996 and is open to teams from Florida organizations. Judging involves a two-step process. The team submits a written application, which is scored by a panel of judges against the Team Excellence Criteria, which mirrors the ASQ Team Excellence Award Criteria. The six top-scoring teams are invited to present their projects live at the annual Team Showcase event in Orlando, Florida. The presentations are judged and scored, and then each team and the champion are recognized at the annual Sterling Awards Banquet. The top-scoring team is automatically eligible to participate at the international-level event. Each team receives written scoring and feedback from the panel of judges.

Sources for more information:
James Sherlock (jsherlock@floridasterling.com);
http://www.floridasterling.com/team-showcase-overview.php.

Location: Cincinnati, Ohio, USA

Program name: ASQ–Greater Cincinnati Health Council Solutions Awards

Description: This program is for healthcare providers in the greater Cincinnati area. It was established in 2008. It is co-sponsored by the Cincinnati ASQ section and Greater Cincinnati Health Council. It uses a simplified version of the ITEA Criteria consisting of 18 items. The initial submission is a report of the team's project. In the preliminary judging the presentation is scored by teams of four to five judges. The applications of the three best teams with the top average scores are then scored by the remaining judges, and a consensus meeting is held to agree on the winner and runner-up. The teams are ranked according to their final scores. All teams are invited to submit a PowerPoint presentation of their projects for display at the annual Solutions Conference and banquet. The conference is attended by healthcare providers from the greater Cincinnati, Northern Kentucky, and Southeast Indiana area. All the teams who submitted presentations receive recognition at the time. The emphasis of the program is to provide opportunities for learning and recognition for all participants.

Sources for more information:
Bruce Johnson, MS, PMP, CQE; brucej@jcsconsultants.com, or call 513-520-2357.

Table 7.1 *Continued.*

Education Team Excellence Recognition (ETER) Program

This program is tailored to educational institutions. It is focused on recognizing and improving achievement in academic excellence at all educational levels through team-based CI.

> Criteria . . . were derived from the world-class standard, the International Team Excellence Award criteria . . . . Not only do these criteria provide a framework for evaluating teams' entries . . . , but they are also useful as an improvement framework for schools that don't have an improvement process. The . . . process involves two rounds, and teams receive a feedback report after the preliminary round that includes a summary score sheet, information on performance against each of the 24 criteria items, and descriptions of strengths and opportunities for improvement. Any educational institution can apply for the award, including public or private schools and districts (individual buildings/schools, grade-level teams, departments, or individual classrooms), higher education/community colleges, trade schools, or day care centers. The team can include any combination of students, staff, administrators, and parent–teacher organization members. The project must have been completed within the past two years. (American Society for Quality 2009, 41)

The finalist teams present live at the annual National Quality Education Conference (NQEC) each fall. According to Glenn Walters, long-time lead judge in the ITEA and ETER programs, the evaluation and recognition is criterion-based, meaning it is tied to the level of performance of each team relative to the criteria. In addition, based on their point scores, teams can earn a Merit, Distinction, or Star Award. Two educational institutions with 2010 finalist teams were Ramaiah Institute of Management Studies (RIMS) from Bangalore, India, and Glenbrook South High School from Glenbrook, Illinois. B. V. Krishnamurthy, who made his team's presentation at NQEC, has observed the following about participating in this program: "For me personally, attending two NQEC events have been memorable experiences. The NQEC provides an unparalleled platform to learn from peer groups. The incisive questions posed by the learned judges and the equally learned audience have led to long hours of reflection followed by purposeful action . . . ." (Walters 2011, 36).

Information about the program, including the criteria, procedures for participation, and presentations from top-scoring teams, can be found at the following site: http://nqec.asq.org/team-award.

RECOGNITION

In Chapter 3 we described the critical role that recognizing employee achievements plays in employee engagement, commitment, development, and overall motivation. Having teams participate in a team excellence assessment and recognition process provides several forms of recognition, and putting them together has a noticeable impact on the team members. It also impacts their organizational peers by communicating that the organization values teams that contribute significant improvements in organizational results. From a team member's perspective, if my management invested the resources to enter my team in an external event, it reinforces that they really:

- Value what I achieved for the organization and want to further celebrate that success
- Appreciate all the hard work I put into the project
- Are so proud of my team that they want outside people to see our achievements
- Value my mental capacity, skills, and the knowledge I have acquired about my work
- Support my continued learning and development
- Value the contributions resulting from teamwork as much as individual contributions
- Encourage me and my fellow employees to engage in CI as part of the organization's culture and routine operations

Recognition Received from Participating in the International-Wide Events

Anyone who has attended the ASQ World Conference on Quality and Improvement in recent years is aware of the outstanding public recognition that is accorded the teams who make it from the preliminary round to the "finals." Each finalist team is recognized at the opening plenary session. During the conference, each team gives their presentation in a dedicated session in front of a judging panel, and any conference participant can attend.

From 2007–2011 a total of 133 teams have made it to the finals. Each of these teams is presented a Finalist Award. Finalist status is, in itself, recognition of a significant achievement. Accompanying the status of finalist is something even more tangible. Organizations with finalists commit to sending their teams to the World Conference at the organizations' expense. The team members spend about four days there. Conference attendees come to listen to their presentations. Many team members have never had a professional experience of this caliber. Teams travel there from all over the globe. This gesture of confidence, pride, and investment by their management is a profound form of professional recognition.

During the closing plenary session all the teams march in to much fanfare. The last official act of the conference is the announcement of the top-scoring teams. These top honors are in the form of Gold, Silver, and Bronze Awards, and each team is brought up on stage to receive their award. While we would like to fully convey how much energy is generated in the room, it is hard to capture in words. Afterward, ASQ issues press releases and helps teams prepare case studies, which are published on the ITEA website under the link http://wcqi.asq.org/team-competition/case-studies.html. Winning companies also have their own press campaigns to capitalize on this testament to their excellent business practices. They also provide recognition and celebration for the teams when they return. Coupling external recognition with internal recognition is especially powerful, a topic covered below.

Table 7.2 lists the organizations with Gold Award–winning teams since the inception of the program. All Gold, Silver, and Bronze Award–winning teams since 2007 have been cited with references to published case studies throughout this book.

An adjunct to the formal awards is the poster competition co-sponsored by ASQ and the Team and Workplace Excellence Forum (TWEF). Mike Whisman, former chair of the ITEA Committee and liaison to the TWEF Leadership Council, referred to it as "a people's choice award" (Whisman 2011). Each team is invited to bring a poster that describes its project. These are displayed in a common area during the conference, and all conference attendees have the opportunity to vote on their top three choices for best project poster. The 2010 winner was the Food and Nutrition Services Key Ingredients Team from the Food and Nutrition Services Department of the School District of Lee County, Fort Myers, Florida, USA. This department provides 61,000 meals a day across 87 schools. The 2011 winner was the Praxair Mexico Team, from Praxair in Nuevo Leon, Monterey, Mexico. Praxair, a Fortune 300 global company, supplies atmospheric, process, and specialty gases, high-performance coatings, and related services and technologies. The poster competition is an additional opportunity for teams to share their achievements.

Recognition Received by Participating in Regional Showcase Events

The award structure in the regional events is set by each program. The general principle is to formally recognize every team for participating because they all have accomplished something with their project and their

1985 Schick/Warner-Lambert
1986 Borg-Warner
1987 Pella Rolscreen Company
1988 Arizona Public Service
1989 Johns Hopkins Applied Physics Lab
1990 Sheller-Globe
1991 National winner not selected
1992 GTE Products
1993 Harris Corporation
1994 Liebert Corporation
1995 Texaco Refining and Marketing Inc.
1996 Uniroyal Chemical Company, Inc.
1997 Daishowa America Co., Ltd.
1998 Honda of America Manufacturing, Inc.
1999 Solectron Technology, Inc.
2000 Emerson Electric Company
2001 Blue Cross Blue Shield of Florida, Inc.
2002 Merrill Lynch
2003 Fidelity Wide Processing
2004 Fidelity Wide Processing
2005 Baxter Healthcare
2006 Reliance Industries Limited, India
2007 The Boeing Company
2008 The Boeing Company
2009 HD Supply Facilities Maintenance
2010 Telefonica Argentina
2011 Telefonica Argentina

Table 7.2 Organizations with ITEA Gold Award–winning teams 1985–2011.

ability to articulate it in terms of the criteria. Also, there can be more leeway in the number of top awards given since the purpose of the Showcase events is to encourage teams to progressively higher levels of achievement. For example, in the CTEA Program every team gets at least an honorable mention, and the number of Gold, Silver, and Bronze Awards is not given by rank; it is by point score within a predetermined range.

CONNECTING INTERNAL AND EXTERNAL TEAM RECOGNITION

It is important for organizations to have an internal system for assessing improvement team performance, recognizing team member accomplishments, and providing continuous learning. This is necessary to grow and sustain a team-based improvement culture. Otherwise the successes are ad hoc, and momentum can fade. Using an externally validated yardstick for providing formal awards and rewards creates the perception of credibility, transparency, and fairness to the selection of teams to receive significant rewards.

A system that ties the internal recognition system to an external one can be even more powerful. The TEF provides an opportunity to do so.

See Box 7.2 for examples of organizations that have successfully used the TEF for internal recognition and also linked it to external recognition through the ITEA and regional Showcase programs.

BOX 7.2: EXAMPLES OF ORGANIZATIONS USING THE TEF TO LINK INTERNAL RECOGNITION AND EXTERNAL RECOGNITION

Sterlite Industries Limited in India has been a repeat participant in the ITEA Process. Sterlite is the leading copper producer in India. Operations include a smelter, refinery, phosphoric acid plant, sulphuric acid plant, and copper rod plants. They also own a copper mine in Tasmania, Australia. According to Ramakrishna Nayak, Head of Business Excellence for Sterlite Copper (pers. comm.), they use the ITEA criteria as part their internal team recognition program. They evaluate team presentations using these criteria, in addition to other criteria that the company believes are important. As a result over time, many people associated with improvement teams have learned about the criteria and use the principles to help guide their projects. The framework fits in well with the PDCA model of continuous improvement that the company adopted for its TQM initiative, based on guidance from the Juran Institute. Part of the internal recognition program involves selecting high-scoring teams to receive awards.

These awards are distributed by the chief operating officer in a public ceremony to which all the team members and their families are invited. From this set of teams, the top one or two teams are invited to submit their presentations to the ITEA Process. The company has had several teams over the past few years be awarded "finalist" status. This has enabled them to attend the ASQ World Conference and present their projects. The team members have found this experience very motivating. They realize the substantial financial investment that management makes by sending them to this conference and see it as a reward for a job very well done. Management and the team members have benefited from the ITEA experience, both from the feedback received and also the opportunity to learn how other successful teams have used tools and techniques to achieve outstanding results.

Baxter International, Inc. is a global healthcare company that develops, manufactures, and markets products that save and sustain the lives of people with hemophilia, immune disorders, infectious diseases, kidney disease, trauma, and other chronic and acute medical conditions. It has had teams involved in the ITEA Process for a number of years and benefited with improved business results and employee engagement. For example, one of its teams, a 2005 Gold Award recipient, succeeded in removing significant amounts of waste from a large-scale production process for one-liter saline IV units. The team reduced cycle time by more than 70%, reduced product carriers by 25%, eliminated 2400 wasteful product moves per day, reduced work-in-process by 30%, increased available floor space by 22,000 square feet, and eliminated two daily production schedules. In addition, "We have created a passion for lean enterprise improvements where all team members have developed genuine 'eyes for value' and 'eyes for waste.'" (Buchanan, Smith, and Williamson 2005, 36) According to Michael Whisman, former director of quality, they leveraged the motivation created by the ITEA experience with internal recognition. For Baxter teams who went to the finals at the ASQ World Conference, internal publicity was generated, especially upon their return. His observation about employee motivation is insightful. It is that the publicity about their achievements should be directed at those people whose opinions the employees value. Most people particularly value the opinions of fellow workers, their families, and outside personal friends. So the channels for delivering the good news of their achievements must be tailored to reach that constituency. In the case of hourly production employees, for example, he arranged for parades and parties on the work floor. Additional means were used to get the word out through informal channels in the local community so that it became a conversation topic in the places those employees spent time outside of work. The point is that, while a press release to a national newspaper is motivating to management because it gains the company excellent performance and brand recognition, if the team members are not members of top management, this audience is not as important as feeling proud in their circle of family and friends.

For more than a decade *Boeing*'s C-17 Program has entered dozens of team projects into ITEA and CTEA events, winning more awards than any other participating organization. After its initial successes using the TEF to achieve business results, the organization integrated its internal and external recognition programs using the TEF. Their formal internal team project recognition program annually bestows specific awards and rewards to teams for successful improvement projects. It applies the TEF criteria to decide which project teams are worthy of this recognition (Rick Payne, pers. comm.). When Howard Chambers led this organization, he also met every month with one of his top teams for breakfast, lunch, or dinner. (Chambers, pers. comm.) Then, top leadership has sent the top-scoring teams to participate in CTEA and/or ITEA programs. This approach reinforces the expectation that all teams are expected to use the TEF as a guide in doing their projects.

Telefonica/Movistar, a more recent participant in the ITEA Process, has evolved in the same direction as Boeing C-17 in tying internal and external recognition through the TEF. Management has been entering their most successful team projects into Argentina's regional team excellence Showcase program where they get assessed and recognized. Those teams that score above a certain level are sent by top leadership to the ITEA finals at the ASQ World Conference. Again, this reinforces the message that addressing the TEF criteria is what defines team excellence.

OTHER OPPORTUNITIES FOR PARTICIPATION

Two types of opportunities exist to participate beyond being on an improvement team. One is to learn what these teams have done. The other is to volunteer in the program. As Janet Jacobsen (2007) observed, "Of course, the success of this international competition is due to the valuable contributions of many volunteer committee members and judges . . . ."

Learn from Participating Teams

Everyone has the opportunity to learn what high-scoring teams have done from two published sources: the presentations that are posted on the ITEA website and the many articles and case studies published by ASQ Quality Press in *Quality Progress* and in the *Journal of Quality and Participation*. We also recommend that you take advantage of the opportunity to listen firsthand to team presentations. These opportunities exist both at the international and regional levels. If you attend the ASQ World Conference, you have an opportunity to see presentations that are extremely well done, both in technical content and in presentation delivery. It is an excellent chance to learn, not only to improve your understanding of CI methodology and the power of teamwork, but also to see how other organizations have applied tools in ways that you might not have previously considered. It enables you to expand your horizons and to benchmark the best of the team projects.

> I had attended team presentations throughout the conference, and had walked away with much more than I expected. Not only did the members showcase the esprit de corps we commonly associate with teams, but they also demonstrated problem-solving techniques that align with the ITEA criteria and incredible results. As a new practitioner in the quality profession, most of my projects involve working with teams, so these concepts weren't new to me, but the team presentations raised my faith in the power of teamwork to an entirely new level (Peotter 2009, 32–33).

Also, TWEF sponsors a feedback system from the audience to the team. It entails a sheet with a list of eighteen categories of impact that a presentation might have on the listener, such as *creative project*, *team spirit*, *persistence in project management*, or *team/vendor relationship*. Each audience member can pick up to three categories from the list. The audience responses are tabulated and given to the team as a way of letting them know how they made a unique impact on the audience.

Volunteer to Support the Assessment and Recognition Process

The ITEA Process depends on its very extensive and dedicated volunteer base. The program could not run without its volunteers. Even if your organization does not enter teams into the events, it does not preclude you from getting involved. Why do people volunteer? Most people who are professionally involved in CI consider it to be more than just a job. It helps improve the standard of living and quality of life of humankind. Improving customer satisfaction and eliminating waste and inefficiency positively impact every area of life. Another reason pertains to professional development. Being involved produces a much better appreciation of what it takes to do a successful project. Even those who are already sophisticated take away new learning. Last, it is personally motivational to see the human side of teams in action. When teams are properly formed and guided by these best practice criteria, they have a very successful experience. The impact of this experience on team members is motivational, and sometimes it is the most meaningful work experience of their lives. Their enthusiasm is contagious and renews one's faith in the power of true teamwork coupled with systematic CI methodology. The ways to volunteer are covered below.

Volunteer As a Judge

Judges are at the heart of this process. They provide the assessment in the form of scoring and feedback comments using the methods described in Chapter 4. While an unlimited number of people can be trained to do good assessment and feedback, the judges for the international-wide events are a carefully selected group. In 2011, 414 people applied to be an ITEA judge, and 208 were selected. All those selected to attend a two-day judging event donate their time to be trained and perform judging. They pay their own travel expenses to these events. They also must participate in pre-training prior to attending the event. "Judges review a mock case, calibrate their sensitivity and listening competencies, and brush up on judging skills. It is always amazing to see a group of relative strangers go from zero to 60 in collaboration in less than 48 hours!" (Zilbershtein 2010, 31). From the preliminary round judges a smaller number of very experienced judges are selected to serve in the final round at ASQ's annual World Conference. There is a larger group of judges who work in the regional Showcase programs. While being an ASQ member is a requirement to qualify as an ITEA judge, there is no such requirement in the regional events. The volunteer commitment of all the judges clearly demonstrates their dedication to the cause of increasing and recognizing team excellence. One experienced ITEA judge, Miles Littlefield (pers. comm.), volunteers because he sees the standard of excellence defined by the ITEA criteria as something that drives teams and organizations to outstanding performance levels. He finds it gratifying to contribute to a process that has such positive implications for achieving business results along with building the capacity of the workforce. Another experienced judge, Mindy Corcoran (pers. comm.) continues to be inspired by the extraordinary accomplishments that she sees teams achieve. Judges benefit in numerous ways:

- They see presentations of outstanding teams and learn best practice information they can often apply to their own organizations.
- They hone their knowledge and skills about what constitutes best practice in team excellence, both by taking the judges' training and applying it during judging.
- They get continuing education units and ASQ recertification units (CEUs/RUs).
- They network with fellow judges from various sectors who are highly competent CI professionals. This expands their knowledge and skill both in depth and breadth.
- They get recognition from their own organization's management for achieving the status of ITEA judge.
- They are energized by seeing the extraordinary results accomplished by teams who use the TEF, as well as the professional and personal impacts these achievements have on team members.

Volunteer in Program Administration

The judging events require volunteers to arrange and run them. This includes obtaining the sites, setting up logistics, delivering judges' training, and running the judging sessions. The annual site support in a New Mexico, USA, location for the preliminary round of ITEA judging is an excellent example. This support has been provided by Dawn Reed and Glenn Walters, dedicated contributors in this state's quality community, who have donated their own time to delivering the judges' training and running the judging sessions, and have cultivated a set of repeat sponsors to provide resources. Reed (pers. comm.) offered several reasons why she continues to donate her time and effort. An important one is to cultivate more and better judges. Not only do high-quality judges contribute to the professionalism of the ITEA recognition process, but they also have another important effect. In her experience, when organizations have employees trained to assess team excellence using ITEA's criteria, two things occur. One is that the employees become more valuable to those organizations because they better understand how using the criteria drives project success. They become more effective in driving CI through teamwork in their own organizations.

The other is that the organization's teams gradually score higher, motivating them to continue refining their improvement methods. Another of her reasons is to continue building the capacity of the quality community in the state of New Mexico. Lastly, as someone also very experienced in the Baldrige program, she sees achieving team excellence as "very complementary" to achieving organizational performance excellence. She remains motivated by seeing the stream of extraordinary team success stories, ones that demonstrate leadership, strategic planning, operational focus, workforce focus, and most important of all, incredible results.

Volunteer to Provide Sponsorship and Other Support

The preliminary round ITEA judging events require meeting places, food, and other support. Showcase regional events require the same support. Various organizations provide financial sponsorship and in-kind contributions. The sponsors for the ITEA judging events for the current year are recognized on the ITEA website at the link http://wcqi.asq.org/team-competition/sponsor-recognition.html.

CONCLUSION

In this chapter we have explained how you can be involved in the external assessment and recognition of TEF-based projects. We also have covered how organizations can leverage both formal external recognition programs and internal recognition programs using the TEF as a validated standard. There are numerous other opportunities to get involved by volunteering. In the next and final chapter we wrap up this book on team excellence by covering next steps that organizations can take to get started using the TEF to great advantage.

8
Next Steps
How to Apply the Team Excellence Framework in Your Organization

The purpose of this final chapter is to provide you with suggested next steps for using the TEF in your organization. These are based on your organization's type. The steps are a generic set of suggestions and should be adjusted to fit your own organization. At the end of the chapter is a closing thought that reinforces the theme of this book—which is how much both the organization and the workforce can benefit from practicing team excellence.

No matter what your type of organization, improvement teams in today's world are increasingly virtual, meaning the members are geographically dispersed. It is beyond this book's scope to cover the methodologies to build and maintain teamwork in a virtual environment, but fortunately the professional literature on this subject is growing (Troutman and Falkowski 2003a, 2003b, 2003c; Gibson and Cohen 2003; Johnson 2002; Troutman 2005). The point here is that virtual teams can be as high-performing as colocated teams provided appropriate means are used to support them. Fortunately, in the emerging Web 2.0 environment, the means for people to collaborate through information technology are rapidly reducing the challenges posed by differences in space and time.

In Chapter 1 we included the ways in which the TEF is useful to all types of organizations. One of the TEF's many advantages is that the criteria are written at several levels of detail. This allows organizations to tailor their use to their organization's level of competency in team-based improvement. Moreover, because it is generic, you have the option of tailoring it to your particular business sector with relevant language. Chapter 1 also explained how it is useful to each of the following three types of organizations:

• Organizations new to either CI methodology or the use of teams

- Organizations already using teams equipped with systematic CI methodology
- Organizations recognized as high in overall performance excellence

ORGANIZATIONS NEW TO EITHER CI METHODOLOGY OR THE USE OF TEAMS

If you are in this type of organization, the TEF benefits you greatly by getting you off on the right foot. Using the framework as a guide to form and manage your improvement teams enables you to avoid common mistakes made with team improvement projects.

Step 1. Start small. Begin with one team doing one project.

Step 2. Engineer the project for success from the outset.

- Pick a project of modest challenge but nevertheless one that is clearly aligned to one or more organizational goals. Do not pick your most intractable problem, as tempting as that may be.
- Pick team members who collectively have all the necessary functional skills and who represent all stakeholders who are directly involved in the problem or process.
- Pick team members who already have good teamwork skills. This is not the time for turning lone rangers into team players.
- Resource the team fully. For example, provide members enough work time to devote to the project, meeting space, technical expertise, access to needed information, and so on.
- Provide unwavering management sponsorship and support from whatever level of leadership is adequate. While top leadership support is always desirable, a middle or frontline manager can also provide the needed sponsorship as long as they control the necessary resources. The history of successful performance improvement initiatives shows that most initial efforts did not start with the top person. They started at lower levels, sometimes as quasi-guerilla efforts viewed as countercultural inside the organization. The best way to get top leadership on board is to show a verifiable track record of project successes.

Step 3. Obtain whatever necessary technical expertise you lack. This includes technical expertise on the analytic tools of CI and on how to turn groups into teams.

- Before turning outside, determine if you have the needed skills inside. You might be pleasantly surprised at what skills reside in your workforce. Do not get more expertise than you need.

- If you require outside expertise, stick with the basics. Some can be obtained from books and online resources. Have key people read this book, especially Chapters 3 and 4. One approach is to have one or two people take introductory courses on CI analytic methodology and/or how to build a team. Such courses are usually three to five days. Generally, the best people to send to such training are the project leader and the direct management sponsor of the project. It would also be beneficial to send the entire team together to a one-day course on best practices in team excellence that includes use of the TEF. Another approach is to employ an expert who is familiar with CI tools, team-building requirements, and the TEF to teach and coach the team. At this point all you need is enough expertise to pull off one successful project. Do not over-invest in expertise until you have built a track record of project successes.

- Have your experts provide just-in-time training and coaching to the rest of the team members. Adult learning principles tell us that people learn best by applying their learning immediately in the workplace. The phases of a CI approach and the tools needed for their particular project can easily be taught as the team moves forward through the project. This approach avoids overwhelming the team members with tools that they do not need for their project and creating anxiety with needless information and complexity. There are over a hundred tools in the CI toolbox, yet useful solutions to most problems can be achieved with a relatively small number of these tools. In other words, keep it simple and comfortable for all members.

Step 4. Require the team to use the Team Excellence Criteria as a checklist, either using the Summary or by turning it into an even simpler checklist. In other words, how the checklist reads should be matched to the level of sophistication of the team members. Using it as a checklist will enable them to avoid missing any necessary requirement. We recommend that you do not use the amplified (detailed) version of the Criteria for your early projects.

If this first project is on a simple problem, then it is likely that not every individual item in the Summary need be applied. The team leader or facilitator should keep tabs to make sure the team doesn't neglect really essential steps to their project, but if they skip some "nice to do" steps as novices, it is acceptable. An even simpler alternative is to use only the topmost level of the criteria. For example, only use the statements in 1A, 1B, and 1C rather than including 1Aa, 1Ab, 1Ac, 1Ba, 1Bb, 1Bc, 1Ca, 1Cb, 1Cc, and so on. The idea is to teach them how to take baby steps but still obtain a minimally acceptable project outcome. Again, keep it as simple as possible to match the readiness of the participants.

Step 5. Execute the project. As the team goes through each phase of its CI methodology (for example, DMAIC, PDC/SA), create PowerPoint slides addressing the criteria items in your checklist. In this way the team will have a completed presentation for management by the project's end rather than having to backtrack and build it from scratch. They will be grateful.

Step 6. Present the project to management using a PowerPoint presentation. During the project it is important at the end of each phase to present the project to the management sponsor so he/she can understand what the team has done and provide any suggestions and redirection before the project moves forward. All team members should have some role in giving presentations. Once the project is completed, give the final presentation to the sponsor. Finally, the team and sponsor together should bring it up the management chain for presentation. Many good projects have died on the vine for the team's lack of a well-articulated presentation that is comprehensible and convincing to top management.

Step 7. Celebrate success. Similarly to step 6, celebration should be an action taken at the end of each phase, not just at the project's end. Its importance is often overlooked in the press of getting the project done. Pick ways to provide recognition to your team members that they find meaningful. Never underestimate how much mileage you can get from free or almost free forms of recognition such as a heartfelt thank-you or a pizza. Publicize project successes internally to the organization. To your management audience highlight the excellent tangible and intangible results achieved. To your workforce audience highlight the sense of achievement and pride of the team members. Add external publicity reaching external stakeholders such as customers, shareholders, and professional organizations. Include the fact that you used the TEF. It adds professional credibility to your project since it represents an internationally recognized standard.

Step 8. Discuss what went well and what needed improvement in how the first project was done. Also, have at least one person score the project presentation using the TEF assessment method described in Chapter 4 and provide a feedback report to the team. Incorporate the learning from both these sources.

Step 9. Repeat steps 1 through 7 with one or two more projects. Pace yourself so the organizational capacity for doing successful projects does not get overextended.

Step 10. Learn, adjust, and repeat with more projects. After you have accomplished enough projects to move beyond the prototype, start institutionalizing the use of the TEF by adding a broader-based training program and other programmatics. Avoid falling into the numbers game trap of measuring success by the number of people trained or the number of projects if they have not been assessed for success using an externally validated yardstick.

ORGANIZATIONS ALREADY USING TEAMS EQUIPPED WITH SYSTEMATIC CI METHODOLOGY

If you are in this type of organization, the TEF benefits you in at least two ways. One is that it increases the true success rate of your team improvement projects. Most organizations in this category lack a validated yardstick, so what is judged as successful lies in the eyes of the beholders: the champions, sponsors, and leadership. Unfortunately, beholders can vary greatly in their expert ability to assess true success. An example of a management mistake is to be satisfied by positive ROI even though the CI methodology and/or teamwork were poor. Good results can be generated by luck, brute force on the backs of the employees, having an expert do most of the work for the "team," or doctoring the numbers. Managers can be hoodwinked if they do not recognize lack of sound methodology. Such projects send a terrible message and undermine the credibility of the approach. The workforce begins to perceive the initiative as a "numbers game," with success judged by how many people have been trained, how many projects have been completed, how much money was saved, and so on. Projects that meet superficial requirements but lack staying power—for example by not taking the steps to ensure stakeholder involvement—will not have long-lasting results; the minute the champion turns his/her back, the process reverts back to the way it was. The TEF provides a yardstick, and adopting it is easier than building and validating a yardstick yourself. Also, because it has been externally validated, it is more credible to customers, shareholders, and outside professional organizations.

The other benefit is that using the TEF makes it more likely that the team-based CI initiative will last beyond the tenure of the leader who is driving it. Typically, in this type of organization the initiative has strong but limited support. The drivers are often top leaders, skilled staff experts, some other committed managers at various levels, and some team leaders and members who have had successful project experiences. The rest of the workforce falls into two categories: (1) those who pay lip-service because the requirement is mandated by the boss, meaning it is not career-enhancing to appear unenthusiastic, and (2) those who remain open skeptics. Sophisticated leaders and staff understand that they need to ingrain the team-based CI culture into the DNA of the organization so that it will continue past their tenure. However, what they lack is a validated approach to make this happen. Using the TEF will spread the source of momentum behind team-based CI beyond just the people who are directly supporting the initiative.

> *Step 1.* Obtain whatever necessary technical expertise you lack. Some organizations are strong in CI but have no systematic methodology for turning groups into teams. Some have the opposite problem. If you need outside expertise, stick with the basics for the prototype. Expertise can partly be obtained from books and online resources. Have key people read this book, especially Chapters 3, 4, and 5. One approach is to have one or two people take introductory courses on the subject matter you lack. Such courses are usually three to five days. Generally, the best people to send to such training are the project leader and the direct management sponsor of the project. It would also be beneficial to send the entire team together to a one-day course on best practices in team excellence that includes use of the TEF. Another approach is to employ an expert who is familiar with CI tools, team-building requirements, and the TEF to coach the team during its project.

Step 2. Apply the yardstick to two or three already completed projects by putting them into a TEF PowerPoint presentation format. In other words, retrofit what was done to show how they met the TEF criteria. Since teams in this type of organization already are using a systematic CI methodology, this should be fairly easy. Have a two- to three-person panel score the presentations using the assessment procedure described in Chapter 4. Have them develop a feedback report for each.

Step 3. Discuss what was learned that can help improve the success rate of future teams.

Step 4. For several new projects (but not all), require the management sponsors and teams to use the TEF Criteria Summary as a checklist for each phase of the project. This will enable them to avoid missing any necessary element. We suggest that you do not use the amplified (detailed) version of the Criteria at this point.

Step 5. Present the projects to management using the TEF-formatted PowerPoint presentation. Again, it should be easy for your teams to put them into this format. Give the sponsors the Criteria Summary to use as a checklist so they can assess how well the team addressed each item. You probably already have established the protocol of presenting the project at the end of each phase to the management sponsor so he/she can understand what the team has done and provide any suggestions and redirection before the project moves forward. All team members should have some role in giving the presentations. Next, present the final, total presentation to the sponsor. Finally, the team and sponsor together should bring it up the management chain for presentation.

Step 6. Celebrate success. Similarly to step 5, celebration should be an action taken at the end of each phase, not just at the project's end. Its importance is often overlooked in the press of getting the project done. Pick ways to provide recognition to your team members that they will find meaningful. Never underestimate how much mileage you can get from free or almost free forms of recognition such as a heartfelt thank-you or a pizza. Publicize the project's success internally to the organization. If you already have an internal team member recognition program, supplement it with use of the TEF as the way to evaluate degree of achievement. Without a documented and independently validated yardstick, the workforce sometimes perceives internal recognition programs as based on popularity or politics. Using the TEF creates transparency and fairness. If appropriate, add external publicity reaching external stakeholders such as customers, shareholders, and professional organizations. Future success is best built on a track record of prior success.

Step 7. Discuss what went well and what needed improvement in how these projects were done. Have a two- to three-person panel assess the project presentation using the TEF scoring system presented in Chapter 4 and provide a feedback report to each team. Incorporate the learning from both these sources.

Step 8. Adjust, and repeat with more projects.

Step 9. After you have accomplished a sufficient number of successful projects, institutionalize the use of the TEF. Take two actions. One is to start using the amplified version of the Criteria rather than the Criteria Summary. When you should make this switch depends on the sophistication of your past projects and the sophistication of each team. The other is to add use of the TEF into your policies, procedures, and training program.

ORGANIZATIONS RECOGNIZED AS HIGH IN OVERALL PERFORMANCE EXCELLENCE

If you are in what is considered a high-performing organization, you are justifiably proud of your achievements. Business history, however, is full of examples of organizations that were best-in-class in their heyday but are no longer with us. Two dangers exist.

One is complacency. While some of your workforce understands the need for continuous improvement, others may not. In today's world, complacency is not an option.

The other danger pertains to organizations that have applied for and won a performance excellence award. They will attest to how much time and energy it takes across a wide swath of the organization. After winning, the typical reaction is to "take a breather." While leadership recognizes that this well-deserved breather is only temporary, the rest of the employees do not always share this perspective. Introducing use of the TEF at this point is a way to reenergize the rank and file by engaging them in continuously generating tangible and intangible benefits. It creates an engine for sustainment that everyone can help power, not just management. The gift it keeps on giving is more and better results.

Step 1. Obtain whatever necessary technical expertise you lack. Chances are good that you have most of the expertise you already need. If you are not already familiar with the TEF, have key people read this book, especially Chapters 3, 4, and 5. Your staff may be able to grasp it simply by reading the book and reviewing ITEA's case material. A way to jump-start TEF implementation is to send someone to a short training course and/or have an expert get you started.

Step 2. Apply the yardstick to two or three already completed projects by putting them into a TEF PowerPoint presentation format. In other words, retrofit what was done to show how they met the TEF criteria. Since teams in this type of organization already are using a systematic CI methodology, this should be fairly easy. Have a two- to three-person panel score the presentations using the assessment procedure described in Chapter 4. Have them develop a feedback report for each.

Step 3. Discuss what was learned that can help improve the success rate of future teams.

Step 4. For several new projects (but not all), require the management sponsors and teams to use the TEF Criteria checklist for each phase of the project. This will enable them to avoid missing any necessary element. Depending on the level of sophistication in team-based CI, you can either start with the Criteria Summary or use the amplified Criteria from the very outset.

Step 5. Present the projects to management using the TEF-formatted PowerPoint presentation. Again, it should be easy for your teams to put them into this format. Give the sponsors the Criteria checklist so they can assess how well the team addressed each item. Use your established protocol of presenting the project at the end of each phase to the management sponsor so he/she can understand what the team has done and provide any suggestions and redirection before the project moves forward. All team members should have some role in giving the presentations. Next, present the final, total presentation to the sponsor. Finally, the team and sponsor together should bring it up the management chain for presentation.

Step 6. Celebrate success. Similarly to step 5, celebration should be an action taken at the end of each phase, not just at the project's end, even if it just involves something simple like a free lunch. Its importance is often overlooked in the press of getting the project done. For recognition of final project success, chances are you already have a well-developed employee recognition program that rewards improvement teams for success. If not, you can create one based on meeting the TEF criteria. If you do, just integrate use of the TEF into it. This means assessing projects against the Criteria to decide which teams deserve to be formally recognized and rewarded at which levels of reward. Pick ways to provide recognition to your team members that they will find meaningful. Chances are you also have effective means for internal and external communications, so utilize these fully to publicize project successes. Without a documented and independently validated yardstick, the workforce sometimes perceives internal recognition programs as based on popularity or politics. Using the TEF creates transparency and fairness. If appropriate, add external publicity reaching external stakeholders such as customers, shareholders, and professional organizations. Continued success is best built on a track record of prior success.

Step 7. Discuss what went well and what needed improvement in the conduct of these projects. Have a two- to three-person panel assess the project presentation using the TEF scoring system presented in Chapter 4 and provide a feedback report to each team. Incorporate the learning from both these sources.

Step 8. Adjust, and repeat with more projects.

Step 9. After you have accomplished a sufficient number of successful projects, institutionalize use of the TEF by adding its use into your policies, procedures, and training program.

CLOSING THOUGHTS ON THE MERITS OF PROMOTING TEAM EXCELLENCE

In an article titled, "Unleashing Positivity in the Workplace" Ann Pace (2010) summarized the findings from the emerging discipline called *positive organizational scholarship*. It focuses on the best of the human condition. It captures organizational work practices that enable employees to feel that they are becoming better people than they ever thought they could be.

The business imperative is not positivity for its own sake; it is for the sake of effectively leading twenty-first-century organizations. Deborah Hopen (2010, 7) reviewed twenty-first-century conditions having implications for leadership. One that is particularly relevant to best practice in team excellence is as follows:

> Technology and global reach make it possible to amass an immense amount of facts and data in a short time, but no individual leader can track all of this new information, let alone absorb and apply it appropriately. This forces modern leaders to accept the reality that they never will have all the knowledge needed to make the best decisions and encourages them to engage associates and other resources in the decision-making process.

During our journey through the world of team excellence we have seen countless examples of people from all walks of life and organizational levels becoming better members of the workforce than they ever thought they could be. They impress and inspire us. Seeing such extraordinary accomplishments, achieved by ordinary people who became extraordinary by practicing team excellence, continues to generate delight and hope for a better future.

Appendix A
International Team Excellence Award Process—Criteria

The Criteria presents each item along with a brief discussion. It is not all-inclusive, and teams should ask for clarification on any item not fully discussed.

The team's presentation is evaluated by the judges based on how well the team demonstrates that they have addressed the criteria. Judges will decide if the team "exceeded the criterion," "met the criterion," provided evidence that was "unclear" to the judges, or if the criterion item was "not covered" at all. Criteria items in sections 1 A, B, and C; 3 A, B, and C; and 4 A, B, and C will receive 3 points for "exceeds," 2 points for "meets," 1 point for "unclear," and 0 for "not covered." Items in sections 2 A and B, and 5 A, B, C, and D will receive 4.5 points for "exceeds," 3 points for "meets," 1.5 points for "unclear," and 0 for "not covered." The following table provides additional information that further clarifies the four judging options for each criterion item.

Judging option	Score
Not covered	0—Totally missing
Unclear	1 (1.5)—Touched upon, but not clear. Not enough information is provided to determine if the team's approach met, or could meet, the criteria requirements.
Meets criteria	2 (or 3)—Sufficient information is provided to determine that the team's approach met the criteria requirements.
Exceeds criteria	3 (or 4.5)—The team's approach goes beyond meeting the criteria and provides additional clarity indicating increased accuracy in the

team's analysis, actions, and/or conclusions. Integration with other criteria items is apparent and enhances the team's overall results. A "best practice" or "role model" approach.

1. Project Selection/Purpose (9 items @ 3 points = 27 points possible)

1. Project Selection/Purpose focuses on both why and how a project was selected, including explaining the importance of the project as it relates both to the organization sponsoring the project and to potential project stakeholders.

1A. Explain the methods used to choose the project. Provide specific examples of techniques and data used. The project may be selected by the team or assigned by management, but the process used to select the project must be clear and well stated.

1Aa. Describe how data and/or tools were used to support the selection, even if the project is assigned to the team. Explain the tools and/or data the organization used and why they used them.

1Ab. Explain how and why the project was selected—what discerned gap or observed opportunity led to the launching of this project? *Note: 1Aa addresses the tools and data used. The emphasis in this item is on the decisions made as a result of the tool usage/data analysis in 1Aa.*

1Ac. Describe the potential stakeholders for the project and how they participated in the selection process. If the stakeholders were not directly involved, then describe how their interests were known and taken into account. *Note: This is intended to be a historical presentation, and the actual/final stakeholders may be different from the potential stakeholders at the time the project was being defined. The goal here is to be sure that the project was not selected in a vacuum without an understanding of the organizational environment.*

Criteria Summary:

1A. Explain the methods used to choose the project. (Provide specific examples of techniques and data used.)

    a. Describe the types of data and/or quality tools used to select the project, and why they were used.

    b. Explain the reasons why the project was selected.

c. Describe the involvement of potential stakeholders in project selection.

1B. Explain how the project supports/aligns with the organization's goals, performance measures, and/or strategies. Organizational goals can vary in type and style, from organization to organization; some companies have vision/mission statements that guide the direction of the business. Some have goals that may be more specific than the vision/mission statements, and still others may have very specific objectives related to their goals and/or strategies. Regardless of how the organization presents its high-level guidance to its associates, this item is looking for the link between the team's project and those goals and/or strategies. The question here is, "Why is this project of importance to the organization?"

1Ba. Identify the affected organizational goals, performance measures, and/or strategies. Goals may be present at various levels in an organization and the team is being asked to identify the goals/performance measures impacted by their project. If the team's project is linked to a lower-level goal, it may be helpful for the team to demonstrate the linkage between the project and the lower-level goal as well as the linkage between the lower-level goal and the organizational-level strategy or goal.

1Bb. Identify *"what"* types of impact the project will have on each goal, performance measure, and/or strategy. "Type" implies a directional impact of some sort. *Examples: increased/decreased costs, efficiencies, safety, associate satisfaction, etc.*

1Bc. Identify the degree of impact (*how much*) the project will have on each goal, performance measure, and/or strategy. To the extent that the team can quantify the predicted degree of impact, it should do so, and explain how it did so. If the team cannot quantify the prediction, it should at least provide a rationale that explains how it decided on the degree of impact. The ability to accurately predict impact (other than high, medium, or low) will be considered in scoring this factor. *Note: If the team characterizes the degree of impact as high, medium, or low impact, and it cannot quantify the degree, it should provide its rationale for deciding "high" vs. "medium" or "low."*

Criteria Summary:

1B. Explain how the project supports/aligns with the organization's goals, performance measures, and/or strategies.

    a. Identify the affected organizational goals, performance measures, and/or strategies.

b. Identify the types of impact on each goal, performance measure, and/or strategy.

c. Identify the degree of impact on each goal, performance measure, and/or strategy, and explain how this was determined.

1C. Identify the potential stakeholders (who may be impacted by the project) and explain how they may be impacted by the project. "Stakeholders" defines anyone who may be affected by the project. Stakeholders might include internal/external customers/clients, suppliers, employees, etc. Stakeholders may refer to a unique group (e.g., "the maintenance department") or one or more individuals.

1Ca. Identify the potential internal and external stakeholders who might be impacted by the team's project. The team should briefly explain how the potential stakeholders were identified.

1Cb. Identify the types of potential impact on stakeholders and explain how these were determined. Stakeholders may be impacted in many different ways by the project, from quality to timeliness. Demonstrating that the team understands how the project may have different impacts on the different stakeholder groups is important. As with 1Bb (type of goal impact), the impact is implied to be directional. *Note: This section could later tie to 4Ab, as correctly predicting potential negative impacts early in the project can help the team prepare to overcome resistance later.*

1Cc. Identify the degree of potential impact on stakeholders and explain how this was determined. Not all stakeholders are impacted to the same degree. Identify how much each stakeholder may be impacted and explain how the team determined that level of potential impact. The ability to accurately predict impact (other than high, medium, or low) will be considered in scoring this item. *Note: As was the case in 1Bc, quantifying the degree of impact or providing the rationale for a qualitative degree of impact is preferred.*

Criteria Summary:

1C. Identify the potential stakeholders and explain how they may be impacted by the project.

a. Identify potential internal and external stakeholders and explain how they were identified.

b. Identify the types of potential impact on stakeholders and explain how these were determined.

c. Identify the degree of potential impact on stakeholders and explain how this was determined.

2. Current Situation Analysis (6 items @ 4.5 points = 27 points possible)

2. Current Situation Analysis focuses on how the team analyzed the current situation including the processes, data, and information; how stakeholders were involved; and how the team validated its final root cause(s)/improvement opportunity(ies).

2A. Explain the approach/process the team used to identify the potential root causes/improvement opportunity(ies).

2Aa. Describe the methods and tools used to identify possible root causes/improvement opportunities. Teams may use a variety of approaches/processes to identify the possible root causes of a problem they face or the improvement opportunities in a given situation. If the organization uses a specific methodology as part of the quality process, the team should clearly describe that methodology and how it was applied to this project in identifying the possible root causes/improvement opportunities. *Note: For "opportunity for improvement teams," describe the methods and tools that were used to generate a list of possible opportunities for improvement.*

2Ab. Describe the team's analysis of data to identify possible root causes/improvement opportunities. Provide clear, specific examples of what data were analyzed (from the tools/methods described in 2Aa), and how they were analyzed, to help identify the possible root causes/improvement opportunities. Teams should attempt to demonstrate the depth and breadth of their analyses as appropriate.

2Ac. Describe how or if any of the stakeholders were involved in identifying the possible root causes/improvement opportunities. Provide supporting information. *Note: "Involved" does not necessarily mean how stakeholders participated directly in the process of selecting the root causes/improvement opportunities. "Involved" can be addressed by describing how the team took the interests of the stakeholders into account in determining the possible root causes/improvement opportunities.*

Criteria Summary:

2A. Explain the approach/process the team used to identify the potential root causes/improvement opportunity(ies).

a. Describe the methods and tools used to identify possible root causes/improvement opportunities.

b. Describe the team's analysis of data to identify possible root causes/improvement opportunities.

c. Describe how or if any of the stakeholders were involved in identifying the possible root causes/improvement opportunities.

2B. Describe how the team analyzed information to identify the final root cause(s)/improvement opportunity(ies). Include any appropriate validation. Having identified a variety of possible root causes/improvement opportunities, in 2A, how did the team go about narrowing down the possibilities to identify the true root cause(s)/improvement opportunity(ies) for this project?

2Ba. Describe the methods and tools the team used to narrow down the list of potential root causes/improvement opportunities (identified in 2A), to the final root cause(s)/improvement opportunity(ies).

2Bb. Describe the team's analysis of data to select the final root cause(s)/improvement opportunity(ies). Provide clear, specific examples of what data were analyzed (from the tools/methods described in 2Ba), and how they were analyzed, to help identify the final root cause(s)/improvement opportunity(ies). Teams should attempt to demonstrate the depth and breadth of their analyses as appropriate.

2Bc. Clearly state what the root cause(s)/improvement opportunity(ies) was/were and explain how the team validated that the final root cause(s)/improvement opportunity(ies) determined in 2Bb was/were in fact the final root cause(s)/improvement opportunity(ies). What tools and/or methods did the team use to validate (prove) to itself (and others if needed) that it identified the true root cause(s)/improvement opportunity(ies)?

Criteria Summary:

2B. Describe how the team analyzed information to identify the final root cause(s)/improvement opportunity(ies). (Include any appropriate validation.)

a. Describe the methods and tools used to identify the final root cause(s)/improvement opportunity(ies).

b. Describe the team's analysis of data to select the final root cause(s)/improvement opportunity(ies).

c. Identify the root cause(s)/improvement opportunity(ies) and explain how the team validated the final root cause(s)/improvement opportunity(ies).

3. Solution Development (9 items @ 3 points = 27 points possible)

3. Solution Development: once the final root cause(s)/improvement opportunity(ies) is/are identified, the team should demonstrate how it developed its solution(s) to/improvement action(s) for the problem.

3A. Explain the methods used to identify the possible solutions/improvement actions.

3Aa. Describe the tools and methods the team used to identify the possible solutions/improvement actions for the root cause(s)/improvement opportunity(ies) identified and verified in 2B. There may be a number of ways to address the root cause(s)/improvement opportunity(ies). The team is being asked here to explain what tools and methods they used to identify these possible solutions/improvement actions.

3Ab. Describe the team's analysis of data to develop possible solutions/improvement actions. Provide clear, specific examples of what data were analyzed (from the tools/methods described in 3Aa), and how they were analyzed, to help identify the possible solutions/improvement actions. Teams should attempt to demonstrate the depth and breadth of their analyses as appropriate.

3Ac. What criteria did the team decide to use to assess the relative effectiveness of the various possible solutions/improvement actions it identified in 3Aa and 3Ab above, so that it can narrow down the list of possible solutions/improvement actions to enable it to identify the best solution(s)/improvement action(s)?

Criteria Summary:

3A. Explain the methods used to identify the possible solutions/improvement actions.

    a. Describe the methods and tools used to develop possible solutions/improvement actions.

    b. Describe the team's analysis of data to develop possible solutions/improvement actions.

c. Indicate the criteria the team decided to use in selecting the final solution(s)/improvement action(s).

3B. Explain how the team selected/determined the final solution(s)/improvement action(s) from the list it generated in 3A above.

3Ba. Describe the methods and tools used by the team to select the final solution(s)/improvement action(s). Now that the team has identified the criteria it used in selecting the final solution(s)/improvement action(s), this item asks the team to describe the tools and methods it used along with the criteria identified in 3Ac above to select the final solution(s)/improvement action(s). For example, if the team's criteria were cost, ease of implementation, and impact on product quality, this item is asking the team to describe the tools and methods it used to weigh the various solutions/improvement actions against its criteria and select the final solution(s)/improvement action(s).

3Bb. Describe what data were analyzed, and how they were analyzed to help identify the final solution(s)/improvement action(s). The team described the methods and tools it used to determine the final solution(s)/improvement action(s) in 3Ba; 3Bb is now asking the team to describe what data were analyzed and how they were analyzed, to support the selection of its final solution(s)/improvement action(s).

3Bc. Describe how stakeholders were involved in determining the final solution(s)/improvement action(s). If the stakeholders were directly involved in the selection of the final solution, the team should describe how they were involved in the process; if they were not directly involved, the team should describe how the stakeholders' interests and concerns were considered.

Criteria Summary:

3B. Explain how the final solution(s)/improvement action(s) was/were determined.

   a. Describe the methods and tools used by the team to select the final solution(s)/improvement action(s).

   b. Describe the team's analysis of data to select the final solution(s)/improvement action(s).

   c. Describe the involvement of stakeholders in the selection of the final solution(s)/improvement action(s).

Appendix A: International Team Excellence Award Process—Criteria

3C. Explain how the team validated the final solution(s)/improvement action(s) and what benefits the team expects the organization to realize once the team's solution(s)/improvement action(s) is/are implemented.

3Ca. The team should describe the solution(s)/improvement action(s) it felt would be most appropriate and then explain how they validated that the solution(s)/improvement action(s) would solve the problem prior to actually proceeding with the implementation of the solution(s)/improvement action(s). "Validation," as used in this item, is not to be confused with "justification" in 3Cc below. "Validation" is simply verifying that the solution(s)/improvement action(s), if implemented, will solve the problem(s)/address the root cause(s)/improvement opportunity(ies) described in 2Bc.

3Cb. Provide a list of benefits that may be realized from the solution(s)/improvement action(s). Tangible benefits include those benefits that lend themselves to being represented by improvements in specific measures or metrics—cycle time, number of defects, production, etc. Intangible benefits include those that may not easily be linked to a specific measure or measurement, but might require demonstration through improvements in a variety of related indicators—morale, employee satisfaction, etc. Teams should attempt to describe what indicators they are looking at when identifying their intangible benefits—what did they see that led them to believe there was an improvement in a given intangible benefit?

3Cc. Explain how the team used data to justify the implementation of the solution(s)/improvement action(s) it determined to be best in 3B. The team should present the data and information it used to demonstrate the value to the organization in implementing its solution(s)/improvement action(s). *Example: the team might conduct and summarize here a cost/benefit analysis to verify that the benefits to be realized are worthwhile in comparison to the costs involved to implement the solution(s)/improvement action(s).*

Criteria Summary:

3C. Explain the final solution(s)/improvement action(s), validation, and the benefits expected to be realized by implementing the team's solution(s)/improvement action(s).

   a. Describe the final solution(s)/improvement action(s) and explain how the team validated the final solution(s)/improvement action(s).

   b. List the types of tangible and intangible benefits that are expected to be realized by implementing the team's solution(s)/improvement action(s).

c. Explain how the team used data to justify the implementation of the team's solution(s)/improvement action(s).

4. Project Implementation and Results (9 items @ 3 points = 27 points possible)

4. Project Implementation and Results addresses how the team sought and secured buy-in, what approaches it used to plan for and implement its solution(s)/improvement action(s), and what results were achieved.

4A. Explain how the team went about securing buy-in, identifying resistance, and convincing itself (and others) that buy-in did, in fact, exist.

4Aa. Indicate how internal and external (as applicable) stakeholders were involved in implementing the solution(s)/improvement action(s). *Note: There are a number of ways in which teams may involve stakeholders and this item is looking for the stakeholder involvement methods used by the team.*

4Ab. Describe how the team identified the various types of resistance encountered (to its project, solution(s)/improvement action(s), and/or implementation plan), what steps were taken to anticipate resistance, and how resistance from any of the stakeholder groups was addressed.

4Ac. Explain how the team ensured that it had stakeholder buy-in. What proof did the team have that stakeholder buy-in existed prior to implementation? If it was not practical to obtain buy-in from all stakeholders, the team should explain why.

Criteria Summary:

4A. Explain how buy-in/agreement was achieved for implementation.

a. Indicate the types of internal and external (if applicable) stakeholder involvement in implementation.

b. Describe how various types of resistance were identified and addressed.

c. Explain how stakeholder buy-in was ensured.

4B. Explain the approach used by the team to implement its solution(s)/improvement action(s) and to ensure the results. The team is asked to provide information regarding how it went about implementing its solution(s)/improvement action(s) and ensuring that the desired results would be achieved and sustained.

4Ba. Describe the methods used by the team to implement its solution(s)/improvement action(s). How did the team plan for the implementation of its solution(s)/improvement action(s), including action plan development, and such items as allocation of resources, time management activities, etc.?

4Bb. Describe the specific procedures, systems, or other changes that occurred as a result of the implementation of the team's solution(s)/improvement action(s). What actions/changes did the team make (or arrange to have made) to ensure that gains realized would be sustained and that new processes, procedures, or systems would not revert to the way they were before the team's solution(s)/improvement action(s) was/were implemented.

4Bc. Describe the system(s) used to measure and manage the team's results over time. What method(s) has the team created or installed to measure the performance of its solution(s)/improvement action(s) over time. *Note: If the measurements used for the improved processes are already reviewed as part of a current measurement system, the team should note that this is the case and describe the existing measurement system in its response.*

Criteria Summary:

4B. Explain the approach used by the team to implement its solution(s)/improvement action(s) and to ensure the results.

   a. Describe the plan developed by the team to implement its solution(s)/improvement action(s).

   b. Describe the procedure, system, or other changes that were made to implement the solution(s)/improvement action(s) and to sustain the results.

   c. Describe the creation and installation of a system for measuring and sustaining results.

4C. Describe the results achieved by implementing the solution(s)/improvement action(s) the team selected in Section 3.

4Ca. Identify the actual results attributable to the implementation of the team's solution(s)/improvement action(s). Tangible results include those results represented by improvements in specific measures or metrics—cycle time, number of defects, production, etc. Intangible results include those that may not easily be linked to a specific measure or measurement, but might be demonstrated through improvements in a variety of related indicators—morale, employee satisfaction, etc. Teams should describe the indicators they used to identify their intangible results and what led them to believe there was an improvement in a given intangible result.

4Cb. Explain how the team's results impacted the organization's goals, performance measures, and/or strategies as identified in 1B. Trail back through the criteria to the organization's goals, measures, and strategies identified early in the improvement process, and demonstrate how the team's results supported the achievement of these organizational goals, measures, and/or strategies.

4Cc. Describe the ways in which the team shared its results with the various stakeholder groups. Throughout the improvement process, the team has described how it identified, communicated, and interacted with internal and external (as applicable) stakeholders to understand their concerns and gain their inputs. Teams should describe how they closed the feedback loop by sharing the project's results with the stakeholders.

Criteria Summary:

4C. Describe the results achieved.

   a. Identify the types of tangible and intangible results that were realized.

   b. Explain how the project's results link with the organization's goals, performance measures, and/or strategies.

   c. Describe how results were shared with stakeholders.

5. Team/Project Management and Project Presentation (4 items @ 4.5 points = 18 points possible)

5. Team Management and Project Presentation covers the people-resource side of the project: how were the most appropriate team members chosen; how were they prepared for this special assignment; and what help did the organization provide to assure they were successful? In addition, how the team communicates the project results through their presentation is also examined.

5A. Explain team member selection and involvement. The team's response should include an explanation of how and/or why the various members of the team were selected including any specific skills, capabilities, knowledge, qualifications, and/or any other criteria used in selecting the team members. The team should also describe how the various team members were involved throughout the project including any specific tasks, roles, responsibilities, etc., they may have had during the project.

5B. Explain team member preparation/development. The team's response should include an explanation of any training or other preparation the team received prior to or during the project to help it operate more effectively as a team, as well as any training it received related to the process improvement methodology/approach used by the team—including the various tools and techniques used throughout the project to collect, analyze, and/or present data and information.

5C. Explain team performance management. Explain how the team members worked together effectively throughout the project. The team's response should include an explanation of how the team capitalized on the skills of its individual members as they carried out their roles and responsibilities, how team members shared data and information throughout the project, how they ensured effective communication within the team, and how the team managed its performance with respect to project deadlines/deliverables/milestones. *Note: Responses might include a description of how meetings were conducted, any electronic means the team may have used, or any other methods it used to share data and information. Regardless of the approach(es) the team used, an explanation of how it ensured effective communication within the team is appropriate.*

5D. Project presentation. The team will be scored on the organization, clarity, and overall effectiveness of its presentation. Effective use of any audio/visual aids and any other presentation aids and/or techniques will also be considered in this item. It is important to note that the judges will assess how clearly and effectively the team communicated the story of its project.

Criteria Summary:

5A. Explain how the team members were selected and how they were involved throughout the project.

5B. Explain how the team was prepared to work together in addressing the project.

5C. Explain how the team managed its performance to ensure it was effective as a team.

5D. The team will also be judged on the clarity and organization of its presentation.

Appendix B
International Team Excellence Award Process
Scoresheet Example

Criteria area	Criteria description	Score	Section average	Section total
1Aa	Describe the types of data and quality tools used to select the project, and why.	2.0	6.0	20.0
1Ab	Explain the reasons why the project was selected.	2.0		
1Ac	Describe the involvement of potential stakeholders in project selection.	2.0		
1Ba	Identify the affected organizational goals, performance measures, and/or strategies.	3.0	8.0	
1Bb	Identify the types of impact on each goal, performance measure, and/or strategy.	3.0		
1Bc	Identify the degree of impact on each goal, performance measure, and/or strategy.	2.0		
1Ca	Identify potential internal and external stakeholders and explain how they were identified.	2.0	6.0	
1Cb	Identify the types of potential impact on stakeholders and explain how determined.	2.0		
1Cc	Identify the degree of potential impact on stakeholders and explain how determined.	2.0		
2Aa	Describe the methods and tools used to identify possible root causes/imp. opps.	1.5	7.5	18.0
2Ab	Describe the team's analysis of data to identify possible root causes/imp. opps.	3.0		
2Ac	Describe how/if any of the stakeholders were involved in identifying the root causes.	3.0		

Appendix B: ITEA Process: Scoreheet Example

Criteria area	Criteria description	Score	Section average	Section total
2Ba	Describe the methods and tools used to identify the final root cause(s)/imp. opps.	4.5	10.5	
2Bb	Describe the team's analysis of data to select the final root cause(s)/imp. opps.	3.0		
2Bc	Identify the root cause(s) and explain how the team validated the final root cause(s).	3.0		
3Aa	Describe the methods and tools used to develop possible solution(s)/actions.	2.0	6.0	19.0
3Ab	Describe the team's analysis of data to develop possible solution(s)/actions.	3.0		
3Ac	Indicate the criteria the team decided to use in selecting the final solution(s)/actions.	1.0		
3Ba	Describe the methods and tools used by the team to select final solution(s)/actions.	2.0	6.0	
3Bb	Describe the team's analysis of data to select the final solution(s)/actions.	2.0		
3Bc	Describe the involvement of stakeholders in the selection of final solution(s)/actions.	2.0		
3Ca	Describe the final solution(s) and explain how the team validated the final solution(s).	2.0	7.0	
3Cb	Indicate the types of tangible and intangible benefits expected from implementation.	3.0		
3Cc	Explain how the team used data to justify the implementation of the solution(s).	2.0		
4Aa	Indicate types of internal and external stakeholder involvement in implementation.	2.0	6.0	19.0
4Ab	Describe how various types of resistance were identified and addressed.	2.0		
4Ac	Explain how stakeholder buy-in was ensured.	2.0		
4Ba	Describe the plan developed by the team to implement its solution(s)/actions.	3.0	7.0	
4Bb	Describe changes that were made to implement solution(s) and sustain the results.	2.0		
4Bc	Describe the creation and installation of a system for measuring/sustaining results.	2.0		

Criteria area	Criteria description	Score	Section average	Section total
4Ca	Indicate the types of tangible and intangible results that were realized.	2.0	6.0	
4Cb	Explain how the project's results link with the organization's goals, etc.	2.0		
4Cc	Explain how results were shared with stakeholders.	2.0		
5A	Explain how the team members were selected and their ongoing involvement.	4.5	15.0	15.0
5B	Explain how the team was prepared to work together in addressing the project.	3.0		
5C	Explain how the team managed its performance to ensure it was effective as a team.	4.5		
5D	The team will also be judged on the clarity and organization of its presentation.	3.0		
	Total score	91.0	91.0	91.0

Appendix C
Assessment Worksheet and Scoring Guidelines

Assessment Worksheet and Scoring Guidelines

Team:_____ Assessor: _____

Organization:_____ Date: _____

Assessment location: _____

Instructions for Completing Worksheet

1. Re-familiarize yourself with the criteria, the scoring guidelines, comment writing guidelines (Assessor).

2. As you conduct the assessment, take notes on the Judges Worksheet (Assessor).
   a. There are three forms used in the assessment process; 1—Assessment Worksheet, 2—Consensus Scoresheet, 3—Final Scoresheet.
   b. Complete the Assessor Worksheet first.
   c. Take notes in each of the sections and items as the assessment proceeds.

3. After the assessment is finished, use your notes to score the team in each area (Assessor).
   a. Refer to the hard copy presentation (with speaker notes) and any supporting documentation.
   b. Use the assessors Option Scoring Guidelines as a reference for scoring each section.
   c. Add the scores for each section and tally on the last page.

   Note: If there is only one assessor skip steps 4 & 5 and proceed to writing feedback comments (Strengths & Opportunities for Improvement) otherwise proceed to steps 4 & 5.

4. Complete the Consensus Scoresheet (Lead Assessor).
   a. There is a column for each assessor's inputs.
   b. Only input scores on the Consensus Scoresheet—when built-in into an Excel spreadsheet, formulas can compute these scores.
   c. Final scores automatically transfer over to the Final Scoresheet.

5. Validate the Final Scoresheet (Assessment Team).
   a. Reach consensus with your assessor team on final scores and feedback.
   b. Inputs from the Consensus Worksheet automatically will populate the Final Scoresheet—no need to enter data.
   c. Develop actionable feedback comments.

Assessment Option Score	
Not Covered	0—Totally missing (No approach evident)
Unclear	1 (or 1.5) points—Touched upon, but not clear. Not enough information is provided to determine if the team's approach met, or could meet, the criterion requirements. (Approach evident)
Meets Criteria	2 (or 3) points—Sufficient information is provided to determine that the team's approach met the criterion requirements. (Approach applied with results evident)
Exceeds	3 (or 4.5) points—The team's approach goes beyond meeting the criterion and provides additional clarity indicating increased accuracy in the team's analysis, actions, and/or conclusions. *Integration with other criterion items is apparent and enhances the team's overall results. A "Best Practice" or "Role Model" approach.* (Approach broadly integrated and evident)

Assessment Worksheet

Section/item	Section/item description	Not covered	Unclear	Meets criteria	Exceeds criteria	Score
1	**Project selection and purpose (9 item requirements at 3 points each = 27 possible)**					
1Aa	Describe the types of data and quality tools used to select the project, and why.	0	1	2	3	0
Strengths						
OFIs						

Appendix C: Assessment Worksheet and Scoring Guidelines

	Assessment Worksheet					
Section/item	Section/item description	Not covered	Unclear	Meets criteria	Exceeds criteria	Score
1Ab	Explain the reasons why the project was selected.	0	1	2	3	
Strengths						
OFIs						
1Ac	Describe the involvement of potential stakeholders in project selection.	0	1	2	3	
Strengths						
OFIs						
1Ba	Identify the affected organizational goals, performance measures, and/or strategies.	0	1	2	3	
Strengths						
OFIs						
1Bb	Identify the types of impact on each goal, performance measure, and/or strategy.	0	1	2	3	
Strengths						
OFIs						
1Bc	Identify the degree of impact on each goal, performance measure, and/or strategy and how determined	0	1	2	3	
Strengths						
OFIs						

Assessment Worksheet

Section/item	Section/item description	Not covered	Unclear	Meets criteria	Exceeds criteria	Score
1Ca	Identify potential internal and external stakeholders and explain how they were identified.	0	1	2	3	
Strengths						
OFIs						
1Cb	Identify the types of potential impact on stakeholders and explain how determined.	0	1	2	3	
Strengths						
OFIs						
1Cc	Identify the degree of potential impact on stakeholders and explain how determined.	0	1	2	3	
Strengths						
OFIs						
				Section 1 Score >		
2	**Current Situation Analysis (6 Item Requirements at 4.5 points each = 27 possible)**					
2Aa	Describe the methods and tools used to identify the final root cause(s)/improvement opportunities.	0	1.5	3	4.5	
Strengths						
OFIs						
2Ab	Describe the team's analysis of data to identify possible root causes/improvement opportunities.	0	1.5	3	4.5	
Strengths						
OFIs						

Appendix C: Assessment Worksheet and Scoring Guidelines

Assessment Worksheet

Section/item	Section/item description	Not covered	Unclear	Meets criteria	Exceeds criteria	Score
2Ac	Describe how/if any of the stakeholders were involved in identifying the root causes.	0	1.5	3	4.5	
Strengths						
OFIs						
2Ba	Describe the methods and tools used to identify the final root cause(s)/improvement opportunities.	0	1.5	3	4.5	
Strengths						
OFIs						
2Bb	Describe the team's analysis of data to select the final root cause(s)/improvement opportunities.	0	1.5	3	4.5	
Strengths						
OFIs						
2Bc	2Bc Identify the root cause(s) and explain how the team validated the final root cause(s).	0	1.5	3	4.5	
Strengths						
OFIs						
	Section 2 Score >					
3	**Solution Development (9 Item Requirements at 3 points each = 27 possible)**					
3Aa	Describe the methods and tools used to develop possible solution(s)/actions.	0	1	2	3	
Strengths						
OFIs						

Assessment Worksheet

Section/item	Section/item description	Not covered	Unclear	Meets criteria	Exceeds criteria	Score
3Ab	Describe the team's analysis of data to develop possible solution(s)/actions.	0	1	2	3	
Strengths						
OFIs						
3Ac	Indicate the criteria the team decided to use in selecting the final solution(s)/actions.	0	1	2	3	
Strengths						
OFIs						
3Ba	Describe the methods and tools used by the team to select final solution(s)/actions.	0	1	2	3	
Strengths						
OFIs						
3Bb	Describe the team's analysis of data to select the final solution(s)/actions.	0	1	2	3	
Strengths						
OFIs						
3Bc	Describe the involvement of stakeholders in the selection of final solution(s)/actions.	0	1	2	3	
Strengths						
OFIs						

Assessment Worksheet

Section/item	Section/item description	Not covered	Unclear	Meets criteria	Exceeds criteria	Score
3Ca	Describe the final solution(s) and explain how the team validated the final solution(s).	0	1	2	3	
Strengths						
OFIs						
3Cb	Indicate the types of tangible and intangible benefits expected from implementation.	0	1	2	3	
Strengths						
OFIs						
3Cc	Explain how the team used data to justify the implementation of the solution(s).	0	1	2	3	
Strengths						
OFIs						
					Section 3 Score	
4	**Project Implementation and Results (9 Item Requirements at 3 points each = 27 possible)**					
4Aa	Indicate types of internal and external stakeholder involvement in implementation.	0	1	2	3	
Strengths						
OFIs						
4Ab	Describe how various types of resistance were identified and addressed.	0	1	2	3	
Strengths						
OFIs						

Assessment Worksheet					
Section/item	Section/item description	Not covered	Unclear	Meets criteria	Exceeds criteria	Score
4Ac	Explain how stakeholder buy-in was ensured.	0	1	2	3	
Strengths						
OFIs						
4Ba	Describe the plan developed by the team to implement its solution(s)/actions.	0	1	2	3	
Strengths						
OFIs						
4Bb	Describe changes that were made to implement solution(s) and sustain the results.	0	1	2	3	
Strengths						
OFIs						
4Bc	Describe the creation and installation of a system for measuring/sustaining results.	0	1	2	3	
Strengths						
OFIs						
4Ca	Indicate the types of tangible and intangible results that were realized.	0	1	2	3	
Strengths						
OFIs						
4Cb	Explain how the project's results link with the organization's goals, etc.	0	1	2	3	
Strengths						
OFIs						

Assessment Worksheet

Section/item	Section/item description	Not covered	Unclear	Meets criteria	Exceeds criteria	Score
4Cc	Explain how results were shared with stakeholders.	0	1	2	3	
Strengths						
OFIs						
					Section 4 Score	
5	**Team/Project management and Project Presentation (4 Item Requirements at 4.5 points each = 18 possible)**					
5A	Explain how the team members were selected and their ongoing involvement.	0	1.5	3	4.5	
Strengths						
OFIs						
5B	Explain how the team was prepared to work together in addressing the project.	0	1.5	3	4.5	
Strengths						
OFIs						
5C	Explain how the team managed its performance to ensure it was effective as a team.	0	1.5	3	4.5	
Strengths						
OFIs						
5D	The team will also be judged on the clarity and organization of its presentation.	0	1.5	3	4.5	
Strengths						
OFIs						
					Section 5 Score	

Appendix C: Assessment Worksheet and Scoring Guidelines

Assessment Worksheet								
Section/ item	Section/item description	Not covered	Unclear	Meets criteria	Exceeds criteria	Score
		\multicolumn{4}{c	}{Total Score >}	
	Total Points Possible	0	41	82	123	
Scoring guidelines > >	No approach evident >	X	^	^	^	
	Approach evident >		X	^	^	
	Approach applied with results evident >			X	^	
	Approach broadly integrated evident >				X	
	Progressive Maturity Score > > > >					

Appendix D
Assessment Team's Consensus Scoresheet

	Assessment Team's Consensus Scoresheet								
Team name:		Lead assessor:							
Item	Criteria	Assessor 1	Assessor 2	Assessor 3	Assessor 4	Assessor 5	Average	Section total	Total
1A.a	Tool types and why used								
1A.b	Reasons for project selection								
1A.c	Stakeholder involvement								
1B.a	Listing of goals								
1B.b	Impact type on goals								
1B.c	Impact degree on goals								
1C.a	Stakeholders/how identified								
1C.b	Impact type on stakeholders								
1C.c	Impact degree on stakeholders								
2A.a	Root cause methods/tools								
2A.b	Root cause data analysis								
2A.c	Stakeholder involvement								
2B.a	Final cause methods/tools								
2B.b	Final cause data analysis								
2B.c	Validation of final cause								
3A.a	Solutions methods/tools								
3A.b	Solutions data analysis								

Appendix D: Assessment Team's Consensus Scoresheet

Item	Criteria	Assessor 1	Assessor 2	Assessor 3	Assessor 4	Assessor 5	Average	Section total	Total
3A.c	Solution selection criteria								
3B.a	Final solution methods/tools								
3B.b	Final solution data analysis								
3B.c	Stakeholder involvement								
3C.a	Final solution and validation								
3C.b	Solution expected benefits								
3C.c	Implementation justification								
4A.a	Stakeholder involvement								
4A.b	ID and address resistance								
4A.c	Buy-in ensured								
4B.a	Implementation plan								
4B.b	Changes made								
4B.c	Measurement system								
4C.a	Actual benefits								
4C.b	Goal linkage								
4C.c	Stakeholder results sharing								
5A	Team selection and involvement								
5B	Team preparation								
5C	Team performance management								
5D	Clarity and organization								

Glossary of Terms and Acronyms

A

American Society for Quality (ASQ)—A professional, not-for-profit association that develops, promotes, and applies quality-related information and technology for the private sector, government, and academia. ASQ serves more than 100,000 individuals and 1100 corporate members in the United States and 108 other countries.

analysis—The systematic decomposition and examination of a current condition used to determine the factors contributing to and/or causing the current performance, state, results, challenges, and so on.

approach—The methods or techniques used to accomplish a given process or processes, or in some cases, a part or step of a process.

assessment—A systematic evaluation process of collecting and analyzing data to determine the current, historical, or projected compliance of an organization to a standard.

B

balanced scorecard—A management system that provides feedback on both internal business processes and external outcomes to continuously improve strategic performance and results.

Baldrige—The Baldrige Performance Excellence Program Award recognizes U.S. organizations in the business, healthcare, education, and nonprofit sectors for performance excellence. The Baldrige Award

---

Note: Many of the terms and acronyms are ASQ, ITEA, open source, or defined by the authors.

is the only formal recognition of the performance excellence of both public and private U.S. organizations given by the President of the United States.

benchmarking—A technique in which a company measures its performance against that of best-in-class companies, determines how those companies achieved their performance levels, and uses the information to improve its own performance. Subjects that can be benchmarked include strategies, operations, and processes.

best practice—A superior method or innovative practice that contributes to the improved performance of an organization, usually recognized as best by other peer organizations.

Black Belt (BB)—Full-time team leader responsible for implementing process improvement projects—define, measure, analyze, improve, and control (DMAIC) or define, measure, analyze, design, and verify (DMAD-V)—within a business to drive up customer satisfaction and productivity levels.

body of knowledge (BOK)—The prescribed aggregation of knowledge in a particular area an individual is expected to have mastered to be considered or certified as a practitioner.

C

checklist—A tool for ensuring that all important steps or actions in an operation have been taken. Checklists contain items important or relevant to an issue or situation.

consensus—A state in which all the members of a group support an action or decision, even if some of them don't fully agree with it.

continuous process improvement (CPI or CI)—An ongoing effort to improve products, services, or processes. These efforts can seek "incremental" improvement over time or "breakthrough" improvement all at once.

criteria—An accepted standard used in making a judgment.

D

data—Per Encarta, data is "information, often in the form of facts or figures obtained from experiments or surveys, used as a basis for making calculations or drawing conclusions."

describe—One of four descriptors (*describe, explain, identify,* and *indicate*) used in each criterion to show the level of information being requested.

- *identify* means that a simple list is all that is necessary to meet the requirements.

- *indicate* means that something needs to have attention drawn to it, such as in a list or possibly by a statement about a single item.

- *describe* looks for sufficient information such that the object or methodology being described would be recognizable to another.

- *explain* goes a step further by giving sufficient information such than an observer would at least be able to understand the usage and implications of what is explained, if not actually be able to use or apply it themselves.

DMAIC-V—A data-driven quality strategy for improving processes and an integral part of a Six Sigma quality initiative. DMAIC-V is an acronym for *define, measure, analyze, improve, control, and validate/verify.*

E

empowerment—A condition in which employees have the authority to make decisions and take action in their work areas without prior approval. For example, an operator can stop a production process if he or she detects a problem, or a customer service representative can send out a replacement product if a customer calls with a problem.

enterprise systems (ES/ERP)—An integrated application-software package that uses the computational, data storage, and data transmission power of information technology to support business processes, information flows, reporting, and data analytics within and between organizations.

ETER—education team excellence recognition.

explain. See *describe.*

F

5S—5S is the name of a workplace organization methodology that uses a list of five Japanese words, which are *seiri (sort), seiton (setting in order), seiso (sweep or clean), seiketsu(standardize),* and *shitsuke (sustain).* The list describes how to organize a work space for efficiency and effectiveness by identifying and storing the items used, maintaining the area and items, and sustaining the new order. Over time, industry has added to the 5S list to include *safety, security,* and *satisfaction.*

G

goals—A future condition or performance level that one intends to attain. Goals can be both short- and longer-term. Goals are targets that guide actions. Goals may be quantifiable and/or descriptive statements of a desired future state or condition. Some companies may use "objectives" interchangeably with "goals."

Green Belt—An employee who has been trained in the Six Sigma improvement method and will lead a process improvement or quality improvement team as part of his or her full-time job.

H

HPT—high-performance team.

I

identify—See *describe.*

indicate—See *describe.*

indicator, lagging—A measurable factor that identifies change(s) after the process or condition has already begun to follow a particular pattern or trend, Lagging indicators are used to predict changes in the process or condition after the fact, but may not always be accurate.

indicator, leading—A measurable factor that identifies change(s) before the process or condition starts to follow a particular pattern or trend. Leading indicators are used to predict changes in the process or condition, but may not always be accurate.

information—Knowledge gained through analysis and study. May include conclusions based on the analysis of groups of facts and data.

intangible results—*Intangible* refers to results or outcomes that may not lend themselves to specific measures. Intangible results may be best measured by specific indicators or a series of indicators related to the intangible performance area/result.

integration—The harmonization of approaches, methods, processes, and analyses to support key organization improvement efforts. In this context, *integration* is the clear linkage through the use of words, symbols, charts, graphs, or other visual reference of one section of the presentation to another in such a way that linkage is clearly shown and the message is reinforced.

ISO 9000 series standards—A set of international standards on quality management and quality assurance developed to help companies effectively document the quality system elements to be implemented to maintain an efficient quality system. The standards, initially published in 1987, are not specific to any particular industry, product, or service. The standards were developed by the International Organization for Standardization (ISO). The standards underwent major revision in 2000 and now include ISO 9000 (definitions), ISO 9001 (requirements), and ISO 9004 (continuous improvement).

ITEA—International Team Excellence Award.

K

key performance indicator (KPI)—A statistical measure of how well an organization is doing in a particular area. A KPI could measure a company's financial performance or how it is holding up against customer requirements.

key process—A major system-level process that supports the mission and satisfies major consumer requirements.

L

lean—Producing the maximum sellable products or services at the lowest operational cost while optimizing inventory levels.

lean enterprise—A manufacturing company organized to eliminate all unproductive effort and unnecessary investment, both on the shop floor and in office functions.

Lean Six Sigma (LSS)—A quality improvement methodology resulting from the combination of the individual lean and Six Sigma methodologies. *Lean* focuses on eliminating waste from processes and increasing process speed by focusing on what customers actually consider quality, and working back from that. *Six Sigma* aims to eliminate process variation and make process improvements based on the customer definition of quality, and by measuring process performance and process change effects.

M

Malcolm Baldrige National Quality Award (MBNQA)—An award established by the U.S. Congress in 1987 to raise awareness of quality management and recognize U.S. companies that have implemented successful quality management systems. Awards can be given annually in six categories: manufacturing, service, small business, education, healthcare, and nonprofit. The award is named after the late secretary of commerce Malcolm Baldrige, a proponent of quality management. The U.S. Commerce Department's National Institute of Standards and Technology manages the award, and ASQ administers it.

Master Black Belt (MBB)—Six Sigma or quality expert responsible for strategic implementations in an organization. An MBB is qualified to teach other Six Sigma facilitators the methods, tools, and applications in all functions and levels of the company and is a resource for using statistical process control in processes.

measure—The criteria, metric, or means to which a comparison is made with output.

metric—A standard for measurement.

O

objectives—An organization's articulated aims or quantifiable targets to address its goals and/or a major change or improvement. May be focused internally and/or externally and are generally more specific than its goals. Some companies may use "goals" interchangeably with "objectives."

OFI—Opportunity for improvement

P

plan–do–check/study–act (PDC/SA) cycle—A four-step process for quality improvement. In the first step (plan), a way to effect improvement is developed. In the second step (do), the plan is carried out, preferably on a small scale. In the third step (check), a study takes place between what was predicted and what was observed in the previous step. In the last step (act), action is taken on the causal system to effect the desired change. The plan–do–check–act cycle is sometimes referred to as the Shewhart cycle, because Walter A. Shewhart discussed the concept in his book *Statistical Method from the Viewpoint of Quality Control*, and as the Deming cycle because W. Edwards Deming introduced the concept in Japan. The Japanese subsequently called it the Deming cycle. Also called the *plan–do–study–act (PDSA) cycle*.

process—Linked activities with the purpose of producing a product, program, and/or service. Several individual or subprocesses may be combined in some fashion to produce more complicated output—see *system*.

process improvement (PI)—See *continuous process improvement* (CPI).

project management—The application of knowledge, skills, tools, and techniques to a broad range of activities to meet the requirements of a particular project.

Q

quality—A subjective term for which each person or sector has its own definition. In technical usage, *quality* can have two meanings: (1) the characteristics of a product or service that bear on its ability to satisfy stated or implied needs, (2) a product or service free of deficiencies. According to Joseph Juran, quality means "fitness for use"; according to Philip Crosby, it means "conformance to requirements."

quality management system (QMS)—A formalized system that documents the structure, responsibilities, and procedures required to achieve effective quality management.

quality tool—An instrument or technique to support and improve the activities of process quality management and improvement.

R

return on investment (ROI)—*Rate of profit*, or sometimes just *return*, is the ratio of *money* gained or lost (whether realized or unrealized) on an *investment* relative to the amount of money invested.

root cause—The initiating cause of a series of activities or a causal chain that leads to a particular outcome or condition. The point in a series of activities or steps (process) where an intervention, change, and/or improvement could be implemented and prevent the undesirable outcome or condition. The primary cause for a given process performance problem, challenge, shortfall, and so on.

S

Shingo Prize for Operational Excellence—The Shingo Prize is named in honor of the late Dr. Shigeo Shingo. Dr. Shingo has been described as an "engineering genius" for his contributions to improving manufacturing processes. As one of the world's leading experts on manufacturing practices, he helped to create and document the renowned Toyota Production System. Many of his improvement principles, such as single-minute-exchange-of-die (quick changeover), poka-yoke (mistake-proofing) and non-stock production (minimum inventory) are described in six books published in the United States.

Six Sigma—A method that provides organizations tools to improve the capability of their business processes. This increase in performance and decrease in process variation leads to defect reduction and improvement in profits, employee morale, and quality of products or services. *Six sigma quality* is a term generally used to indicate that a process is well controlled (±6 sigma from the centerline in a control chart).

stakeholder—The term *stakeholder* refers to all groups that are or might be affected by an organization's process. *Stakeholders* might include employees, including senior management and board of directors, as well as suppliers, customers, and partners. In the broader sense and depending on the process, municipalities and general citizens in the immediate vicinity of the process could also be considered stakeholders.

statistical process control (SPC)—The application of statistical techniques to control a process; often used interchangeably with the term "statistical quality control."

sustain/sustainability—Sustainability is a system that demonstrates the capacity to endure.

strengths, weaknesses, opportunities, threats (SWOT) analysis—A strategic technique used to assess what an organization is facing.

system—A set of integrated, interdependent components and/or processes that interact to produce another component, product, or service.

T

tangible results—Specific, measurable, observable, and so on, results from the organization's process improvement efforts.

team—A group of individuals organized to work together to accomplish a specific objective.

TEF—Team Excellence Framework.

theory of constraints (TOC)—A lean management philosophy that stresses removal of constraints to increase throughput while decreasing inventory and operating expenses. TOC's set of tools examines the entire system for continuous improvement. The current reality tree, conflict resolution diagram, future reality tree, prerequisite tree and transition tree are the five tools used in TOC's ongoing improvement process. Also called *constraints management.*

top management commitment—Participation of the highest-level officials in their organization's quality improvement efforts. Their participation includes establishing and serving on a quality committee, establishing quality policies and goals, deploying those goals to lower levels of the organization, providing the resources and training lower levels need to achieve the goals, participating in quality improvement teams, reviewing progress organization-wide, recognizing those who have performed well, and revising the current reward system to reflect the importance of achieving the quality goals.

total quality management (TQM)—A term first used to describe a management approach to quality improvement. Since then, TQM has taken on many meanings. Simply put, it is a management approach to long-term success through customer satisfaction. TQM is based on all members of an organization participating in improving processes, products, services, and the culture in which they work. The methods for implementing this approach are found in the teachings of such quality leaders as Philip B. Crosby, W. Edwards Deming, Armand V. Feigenbaum, Kaoru Ishikawa, and Joseph M. Juran.

TWEF—Team and Workplace Excellence Forum.

V

voice of the customer (VOC)—The expressed requirements and expectations of customers relative to products or services, as documented and disseminated to the providing organization's members.

References

Adrian, N. 2007. "Quality Tools, Teamwork Lead to a Boeing System Redesign." *Quality Progress* (November): 43–48
———. 2008a. "A Gold Medal Solution: Boeing Team Uses Quality to Create a Safer Working Environment." *Quality Progress* (March): 44–50.
———. 2008b. "It All Ties Together: CSX Team's Project Curtails Fuel Consumption, Saves Company Millions." *Quality Progress* (May): 20–27.
———. 2008c. "Incredible Journey: Injuries, Costs Persuade a Boeing Team to Develop a Safety Plan." *Quality Progress* (June): 36–41.
———. 2009. "Keep on Truckin': Team Uses Quality Tools to Realize Cost Savings, Simplify Processes." *Quality Progress* (April): 55–58.
———. 2010. "Seamless Transactions: Finance Company Uses Service Quality Tools to Drive Excellence." *Quality Progress* (April): 45–51.
American Society for Quality. 2009. "A Showcase for Teams from Educational Institutions." *The Journal for Quality and Participation* (January): 40–41.
Baldrige Performance Excellence Program. 2011. NIST. Accessed October 12. http://www.nist.gov/baldrige/index.cfm.
Benko, C., and F. W. McFarlan. 2003. *Connecting the Dots: Aligning Projects with Objectives in Unpredictable Times.* Boston: Harvard Business School Press.
Besterfield, D., C. Besterfield-Michna, G. H. Besterfield, and M. Besterfield-Sacre. 2003. *Total Quality Management.* Upper Saddle River, NJ: Pearson Education International.
Beyerlein, M. M., and C. L. Harris. 2003. "Critical Factors in Team-Based Organizing: A Top Ten List." In *The Collaborative Work Systems Fieldbook*, edited by M. M. Beyerlein, C. McGee, G. Klein, J. Nemiro, and L. Broedling. San Francisco: Jossey-Bass.
Bhatt, H., N. Dhingra, A. Jain, S. Akhilesh, K. Sachin, and S. Vakil. 2006. "Reliance Industries Limited Wins Team Excellence Award Competition." *The Journal for Quality and Participation* (Summer): 33–51.

Bodinson, G., and K. Kendall. 2010. "The Power of People in Achieving Performance Excellence." *Journal for Quality and Participation* (July): 10–14.

Brassard, M. 1996. *The Memory Jogger Plus+*. Salem, NH: GOAL/QPC.

Brassard, M., and D. Ritter in partnership with Kent Sterett and the Premier Performance Network. 2001. *Sailing through Six Sigma*. Marietta, GA: Brassard & Ritter LLC.

Broedling, L. 2003. "The Team Excellence Award Program: Recognizing Successful Team Problem Solving and Process Improvement." In *The Collaborative Work Systems Fieldbook*, edited by M. M. Beyerlein, C. McGee, G. Klein, J. Nemiro, and L. Broedling. San Francisco: Jossey-Bass.

Brown, M. G. 2007. *Beyond the Balanced Scorecard: Improving Business Intelligence with Analytics*. New York: Productivity Press.

Brush, M. K. 2009a. "M.A.G.I.C. Huddles: Handbook Motivates Staff and Improves Customer Service." ASQ Knowledge Center. Accessed November 11, 2011. http://asq.org/2009/06/quality-tools/magic-huddles.html.

———. 2009b. "Quality Tools Help Singapore Housing and Development Board Develop Award-Winning New Product." ASQ Knowledge Center. Accessed November 11, 2011. http://asq.org/2009/06/quality-tools/develop-award-winning-product.html.

———. 2009c. "Singapore Housing and Development Board MoJet Pack: Using Quality Tools for Product Development." ASQ Knowledge Center. Accessed November 11, 2011. http://asq.org/2009/06/quality-tools/mojet-pack-product-development.html.

Bryant, R. 2011. Keynote address. ASQ World Conference, May 2011.

Buchanan, J., B. Smith, and A. Williamson. 2005. "Baxter International Wins Team Excellence Award Competition." *The Journal for Quality and Participation* (Summer): 32–36.

Cameron, K. S., and R. E. Quinn. 2010. *Diagnosing and Changing Organizational Culture: Based on the Competing Values Framework*, 3rd ed. New York: John Wiley & Sons.

Camp, R. C. 2006. *Benchmarking: The Search for Industry Best Practices That Lead to Superior Performance*. New York: Productivity Press.

Chircop, J. 2009. "It's a Matter of Time: Ship Servicers Use Quick Kaizen to Shorten Long Turnaround." ASQ Knowledge Center. Accessed November 11, 2011. http://asq.org/2009/11/lean/kaizen-to-shorten-long-turnaround.html.

Daniels, S. E. 2007. "Agency Files Away Inefficiency, Saves Taxpayers a Bundle." *Quality Progress* (October): 41–44.

———. 2009. "Contacts That Count." *Quality Progress* (January): 42–27.

Deming, W. E. 1982. *Out of the Crisis*. Cambridge, MA: MIT Press.

Edmund, M. 2009. "Off the Ground: Boeing Project Team Takes C-17 Manufacturing Process to New Heights." *Quality Progress* (March): 44–59.

———. 2010. "In It for the Long Haul: HD Supply Unit Uses VOC Project to Keep Customers Loyal." *Quality Press* (May): 48–51.

Ellifson, V. F. 2010. "Customer Focus Sparks Invention." *Quality Progress* (March): 49–51.

Gadda-Thompson, M., and L. Barrera. 2010. "Movistar: A Decade of Sustained Excellence Developing an Innovative Quality Management Model." ASQ World Conference on Quality and Improvement, May 2010.

George, M., D. Rowlands, and B. Kastle. 2004. *What Is Lean Six Sigma?* New York: McGraw-Hill.

Gibson, C., and S. G. Cohen. 2003. *Virtual Teams That Work*. San Francisco: Jossey-Bass.

Goldratt, E. M. 2004. *The Goal*, 3rd ed. Great Barrington, MA: North River Press.

Hayen, R. 2006. *SAP R/3 Enterprise Software: An Introduction*. New York: McGraw-Hill/Irwin.

HD Supply. 2009. "HD Supply Facilities Maintenance Wins Team Excellence Award from American Society for Quality." HD Supply. Accessed November 11, 2011. http://www.hdsupply.com/pressroom/awards-recognition.asp.

Hopen, D. 2010. "The Changing Role and Practices of Successful Leaders." *The Journal for Quality and Participation* 33 (1): 4–9.

Ishikawa, K. 1985. *What Is Total Quality Control? The Japanese Way*. Englewood Cliffs, NJ: Prentice-Hall

International Organization for Standardization (ISO). 2011. ISO home page. Accessed November 10, 2011. http://www.iso.org/iso/home.htm.

Jacobsen, J. 2007. "Teaming Up for Process Improvement and Cost Savings." *The Journal for Quality and Participation* (Winter): 4–16.

———. September 2008a. "On the Right Track: Rail Company Reduces Expenses with Six Sigma." ASQ. Accessed November 11, 2011. http://wcqi.asq.org/team-competition/case-studies.html.

———. 2008b. "Teamwork Makes the Difference." *The Journal for Quality and Participation* (October): 30–38.

———. 2009a. "Streamlined Enrollment Nets Big Results for Healthcare Leader." ASQ Knowledge Center. Accessed November 11, 2011. http://asq.org/2009/01/lean/streamlined-enrollment-nets-big-results-for-healthcare-leader.html.

———. 2009b. "Improving Productivity Through Lean Six Sigma Warehouse Design." ASQ Knowledge Center. Accessed November 11, 2011. http://asq.org/2009/02/lean/improving-productivity-lean-six-sigma-warehouse-design.html.

———. 2009c. "Medical Device Manufacturer's Continuous Improvement Approach Reduces Errors in Records." ASQ Knowledge Center. Accessed November 11, 2011. http://asq.org/2009/02/continuous-improvement/medical-device-manufacturer-reduces-errors.html.

———. 2009d. "Optimizing Purchasing Processes Saves $1 Million." ASQ Knowledge Center. Accessed November 11, 2011. http://asq.org/2009/07/six-sigma/optimizing-purchasing-processes-saves-1-million.html.

———. 2009e. "Texas District Uses Peer Assessments to Measure Scorecard Achievement." ASQ Knowledge Center. Accessed November 11, 2011. http://asq.org/2009/10/continuous-improvement/peer-assessments-measure-scorecard-achievement.html.

———. November 2010a. "Quality Revolution Reduces Defects, Drives Sales Growth at 3M." Quality Magazine. Accessed November 11, 2011. http://www.qualitymag.com/Articles/Web_Exclusive/BNP_GUID_9-5-2006_A_10000000000001104980.

———. 2010b. "Six Sigma Improves Productivity, Adds Financial Value." ASQ Knowledge Center. Accessed November 11, 2011. http://asq.org/2010/11/six-sigma/improve-productivity-financial-value.html.

———. 2010c. "Teaming Up with Six Sigma to Improve Accuracy and Customer Satisfaction." ASQ Knowledge Center. Accessed November 11, 2011. http://asq.org/2010/09/six-sigma/teaming-improve-customer-satisfaction.html.

———. 2011a. "Reducing Check Returns with Six Sigma." ASQ Knowledge Center. Accessed November 11, 2011. http://asq.org/2011/04/six-sigma/reducing-check-returns.html.

———. 2011b. "Service Provider Improves Client's Metrics with Six Sigma." ASQ Knowledge Center. Accessed November 11, 2011. http://asq.org/2011/04/six-sigma/service-provider-improves-clients-metrics.html.

Johnson, C. 2002. "Managing Virtual Teams." *HR Magazine* (June): 69–73.

Joiner, B. L. 1994. *Fourth Generation Management: The New Business Consciousness*. New York: McGraw-Hill.

Juran, J. M. 1995. *Managerial Breakthrough*, 3rd ed. New York: McGraw-Hill.

Kaplan, R. S., and S. Anderson. 2007. *Time-Driven Activity-Based Costing: A Simpler and More Powerful Path to Higher Profits*. Boston: Harvard Business School Press.

Kaplan, R. S., and D. P. Norton. 1996. *The Balanced Scorecard*. Boston: Harvard Business School Press.

———. 2007. *The Balanced Scorecard: Translating Strategy into Action*. Boston: Harvard Business Publishing.

Katzenbach, J. R., and D. K. Smith. 1994. *The Wisdom of Teams*. New York: Harper Business.

Kerr, J., and J. W. Slocum Jr. 2005. "Managing Corporate Culture Through Reward Systems." *Academy of Management Executive* 18 (4): 130–38.

Kincade, S., and L. Wolf. 2010. "Barnes-Jewish Hospital Enhances Quality Patient Care by Embracing Lean." ASQ Knowledge Center. Accessed November 11, 2011. http://asq.org/2010/11/lean/enhance-patient-care.html.

Kotter, J. P. 1996. *Leading Change*. Boston: Harvard Business School Press.

Krzykowski, B. 2010. "What Do You Say?" *Quality Progress* (May): 45–47.

———. 2011. "Walking the Talk." *Quality Progress* (June): 41–45.

Lencioni, P. 2002. *The Five Dysfunctions of a Team*. San Francisco: Jossey-Bass.

Liker, J. K. 2003. *The Toyota Way*. New York: McGraw-Hill.

Lindborg, H. J. 2011. "The Missing Links: Tying Baldrige, Quality Values to Increased Employee Engagement." *Quality Progress* (April): 58–59.

Norausky, P. H. 2000. *The Customer–Supplier Innovation Team Guidebook.* Milwaukee: ASQ Quality Press.

Nourse, L., and P. Hays. 2004. "Fidelity Wide Processing Wins Team Excellence Award Competition." *The Journal for Quality and Participation* (Summer): 42–48.

O'Dell, C., and C. Hubert. 2011. *The New Edge in Knowledge: How Knowledge Management Is Changing the Way We Do Business.* Hoboken, NJ: John Wiley & Sons.

Pace, A. 2010. "Unleashing Positivity in the Workplace." *T&D* (January): 41–44.

Passion, V., and G. Gotsill. 2010. "Learning Lessons As a Team." *T&D* (August): 61.

Peotter, E. 2009. "Teamwork Remains the Great Key to Success." *The Journal for Quality and Participation* (July): 32–36.

Perez, A., and I. Vasquez. 2007. "Siemens VDO Guadalajara Captures Bronze at Team Excellence Award Competition." *The Journal for Quality and Participation* (Spring): 38–41.

Pfeffer, J. 2005. "Producing Sustainable Competitive Advantage Through the Effective Management of People." *Academy of Management Executive* 19 (4): 95–108.

Pfeffer, J., and R. I. Sutton. 2006. "Evidence-Based Management." *Harvard Business Review* (January): 63–74.

Project Management Institute. 2008. *Project Management Body of Knowledge (PMBOK Guide)*, 4th ed. Newtown Square, PA: PMI.

Schaar, T. 2010a. "Critical Elements for Major Improvements." ASQ Knowledge Center. Accessed November 11, 2011. http://asq.org/2010/09/six-sigma/critical-elements-major-improvements.html.

———. 2010b. "Negative Press Motivates Impossible Mission." ASQ Knowledge Center. Accessed November 11, 2011. http://asq.org/2010/11/six-sigma/impossible-mission.html.

———. 2011. "No Evil Lasts More Than 96 Hours." ASQ Knowledge Center. Accessed November 11, 2011. http://asq.org/2011/03/six-sigma/no-evil-lasts.html .

Schein, E. H. 2010. *Organizational Culture and Leadership*, 4th ed. New York: John Wiley & Sons.

Scholtes, P. R., B. L. Joiner, and B. J. Streibel. 2003. *The Team Handbook*, 3rd ed. Madison, WI: Oriel Incorporated.

Schroeder, K. 2009. "R. O. Polk & Co.: Making Every Issue the Only Issue." ASQ Knowledge Center. Accessed November 11, 2011. http://asq.org/2009/02/customer-satisfaction-and-value/polk-making-every-issue-the-only-issue.html.

Shewhart, W. A. 1931. *Economic Control of Quality of Manufactured Product.* New York: Van Nostrand.

Shingo, S., and A. P Dillon. 1989. *A Study of the Toyota Production System: From an Industrial Engineering Viewpoint.* New York: Productivity Press.

Shingo, S., T. Epley, C. McLoughlin, and N. Bodek. 2007. *Kaizen and the Art of Creative Thinking: The Scientific Thinking Mechanism.* New York: PCS Inc. and Enna Products Corporation.

Shingo, S., C. McLoughlin, N. Bodek, and T. Epley. 2009. *Fundamental Principles of Lean Manufacturing.* New York: PCS Inc. and Enna Products Corporation.

Shingo Prize for Operations Excellence, The. 2011. Accessed November 10. http://www.shingoprize.org/.

Spong, E. D., and D. J Collard. 2009. *The Making of a World-Class Organization.* Milwaukee: ASQ Quality Press.

Tapping, D. 2003. *Lean Pocket Guide.* Chelsea, MI: MCS Media Inc.

Troutman, S. 2005. "Technology in Virtual Teaming." *IHRIM Journal* (January/February): 38–44.

Troutman, S., and G. Falkowski. 2003a. "Creating and Leading Virtual Teams Using a 'Team Capital' Model and Rudimentary Project Management." *IHRIM Journal* (May/June): 41–45.

———. 2003b. "Creating and Leading Virtual Teams Using a 'Team Capital' Model, Elementary Team Building, and Facilitation." *IHRIM Journal* (July/August): 43–49.

———. 2003c. "Creating and Leading Virtual Teams Using a 'Team Capital' Model, Elementary Team Building, and Some Change Management." *IHRIM Journal* (September/October): 57–62.

Ulrich, D., S. Kerr, and R. Ashkenas. 2002. *The GE Work-Out.* New York: McGraw-Hill.

Walters, G. 2011. "Education Team Excellence Recognition Spotlights Schools." *Journal for Quality and Participation* (January): 35–38.

Whisman, M. 2011. Remarks in Plenary Session, ASQ World Conference on Quality and Improvement, May 18, 2011.

Whisman, M., and M. Levenhagen. 2011. "Maximizing Impact: The International Team Excellence Award." ASQ World Conference on Quality and Improvement, May 17, 2011.

Zilbershtein, D. 2010. "International Team Excellence Award: A Judge's Behind-the-Scenes Perspective of the Teams." *The Journal for Quality and Participation* (July): 30–34.

Index

A

activity-based costing (ABC), 136
after action reviews, 90
Aldine Independent School District, tools and techniques used, 106
Allegheny Energy Incorporated
 use of TEF, 33
 summary of project presentation, 63–71
American Society for Quality (ASQ)
 and ITEA Process, 7
 quality tools, 94–96, 100–101
 World Conference on Quality and Improvement, 147, 151–52, 157, 158
Anheuser-Busch InBev Metal Container Corporation, use of TEF, 25, 43, 44
assessment, in TEF, 11–12
Assessment Team's Consensus Scoresheet (Appendix D), 201–2
Assessment Worksheet, 84
 and scoring guidelines, 191–200 (Appendix C)
assessors, expectations of, 115–16
Association of Quality and Participation (AQP), 142

B

balanced scorecard, 57
 integrating TEF with, 137–38
Baldrige Criteria for Performance Excellence, 120
 implications for integrating TEF with, 128
 integrating TEF with use of, 125–29
Baldrige Organizational Profile, 120, 125–26
Baldrige Performance Excellence Award, 14–15
Baldrige Performance Excellence Program, 10
 criteria, 12–13
Barnes–Jewish Hospital
 tools and techniques used, 111–12
 use of TEF, 42
Barrera, Luciana, 6
Baxter International, Inc., recognition program, 155–56
Bayer Health Care, use of TEF, 41
Bayer MaterialScience, tools and techniques used, 109
benchmarking, 144
 benefits of, 3
Boeing Company

220　Index

Airlift and Tanker Program, use of TEF in, 3–5
C-17 aircraft program
　integration of TEF and Baldrige in, 128–29
　recognition program, 156
　tools and techniques used, 107, 109, 110, 111
　use of TEF in, 3–4
　employee engagement in, 61
　Ramp Operations Improvement Team, use of TEF in, 17
　Support Services Center (BSS), tools and techniques used, 106
　use of TEF, 40–41
bonding, in teamwork, 58

C

California Council for Excellence, 75
California Team Excellence Award (TEA), 75
Caride, Eduardo, 5–6
celebration, 143
CGI Federal, use of TEF, 38
Chambers, Howard, 3–5
clarity, in Feedback Report, 91
collaboration, 57–59
comment guidelines, in feedback, 86–87
consensus, methods for reaching, in assessment, 84–86
Consensus Scoresheet, 85
Continental Guadalajara Services Mexico S.A. De C.V., use of TEF, 43
continuous improvement (CI), xx
　models, 54–57
　and TEF, 13, 14–15
continuous learning, 143
continuous process improvement, 117–18
criteria, in TEF, 11–13
　emphasis on CI, 62–63
　organization of, 45–71
　rationale for, 45–46
　rationale for in terms of CI approaches, 54–57
　rationale for in terms of teamwork and collaboration, 57–59
　using tools to exceed, best practice examples, 102–12
Criteria, Team Excellence. *See* Team Excellence Criteria
criteria integration and cross-linking, 81
criteria scoring guidelines dimension, of TE criteria, 81–83
Criteria Summary. *See* Team Excellence Criteria Summary
criterion amplification, 80–81
criterion discussion dimension, of TE criteria, 78–80
criterion footnotes, 81
criterion structure, Baldrige, 126
criterion summary dimension, of TE criteria, 78–81
cross-linking
　in criteria, 81, 82–86
　criteria items and slide graphics, 115
C-17 aircraft program, Boeing
　employee engagement in, 61
　integration of TEF and Baldrige in, 128–29
　recognition program, 156
　tools and techniques used, 107, 109, 110, 111
　use of TEF, 3–4
CSX Transportation
　tools and techniques used, 108, 110–11
　use of TEF, 37
culture, organizational, changing through use of TEF, 29–30
current situation analysis (Criteria Summary Section 2), 51
　Healthways, Inc. example, 103–4
Customer–Supplier Innovation Team Guidebook, The, 58

D

dashboards, integrating TEF with, 138
data, 101–2

define–measure–analyze–improve–control (DMAIC) methodology, 55–56, 96
Deming, W. Edwards, 54, 55, 62, 101
Deming cycle, 54
descriptors, in criteria, 79–80
DMAIC-V, 100–101

E

Education Team Excellence Recognition (ETER) program, 149–50
employee engagement
  in Boeing Company, 61
  improving level of with TEF, 10–11, 28–29
enterprise management, 123
enterprise resource planning (ERP) systems, 134–35, 136
enterprise sustainability
  best practices for, 118–24
  value creation chain framework for, 122–23
enterprise sustainability tree, 122–23
enterprises system software, 135
exceeds criteria level, scoring integration and cross-linkage, 82–86

F

Fabrinet Co. Ltd., use of TEF, 40
feedback
  customers for, 89–90
  how organizations and teams can best use, 89–92
  how to write, 85–88
  sources of, 90–91
  in TEF, 12
Feedback Report
  how to write effective, 86–88
  understanding and applying, 91–92
Fidelity Wide Processing, tools and techniques used, 107
Firstsource, use of TEF, 22–23
Firstsource Advantage LLC, use of TEF, 31, 32

Firstsource Solutions Limited, use of TEF, 31, 32
Five Dysfunctions of a Team, The, 57–58
5S methodology, 56
Florida Department of Children and Families, SunCoast Region, tools and techniques used, 109
Ford Motor Company, use of TEF, 19, 36
form–storm–norm–perform model, of team formation, 52

G

Gadda-Thompson, Matias, 7
General Electric Company, 142
goals, organization, and use of TEF, 28

H

HD Supply Facilities Maintenance Team Excellence Award, 144
  use of TEF, 21–22
Healthways, Inc., tools and techniques used by improvement team (example), 103–5
high-performance team (HPT), 11
hoshin planning template, 63
hoshin process, 63–64
Housing and Development Board, Singapore
  tools and techniques used, 106, 108, 110
  use of TEF, 40
Humana, Inc., use of TEF, 24, 33, 34

I

IGD, Bogotá, use of TEF, 37
improvement teams
  definition of, 10–11
  improving results from, with TEF, 8–9

reasons for failure of, 9
information and knowledge management system (IKMS), 136
information management, 123–24
  integrating TEF with, 134–35
integration
  in projects, 53–54
  in team excellence criteria, 81, 82–86
International Team Excellence Award (ITEA) Process, 1–3
  Criteria (Appendix A), 173–85
  foundation of, 7
  history, 142
  participation in, 141–60
    opportunities for, 156–60
  scoresheet example (Appendix B), 187–89
  structure, 145–50
  volunteer program, 157–60
international-wide process, ITEA, 145–47
  recognition from participation in, 151–52
ISO 9001:2008, 132–33
  clauses, 133
  integrating TEF with, 131–34
ITEA Committee, 7, 141–42, 152
ITEA-sponsored event
  reasons to attend, 145
  reasons to enter, 142–44

J

judge, ITEA Process, volunteering as, 158–59
Juran, Joseph M., 55

K

Kaiser Permanente Colorado, tools and techniques used, 107
key performance indicators (KPIs), integrating TEF with, 137
knowledge management (KM), 123–24, 136
  integrating TEF with, 134–35

L

lagging indicators, 62
leading indicators, 62
lean methodology, 56
Lean Six Sigma methodology, 56
lean tools, 96
learning, organizational, improving through use of TEF, 29
lessons learned, 90
line of sight, in organizational performance, 50
linear price performance (LPP), 23
Littelfuse Phils, Inc.
  tools and techniques used, 106
  use of TEF, 31
Lockheed Martin, use of TEF, 36

M

MEDRAD, Inc., tools and techniques used, 108, 111
Memory Jogger Plus+, The, 51
Metal Container Corporation, Anheuser-Busch InBev, use of TEF, 25, 43, 44
metrics, 101–2
  integrating TEF with, 137
metrology, 136
Ministry of Defence (MINDEF), Singapore, use of TEF, 33
Movistar Argentina
  quality management model, 59–60
  recognition program, 156
  use of TEF, 34–36
muda, 56
MWM International Motores, use of TEF, 23–24

N

National Quality Education Conference (NQEC), 150
Naval Surface Warfare Center—Crane Division, use of TEF, 40
New Breed Logistics, tools and techniques used, 111

Nextel Argentina SRL, use of TEF, 42
non-value-added activity, 56
North Broward Medical Center, use of TEF, 31

O

on time and in full (OTIF) indicators, 33
operations, of organization, 121
operations management, 123–24
opportunities for improvement, 53
    in assessment, 85–87, 92
        examples of good, 88–89
organizational profile, Baldrige, 120, 125–26
organizations
    benefits to, through use of TEF, 28–30
    new to use of CI methodology or teams, application of TEF in, 162–65
    and recognition, 150–51
    recognized as high in performance excellence, application of TEF in, 168–70
    types of, and TEF, 14–15
    using CI methodology and teams, application of TEF in, 165–68

P

Parrish Medical Center, use of TEF, 38–39
Payne, Rick, 4–5
performance data, 137
performance management, 124
performance metrics, 137
performance system, Baldrige, 126
Pershing LLC
    tools and techniques used, 105–6
    use of TEF, 42
Pitcher, Don, 5
plan–do–check–act (PDCA) cycle, 54–55, 100–101
plan–do–study–act (PDSA) cycle, 54–55, 100–101
PMW 160 Tactical Networks, use of TEF, 41
Polk, R. L., & Co., tools and techniques used, 109–10
positive organizational scholarship, 170–71
postmortems, project, 90
Praxair Mexico, use of TEF, 32–33
process, definition of, 133
process approach, 133
process management, 123–24
    with ISO 9001:2008, 132–33
program administration, ITEA Process, volunteering in, 159–60
project implementation and results (Criteria Summary Section 4), 51–52
    Healthways, Inc. example, 104
project management, 102
Project Management Body of Knowledge (PMBOK Guide), 52
Project Management Institute, 52
project presentation
    Allegheny Energy, Incorporated, summary example, 63–71
    how to assess, 76–89
    must-do's for effective, 112–15
    scoring, basic elements, 76–77
project results and benefits, through use of TEF, 26–27
project selection and purpose (Criteria Summary Section 1), 50–51
    Healthways, Inc. example, 103

Q

quality circles, 142
quality management system, ISO 9001:2008, 132–33

R

Ramaiah Institute of Management Studies, use of TEF, 19, 38

raw data, 137
recognition, external, 142–43, 150–54
    connecting to internal recognition, 154–56
recognition, internal, connecting to external recognition, 154–56
Reliance Industries Limited, use of TEF, 19–21, 38
replication, of improvements, through use of TEF, 30
return on investment (ROI), 8–9, 123
root cause(s), 53

S

School District of Lee County, Fort Myers, Florida, use of TEF, 39–40
SGS Canada Inc., use of TEF, 36
Shewhart, Walter, 54, 55, 101
Shewhart cycle, 54
Shingo, Shigeo, 129–30
Shingo Prize model, integrating TEF with, 129–31
Showcase programs, regional, ITEA, 145–46, 147
    feeder programs, 148–49
    recognition received by participation in, 152–54
Siemens VDO, tools and techniques used, 108–9
Singapore Housing and Development Board
    tools and techniques used, 106, 108, 110
    use of TEF, 40
Six Sigma methodology, 55–56
Six Sigma quality level, 136
slides, presentation, guidelines, 112–15
solution development (Criteria Summary Section 3), 51
    Healthways, Inc. example, 104
Southern California Edison, use of TEF, 19, 42–43
stakeholders, 26, 27, 50–52, 53–54, 84
standardization, achieving, through use of TEF, 30

statistical process control (SPC), 55
Sterlite Industries India Ltd.
    recognition program, 154–55
    use of TEF, 43
strategy, enterprise, 119–20
strengths, in assessment, 85–87, 92
    examples of good, 88
style guidelines, in feedback, 87–88
sunset reviews, 90
sustainability
    best practices for, 123–24
    enterprise, best practices for, 118–24
    enterprise architecture for, 119–20
    enterprise strategy for, 120–22
system foundation, Baldrige, 126

T

Taguchi, Genichi, 55
Team and Workplace Excellence Forum (TWEF), 58, 152, 157
team excellence
    best practices for, 118–24
    merits of promoting, 170–71
team excellence assessment, 73–92
Team Excellence Criteria (Appendix A), 173–89
    application of, 93–116
    four sections of, 93–94
    how to use as project checklist, 94
    organization of, 45–71
    techniques and tools to meet and exceed, 94–102
    three dimensions of, 77–83
    understanding dimensions of, 77
Team Excellence Criteria Summary, 45
    description of, 46–54
Team Excellence Framework (TEF)
    applying in organizations high in performance excellence, 168–70
    applying in organizations new to CI or teams, 162–65
    applying in organizations using CI and teams, 165–68

applying in your organization, 161–71
background, xix, xxi, 1
benefits of using, 2–3, 17–44
 types of, 18–19
components of, 11–12
continuous improvement (CI) and, 13
integrating with balanced scorecards, 137–38
integrating with dashboards, 138
integrating with information management, 134–35
integrating with ISO 9001:2008, 131–34
integrating with key performance indicators (KPIs), 137
integrating with knowledge management, 134–35
integrating with metrics, 137
integrating with Shingo Prize model, 129–31, 134
integrating with use of Baldrige criteria, 125–29
organization-wide results and benefits through use of, 28–30
overview of, 11–13
project results and benefits through use of, 26–27
reasons to use, 8–11
relationship to broader performance excellence programs, 117–39
and types of organizations, 14–15
when to use, 8
Team Handbook, The, 56, 58
team management, 52–54
team management and project presentation (Criteria Summary Section 5), 52–54
Healthways, Inc. example, 104–5
teams
 learning from, 157
 starting new, 102
 types of, and project results through use of TEF, 26–27
teamwork, xxi, 57–59

changing organizational culture to support, through use of TEF, 30
Telefonica Argentina/Movistar quality management model, 59–60
recognition program, 156
use of TEF in, 5–7, 34–36
theory of constraints, 56–57
3 × 3 dimension tree, 77
3M Company, use of TEF, 39
three wide three deep, criteria dimensions, *73*
tools
 lean, 96
 using to exceed criteria, best practice examples, 102–12
total quality management, 56–57
Toyota Production System, 10
traceability, in metrology, 136

U

United Auto Workers (UAW), 61
Urology Group, The, use of TEF, 44
U.S. Naval Ship Repair Facility and Japan Regional Maintenance Center, tools and techniques used, 107

V

vision, enterprise, 119–20
voice of the business (VOB), xix–xx
voice of the customer (VOC), xix–xx
voice of the employees (VOE), xix–xx

W

waste, 56
West Paces Hotel Group, The, use of TEF, 37
Wipro BPO, use of TEF, 42
Work-Out methodology, 142
Wyndham Consumer Finance, use of TEF, 44

Belong to the Quality Community!

Established in 1946, ASQ is a global community of quality experts in all fields and industries. ASQ is dedicated to the promotion and advancement of quality tools, principles, and practices in the workplace and in the community.

The Society also serves as an advocate for quality. Its members have informed and advised the U.S. Congress, government agencies, state legislatures, and other groups and individuals worldwide on quality-related topics.

Vision

By making quality a global priority, an organizational imperative, and a personal ethic, ASQ becomes the community of choice for everyone who seeks quality technology, concepts, or tools to improve themselves and their world.

ASQ is...

- More than 90,000 individuals and 700 companies in more than 100 countries
- The world's largest organization dedicated to promoting quality
- A community of professionals striving to bring quality to their work and their lives
- The administrator of the Malcolm Baldrige National Quality Award
- A supporter of quality in all sectors including manufacturing, service, healthcare, government, and education
- YOU

Visit www.asq.org for more information.

ASQ

ASQ Membership

Research shows that people who join associations experience increased job satisfaction, earn more, and are generally happier*. ASQ membership can help you achieve this while providing the tools you need to be successful in your industry and to distinguish yourself from your competition. So why wouldn't you want to be a part of ASQ?

Networking

Have the opportunity to meet, communicate, and collaborate with your peers within the quality community through conferences and local ASQ section meetings, ASQ forums or divisions, ASQ Communities of Quality discussion boards, and more.

Professional Development

Access a wide variety of professional development tools such as books, training, and certifications at a discounted price. Also, ASQ certifications and the ASQ Career Center help enhance your quality knowledge and take your career to the next level.

Solutions

Find answers to all your quality problems, big and small, with ASQ's Knowledge Center, mentoring program, various e-newsletters, *Quality Progress* magazine, and industry-specific products.

Access to Information

Learn classic and current quality principles and theories in ASQ's Quality Information Center (QIC), *ASQ Weekly* e-newsletter, and product offerings.

Advocacy Programs

ASQ helps create a better community, government, and world through initiatives that include social responsibility, Washington advocacy, and Community Good Works.

Visit www.asq.org/membership for more information on ASQ membership.

*2008, The William E. Smith Institute for Association Research

ASQ Certification

ASQ certification is formal recognition by ASQ that an individual has demonstrated a proficiency within, and comprehension of, a specified body of knowledge at a point in time. Nearly 150,000 certifications have been issued. ASQ has members in more than 100 countries, in all industries, and in all cultures. ASQ certification is internationally accepted and recognized.

Benefits to the Individual

- New skills gained and proficiency upgraded
- Investment in your career
- Mark of technical excellence
- Assurance that you are current with emerging technologies
- Discriminator in the marketplace
- Certified professionals earn more than their uncertified counterparts
- Certification is endorsed by more than 125 companies

Benefits to the Organization

- Investment in the company's future
- Certified individuals can perfect and share new techniques in the workplace
- Certified staff are knowledgeable and able to assure product and service quality

Quality is a global concept. It spans borders, cultures, and languages. No matter what country your customers live in or what language they speak, they demand quality products and services. You and your organization also benefit from quality tools and practices. Acquire the knowledge to position yourself and your organization ahead of your competition.

Certifications Include

- Biomedical Auditor – CBA
- Calibration Technician – CCT
- HACCP Auditor – CHA
- Pharmaceutical GMP Professional – CPGP
- Quality Inspector – CQI
- Quality Auditor – CQA
- Quality Engineer – CQE
- Quality Improvement Associate – CQIA
- Quality Technician – CQT
- Quality Process Analyst – CQPA
- Reliability Engineer – CRE
- Six Sigma Black Belt – CSSBB
- Six Sigma Green Belt – CSSGB
- Software Quality Engineer – CSQE
- Manager of Quality/Organizational Excellence – CMQ/OE

Visit www.asq.org/certification to apply today!

ASQ Training

Classroom-based Training

ASQ offers training in a traditional classroom setting on a variety of topics. Our instructors are quality experts and lead courses that range from one day to four weeks, in several different cities. Classroom-based training is designed to improve quality and your organization's bottom line. Benefit from quality experts; from comprehensive, cutting-edge information; and from peers eager to share their experiences.

Web-based Training

Virtual Courses

ASQ's virtual courses provide the same expert instructors, course materials, interaction with other students, and ability to earn CEUs and RUs as our classroom-based training, without the hassle and expenses of travel. Learn in the comfort of your own home or workplace. All you need is a computer with Internet access and a telephone.

Self-paced Online Programs

These online programs allow you to work at your own pace while obtaining the quality knowledge you need. Access them whenever it is convenient for you, accommodating your schedule.

Some Training Topics Include
- Auditing
- Basic Quality
- Engineering
- Education
- Healthcare
- Government
- Food Safety
- ISO
- Leadership
- Lean
- Quality Management
- Reliability
- Six Sigma
- Social Responsibility

Visit www.asq.org/training for more information.